T0311698

"*Health Tech: Rebooting Society's Software, Hardware and Mindset* provides a historical context around the evolution of digital health technologies to better understand where we are heading next. As it also helps us peek into the near future of medicine and healthcare, it asks the right questions so we can make our own assumptions about what we expect from technologies in our care."

—*Dr. Bertalan Meskó, Director of The Medical Futurist Institute*

"Trond Undheim brings a well-needed fresh perspective to the challenges surrounding the integration of technology into healthcare delivery. This book should be required reading for anyone who is embarking on the slippery journey of technology innovation as applied to healthcare."

—*Dr. Joe Kvedar, Professor of Dermatology, Harvard Medical School, author, editor, advisor and telehealth evangelist*

"Simplicity is always an important goal to achieve innovation. Trond is a great synthesizer of insights and presents complex ideas clearly and concisely. One of the core ideas is that if we simplify the delivery of healthcare, we increase its overall impact. To do so requires rethinking who delivers care, what the technology looks like, and how we measure progress. *Health Tech* captures the pivotal moment where health tech innovation can transform the world if we can competently align incentives with value creation."

—*Jeff Karp, Distinguished Chair in Clinical Anesthesiology, Perioperative and Pain Medicine. Professor of Anesthesiology, Brigham, and Women's Hospital, Harvard Medical School, principal faculty at the Harvard Stem Cell Institute, affiliate faculty at the Broad Institute and at the Harvard-MIT Division of Health Sciences and Technology*

"Health tech is a big part of the future of healthcare, and Trond Arne Undheim ranks among the foremost technologists that will make it happen. As a citizen concerned about how pandemics will change our world, you should not wait a minute more to read *Health Tech: Rebooting Society's Software, Hardware and Mindset.*"

—*Thomas Clozel, M.D., CEO & co-founder, Owkin, the AI-powered life science company*

"Trond Arne Undheim takes readers on a cutting-edge exploration to understand what individuals can do now to prepare for the upcoming paradigm shift in the future of healthcare. *Health Tech: Rebooting Society's Software, Hardware and Mindset* also paves the way for the future of employment and includes specific calls to action! This book is a buzzer-beater for any entrepreneur looking to gain the insight and edge required to stay ahead!"

—*Scott E. Burgess, Founder & CEO, Healthcare360 Media, LLC*

Health Tech

Health Tech
Rebooting Society's Software, Hardware and Mindset

Trond Arne Undheim, PhD

Routledge
Taylor & Francis Group

A PRODUCTIVITY PRESS BOOK

First published 2022
by Routledge
600 Broken Sound Parkway #300, Boca Raton FL, 33487

and by Routledge
2 Park Square, Milton Park, Abingdon, Oxon, OX14 4RN

Routledge is an imprint of the Taylor & Francis Group, an informa business

ISBN: 9781032012933 (hbk)
ISBN: 9781032012926 (pbk)
ISBN: 9781003178071 (ebk)

DOI: 10.4324/9781003178071

Typeset in Garamond
by codeMantra

This book is dedicated to those excluded from exercising their basic human rights to high quality healthcare by the simple fact of living in the wrong place.

Contents

Acknowledgments

To Kristine Rynne Mednansky, Senior Editor, Business Improvement, Healthcare Management at Taylor & Francis for instantly believing I had something of value. To Samantha Dalton, editorial assistant, for helping me submit my manuscript properly. Finally, to Brianna Ascher, commissioning editor, Business & Management also at Taylor & Francis for immediately answering my initial outreach request. A 6 month process from proposal to finished book is near a record.

To my developmental editor, Kyle McCord with Atmosphere Press who generously poured through the manuscript, tightened up the narrative, and helped me straighten out my metaphors and vignettes, and to Executive Editor Nick Courtright for arranging it. To Karthikeyan Subramaniam, Project Manager at codeMantra U.S. LLC for diligently following up with me at all stages of the copyediting process.

To my PCP, Mark Pasternack, Internist and Chief, Pediatric Infectious Disease Unit, Massachusetts General Hospital, for taking care of my health for nearly 20 years and for bearing with my many questions about the healthcare system we are all part of.

To guests on the Futurized podcast who were guinea pigs for my many questions about health and wellness, including Professor Joe Kvedar, Harvard Medical School, Luci Gabel, author of *Eat To Lead*, Jesse Boehm, Chief Science Officer, Break Through Cancer, Greg Licholai, Chief Medical Information Officer, PRA Health Sciences, Ken Accardi, CEO & Founder, Ancota, and Dmitry Kaminskiy, General Partner at Deep Knowledge Group, Giuseppe Perale, Professor of Regenerative Medicine, USI, Thomas Clozel, CEO & Founder, OWKIN, British futurist Nick Jankel, and many others.

Author

 **Trond Arne Undheim** is a futurist, podcaster, venture partner at Antler, ecosystem evangelist at Tulip, nonresident Senior Fellow at the Atlantic Council, and co-founder of Yegii. He has experience from public health consulting, including projects on infectious disease like Ebola and HIV/AIDS.

He was a Senior Lecturer in Global Economics and Management at the MIT Sloan School of Management and has conducted foresight work at the Norwegian Board of Technology and at the EU. A former Director of MIT Startup Exchange, Director of Standards Strategy & Policy at Oracle, and National Expert for e-Government at the European Commission, he holds a Ph.D. on the future of work and the role of artificial intelligence and cognition. He is a 5x author, having penned *Future Tech* (2021), *Pandemic Aftermath* (2020), *Disruption Games* (2020), and *Leadership From Below* (2002), before he wrote *Health Tech* (2021). Trond is also a serial entrepreneur who founded a business incubator, a think tank, and a consulting firm. He hosts two podcasts, Augmented—the industry 4.0 podcast—and Futurized—thoughts on our emerging future. Trond is based in Wellesley, MA.

Introduction— Why Health Tech Is Beginning to Transform Public Health

Global healthcare will change drastically in the next decade due to key technologies, social dynamics, and systemic shifts that are already in motion. However, shaping the future requires being aware of the opportunities and able to capitalize on them to one's family and the community's benefit.

Health tech can be part of the solution, but tracking the right startups and influencers takes know-how. The grand challenges of our time demand that we coordinate better than ever before. Social movements can both accelerate and slow down change.

Health systems across the world need a reboot, with private partnerships and new governance paradigms that have global reach but local legitimacy, but exactly how can this be done considering the collective action problem and complexity involved?

Thomas Jefferson writes: "...No society can make a perpetual constitution, or even a perpetual law. The earth belongs always to the living generation" (Jefferson, 1789). Jefferson believed that a country's constitution should be rewritten, or at least fundamentally re-examined and adjusted, every 19 years. A constitution has a sort of planned obsolescence. This is analogous to how we might better approach health tech. It needs to be reconsidered holistically. In fact, a health tech reboot might be needed more often than that. This book will explore how and why such an overhaul might benefit health systems.

1. The Complex History of Public Health

In Chapter 1, I take you on a brief tour of the complex history of public health. In the process, I raise a set of questions: what is the legacy of public health throughout human history and where are we at this moment? Why is public health so complicated to get right? What are the major challenges right now? What are the causes of disease? How have humans attempted to prevent it? What are the major successes?

For the latter part of this century, public health efforts have largely gone into efforts around vaccination to reduce epidemics, attempting to control infectious diseases, intervening in family planning (through encouraging and developing contraceptives), and monitoring and curbing tobacco use, mostly because of the strain it puts on the health system. These efforts have largely (with some notable exceptions) been carried out with little concern for the cultural practices surrounding human choices. That approach, while, at times, effective in medical terms, has faced backlash in terms of social dynamics. There are signs that new approaches are needed, even to solve these classical problem sets, let alone to solve emerging challenges of even more far-reaching consequences.

Historically, the largest global public health efforts have been applied to infectious diseases such as HIV/AIDS, tuberculosis, malaria, childhood immunizations, cholera, Ebola, yellow fever, measles, polio and Zika and pandemics (influenza, coronavirus). However, other notable foci are antibiotic resistance, the prescription drug/opioid crisis, and access to fresh water. It is not immediately obvious how each of these topics rose in prominence. In Chapter 1, I explain why they are linked to national public health and how these issues also have risen and sunk in importance due to a host of other factors such as lobbying by the industry, social movements, political concerns, as well as technological developments.

It is far too easy to think of public health as the history of national health priorities. However, that would be revisionist history. Of key importance, although typically under-communicated, is the community health efforts (by doctors, nurses, educators, volunteers, organizations, and health advocates).

How public health ties in with promoting good health, quality of life, and longevity is another, more emerging story. There, again, historically, the state has had a lot to say about it, but these days, there is a wide-ranging awareness of the many choices that are becoming available—at least among the affluent.

Conventional wisdom is that there are eight or so core functions of public health (monitor, diagnose, plan, educate, mobilize, assure, enforce, and assess). How is that so? I assess these functions particularly as it begins to intersect (and sometimes not at all) with emerging behavioral insight. When there is no match, public health efforts run the risk of being not only questioned but even quelled.

2. Digital Health Tech

In Chapter 2, I discuss to what extent digital health tech has solutions for the wide set of public health challenges identified so far. Then, I briefly identify each of the technologies of the moment. This chapter hones-in on five specific technologies: AI, wearables, digital therapeutics, social media, and telemedicine. Each is highly software enabled—somewhat connected—and have the potential to increasingly interact in life-changing ways. I describe how each technology is embedded with a complex set of forces of disruption (sci-tech, business models, policy & regulation, social dynamics, and the environment). I assess what each technology is capable of today, and what it might achieve in the next 3–5 years, when applied to public health challenges. I include a brief investor's guide to each technology section. Lastly, synthetic biology (CRISPR-CaS, personalized medicine, mRNA vaccines, etc.), sensors, robots, and neutraceuticals will be handled in other chapters.

3. The Health Innovation Players of the Next Decade

In the current healthcare system, the established professions (doctors, nurses) and institutions (hospitals, insurers, and pharma industry) rule the scene. However, in the emerging healthcare landscape, a new set of actors emerge as reformers, innovators, and game changers. In Chapter 4, I portray the movers and shakers in the healthcare system of the future: startups, intrapreneurs, engineers, patients, and service providers. First off, once the frustrations with the existing system become too hard to bear, intrapreneurs start to emerge on the scene, challenging status quo and suggesting ideas, concepts, and even technologies to remedy or even gradually transform healthcare from the inside. Second, startups are starting to truly chip at healthcare, not from one angle but from literally hundreds of angles, everything from the ways certain procedures are carried out, to the relationship between various providers, to the patient relationship itself. To some extent startups partner with the industry, whether pharma, medical device, or other types of service providers in the health field. Research hospitals have become playgrounds for change, given that they stand at the intersection of the hospital world and the innovation spinout activity of engineering and medical labs.

Lately, patients, or patient organized input, has emerged as a third force. No longer content just to pick providers, patients to a greater extent come with their own suggested treatment plans and detailed knowledge of the entire chain of events in a healthcare career. Which startups are breaking new ground in technology? Who are the tech influencers, emerging scientists, and experts? Which think tanks are influential? What research hospitals and university laboratories are driving the field forward?

4. The Disruption of Healthcare and Emerging Health Tech Solutions

In Chapter 4, I look in-depth at the health tech solutions that work and those that do not. Certain health tech measures, tools (basic medical devices gradually being upgraded and digitally enhanced), processes, and innovations are already working well, and others are still in their infancy (AI, wearables, robotics, sensors, and digital therapeutics). This brings the controversial yet important question: to what extent is health tech the solution? Because: if health tech is more of the solution, why aren't we investing even more in it to make quicker gains? The technologies of the moment include AI, digital therapeutics, synthetic biology including mRNA vaccines, sensors, robots, wearables, population health, personalized medicine, neutraceuticals, electronic health records (EHRs), and telehealth.

Transformational innovation is underway both due to hardware and software upgrades and mostly their interaction. Operating this new equipment and managing new workflows are complex. Realizing what the opportunities are is important, whether as healthcare professionals, patients, or as health wellness consumers. Evaluating the healthcare you are being given to see if it really is the best there on the market is also becoming an important patient and caregiver skill, at times professionalized to family healthcare consultants. However, not all can afford to hire such a function or would want to outsource such a key competency.

The chapter provides a way to navigate the emerging technologies and make the best choices, looking at what startups and corporate providers have available now and in the next few years, across a plethora of disease areas and domains of healthcare, including primary care, surgery, and non-acute care, including elderly care.

5. Grand Health Challenges

In Chapter 5, I take you through the grand health challenges of our time: pandemics, aging, and preventive healthcare. We may not agree on the priorities between them and what to do about it, but most of the grand health challenges of our time are well established. Pandemics, aging, health system complexity, building or maintaining a welfare state, each is an exceedingly difficult challenge. However, there are promising paths to take in each area, guided by tech, innovation, and emerging healthcare domain knowledge.

Emerging actors and public health initiatives that matter a lot include these foundations, among others: Gates Foundation, Kaiser Foundation, Novo Nordisk Foundation, and the Wellcome Trust. Each has a plethora of future-oriented activity and examples of demonstrable impact on many of these grand challenges. But the question still remains, given all the negative fallout on a societal level—and obviously for individuals as they are waiting for breakthroughs—is the existing activity enough? What is the real challenge here—technology, policy, or individual choices?

6. The Gargantuan Global Fight for Interoperability

In this chapter, I tackle the single most important technology battle in healthcare, that of interoperability. For 30 years, public health advocates, startups, non-profits, and others, have been arguing that there are too many barriers to sharing health information. During this time, a few vendors have pushed back, stating privacy concerns but even more protecting their monopolies. Will this battle be resolved in this decade? What are the consequences if it is not resolved? First, I outline the various standardization alternatives available and explain how standardization has been used as a tool in every other industry. I particularly look at the US and Europe. Second, I explore the global fight for interoperability in EHRs, digital health apps, and beyond. Finally, I outline some principles that should constitute the backbone of any future-oriented health tech strategy, whether they pertain to EHRs, mobile apps, or other solutions that require interoperability.

7. Natural Wellness—An Individual Path?

In Chapter 7, I look at the opportunities and pitfalls of the natural wellness approach. Can we fight off disease by being attentive, eating well, getting exercise, and living supremely healthy lives?

Natural wellness has emerged as a formidable force of consumer-oriented health power. Natural immunity. Neutraceuticals. Microbiome. Autogenous training. The power of positive thinking. Where are we with these at this point in time? What does the evidence show? Who are the key actors? What are the pathbreaking products to watch out for?

All of these are interesting and provide, perhaps needed, corrective to static and conventional thinking. But is it enough? And what are the downsides?

Even more importantly, how can some of the lasting lessons of natural wellness start to seep into public health efforts (and not remain as merely individual responses from the wealthy)? How can the segments of the global population in greatest need also benefit from natural wellness—and are they already?

Lastly, can natural wellness be combined with traditional medical science in the way that many previously alternative medicine treatments have been (somewhat) incorporated in contemporary medicine (e.g. acupuncture and physical therapy).

8. How to Come to Grips with Anti-Vaxxers without Becoming One?

In Chapter 8, we handle the urgent and sensitive questions surrounding vaccines and anti-vaxxers.

Vaccines are an old remedy that has got miles to go and new approaches will be in the clinic shortly, due to COVID-19, notably Moderna's and Pfizer's mRNA vaccines which build on advances in synthetic biology. However, vaccine skepticism has arguably never been higher, and some of the reasoning behind this is sound, due to political influence and incentive that may currently trump sanguine regulatory considerations under more normal circumstances.

What is the track record of vaccines throughout human history? Smallpox. Flu. Polio. Cholera. Emerging vaccine types. Viruses with no current vaccines. A brief synopsis of the history and current status of vaccines around the world reveal a mixed picture—from the relative success of the polio vaccine to the mixed success of the tuberculosis vaccine and others.

Governments such as Russia, China, and the US are each about to (or have already) issued vaccines before the traditional safety protocols have been carried out, citing emergency use provisions. Does this help or hurt the cause? What is the social dynamics around vaccines and anti-vaxxers in this decade?

The anti-vaxx movement has gone from a relatively fringe phenomenon to, quite possibly, a double-digit force in the population. How did this happen? Will it be sustained? If so, what are the consequences?

Who are the anti-vaxxers of today? What types do they fall into? What is the research on this social movement (and individual attitude)?

9. Platforms of Health—The Urgency of a Health System Reboot

In Chapter 9, we look at the need and prospects for a system reboot in health governance and a shift in emphasis toward the edge, meaning a distributed delivery of healthcare where the end consumer is empowered by interoperable platforms and applications that require few or no software coding skills to build and operate. System reboot is a proposal for systemic change in national and global health based on public/private partnerships and new governance paradigms that have global reach but local legitimacy. The chapter charts a health policy proposal that encompasses how global health now must be part of national security policy.

However, to enact this reboot, which will allow certain changes to take place, but will reinvigorate other elements, the medical profession needs to allow it (or be convinced) and technology needs to become fully self-service while still connected to the major institutional nodes that will make sensors and monitoring effective and connected. Healthcare needs highly advanced multi-level governance to work well, at global national, regional, and local levels. Global healthcare needs to be connected to diplomatic, foreign aid, security, research, and military capability in a networked fashion, with immediate response capability worldwide, regardless of where the health infraction occurs and from whom or what. National healthcare needs to be decoupled from short-term political concerns and needs to go into a decade plus long planning cycle that is protected from election friction. Regional healthcare needs to be viewed in connection with, and should be run by, the institutions that deliver the care, not as an administrative level.

Local healthcare must be upgraded to certain minimum requirements around the world, with sensory and alert capability at speeds and sophistication that almost matches that of the most advanced healthcare system. Otherwise, we get a race to the middle where nobody is happy with the level of care or the ability to respond to public health crises. For this to work, highly advanced technology sensor networks as well as financial incentives need to be put in place, that bypass existing local, regional, or national constraints.

Finally, distributed healthcare ("the edge") must be highly tech enabled so that personalized responsibility for one's own health is not only an option for the wealthy but for anyone. To make that happen, we need to make progress in Augmented Reality, IoT-enabled health devices, Personalized medicine, and Remote population health monitoring specifically. Costs for the above need to be drastically brought down through financing R&D, collaboration, and executing joint procurement initiatives across countries and governance levels.

Capturing the Opportunity Window before It Closes

In the conclusion, I ask how can we capture the opportunity window of a healthcare system reboot before it closes? While it's true that we have an enormous opportunity at hand, that could also have been said for earlier phases in human history, only to experience the change window closed. Health tech may this decade alone provide the biggest opportunity to transform healthcare that we have seen in a century. That window may also close, and once it does, we are stuck with pockets of excellence and pockets of mediocrity (or worse), which is only damaging to the whole system over time.

The system reboot suggested will encompass changes to governance structures and processes at all levels—global, national, and regional—and will take participation from all sectors (government, private, and nonprofit). It takes the admission that we have previously been on the wrong path.

Fortunately, the possibility to conduct a reasonable amount of healthcare implementation "magic" is very real. This opportunity for a dynamic revamp hinges on the technology-enabled business models and incentives that must be put into place. Any creative health tech solutions must have short-time horizons for visible return of investment. The plenty for investors—governments, high net worth individuals, startups—will be financial, but socially these rewards will be measurable in millions of lives, billions of health span years, and increased lifespan for the world population as a whole. In the case of the current coronavirus pandemic, this could hasten a return to a new normal.

Reference

Jefferson, T. (1789) 'Letter from Thomas Jefferson to James Madison', Paris, 6 September 1789. Available at: https://jeffersonpapers.princeton.edu/selected-documents/thomas-jefferson-james-madison (Accessed 15 February 2021).

Chapter 1

The Complex History of Global Public Health Tech Innovation

Can Public Health Be Defined—And What If Not?

According to the *Oxford Textbook of Global Public Health* (2015), public health is the art and science of preventing disease, prolonging life, and promoting health through the organized efforts of society. The goal of public health, correspondingly, is the biological, physical, and mental well-being of all members of society. Sound right? Unfortunately, that is not the whole picture. Arguably, public health is both more and less than that.

First off, there is not necessarily anything particularly *public* about health. Wellness has become a major thrust in health and can be an entirely private endeavor even though it may be influenced by the (public and private) forces of disruption surrounding it. Huge swaths of public health systems are also privatized, which complicates the notion of the "public" aspects, notably in the US. Hygiene, which plays a massive role in health, is also largely a private choice, although it is socially conditioned.

Second, public health has always been connected to innovative technologies, which is arguably interlinked with art and science, but is also its own thing entirely because it emphasizes the application and implementation of specific approaches more than "art" (which juxtaposed with science makes health sound fanciful, magical, and difficult) and "science" (which makes it sound so theoretical and complex).

DOI: 10.4324/9781003178071-1

1

In reality, public health is neither magical nor theoretical. Instead, it is emergent, contingent, and ever-changing. I am not sure pretending it is not so is such a fruitful approach. The challenge with that fact is, among other things, that it flies in the face of any traditional strategic goal of focusing resources on specific targets. That also backfires for other reasons because once you focus on a specific disease, you are bound to interfere with national priorities which undoubtedly are (trying) to encompass and target a much wider set of diseases that are prevalent across their population.

Third, there is absolutely no agreement on which diseases to prevent, whether prolonging life is a goal in and of itself, and exactly what "promoting health" would mean across different cultures. At times in the history of public health, government or even powerful non-state actor's promotion of health has been moralistic and demeaning, it has adversely affected (or ignored) specific populations (the poor, blacks, children, women, LGBTQ, the elderly, the African continent, the mentally ill, etc.).

Fourth, and very importantly, health is rarely (or has at least rarely been in a historical context) about all of society. In fact, health is all about wealth in more than one sense. It is, arguably, the biggest economic machine in the world. As such, its successful implementation skews toward the wealthier states, groups, and is also a source of both massive (and necessary) investments and running expenses on behalf of governments and large employers as well as a tremendous source of income for the same. Health is, in that sense, the biggest boon in the history of mankind. The healthy are wealthy and the wealthy are healthy.

Lastly, public health is often so more concerned with the short-term because health problems are urgent, affect human lives, and immediate actions are required to cope with them, yet, the causes of disease, and doctrines about how to deal with them, or live with or around them, have evolved over years, even decades (Perdiguero et al., 2001). In fact, actions carried out in the name of public health can be highly controversial, can have differential effect on each subpopulation affected, and are highly culturally and contextually sensitive.

During the influenza epidemic in 1918, a public health-oriented action taken in Alicante, a Spanish city located in the Mediterranean coast, ended with the demolition of an entire area of the city and the expulsion of its inhabitants. In November 2020, the entire mink population of Denmark (home of the largest mink industry in the world) was about to be killed off by the Danish government. This was due to the fear of a mutation of COVID-19 that would render vaccines inefficient. However, the government had to reverse course having killed off all infected minks only when realizing this may have been an overreaction.

At the end of the day, that Oxford definition which seemed so simple, contains within it a huge element of vision and is slightly unrealistic as a description of the history of public health, of its contemporary form, and perhaps even misleading in terms of its future. I will need a whole book to unpack why this happened and how and which innovations potentially can change the picture in the decade ahead of us. I am not too worried about the lack of a clear definition—this is what characterizes most fields of rapid innovation. I do, however, worry for folk who spend so much time looking for a definition or the perfect policy approach, that they have no time to innovate. That is why I wrote this book, which I hope will provoke and inspire innovation and change, not just among startups and founders but also spike intrapreneurs in governments, among non-state actors and corporations—as well as social innovation from the ground up.

How Old Is Public Health as an Approach?

International health diplomacy is certainly not new. The quarantine practices of European states in the 14th century might have marked the beginning of modern public health. However, there was broader Eurasian awareness that health effects crossed national borders throughout the Middle Ages. What is also the case is that true international coordination and cooperation on health did not begin that early (Fidler, 2001). But before diplomacy, there was dominance. The colonial period was one of the internationalist expansion with a quite different aim, that of territorial and demographic dominance. Coupled with that often came a countercurrent of humanism, interspersed with patriarchal ideas of applying Western "quick fixes" to the world's health problems. Typically, this mix of altruism, compassion, and (at times) well-meaning intervention, ended up badly, for a myriad of reasons. Either way, such paternalistic interventions meant that innovation has not always been a force for good, which is a reminder for contemporary exploits as well, whether they occur in emerging economies or in poorer neighborhoods closer to home (Figure 1.1).

Colonial Period—Using the Colonies as Laboratories for Tech Experimentation

It has been convincingly argued that the colonial period was characterized by outsourcing testing of new approaches to the "laboratory of the colonies" (Keller, 2007, p. 65). In the extreme, in French Muslim colonies in North Africa, it has meant using psychiatry as a weapon in the arsenal of colonial racism to tame and treat "savages". The conventional view at the time was to clearly distinguish between moderns and primitives, an idea which now largely is debunked, although it pops up now and again in race discussions and debates

COLONIAL MEDICINE

HYGIENE FOCUS
DISCRIMINATION
TECH EXPERIMENTATION

INTERNATIONAL HEALTH

BASIC STANDARDIZATION
DISEASE FOCUS
EPIDEMICS

GLOBAL HEALTH

GRAND CHALLENGES
INTEROPERABILITY
DIGITALIZATION

Figure 1.1   The history of public health tech.

over immigration and France's postcolonial legacy. Arguably, there are also remnants of this logic in the US when you consider the blatant health discrimination in terms of legacy effects, access, and healthspan still faced by blacks or Hispanic immigrants. Whichever way you look at it, colonial medicine was heavily focused on broad sweep, ethically questionable measures addressing public hygiene as a path to lessening disease burdens.

The Birth of International Public Health in the Mid-19th Century

International regimes for public health were set up beginning in the mid-19th century, starting with the International Sanitary Conference of 1851 which was centered on whether to support and standardize cholera quarantine measures.

At the time, the understanding of infectious disease was quite limited. There was widespread belief that plague, yellow fever, cholera, malaria, and typhus were all the same disease manifesting itself in different ways. The 1851 event did lead to a majority decision to affirm cholera quarantines, but few countries ratified the agreement, so on paper, the effect was nil. However, the seed was sown that health was an appropriate topic for international discussions and treaties. The Venice Conference of 1897 was exclusively concerned with plague. A full 14 of these conferences were held until the World Health Organization (WHO) finally was established in 1948 (Howard-Jones, 1975).

Other topics that have been of importance to international health policy throughout the past 150 years, beyond infectious diseases, include labor conditions, transboundary water pollution, international trade in narcotic drugs and alcohol, and occupational health and safety.

As can be readily understood from that variety, developing any kind of sustained competency in public health or health policy has meant straddling impossibly diverse domains that require different types of expertise to succeed. Predictably, and for these reasons, even though it represents potentially the biggest business of all, health policy is often viewed as disjointed, at times disconnected from economic policy by the decision makers "that matter". Creating a shift in understanding would be fundamental if we believe that health is to become a top political and economic priority and if we want to see a sea change in outcomes.

Influential Non-state Actors Begin to Appear

Throughout this early period of internationalization of (public) health, non-state actors, such as the Rockefeller Foundation, the International Union Against Tuberculosis, and the International Bureau Against Alcoholism, have had pivotal impact, too (Fidler, 2001). That trend continues throughout the next century as well, with new actors entering the stage.

The limiting factor of international efforts of any kind, or of the wish for global mandates, is of course the threat (to nation states) of reducing or at least (potentially) eroding their sovereignty. However, there have (at times) been voices advocating for starting to see health as a human right which got enshrined in WHO's constitution, although that vision remains unfulfilled (Fidler, 2001).

Bismarck's imperial Germany first introduced mandatory social insurances on a grand scale (Kuhnle & Sander, 2010), including sickness insurance in 1883, an industrial accident scheme in 1884 and old age and invalidity insurance in 1889. Other European countries followed, some early on (Austria) while others comparatively late (the Netherlands), and in Scandinavia, it has become a key part of their national identity (Van Kersbergen, 2016). In fact, welfare states can be characterized as generous institutions that allocate rights and responsibilities in quite distinct ways, albeit with at least three different models, the liberal

(Australia, US, and UK), social democratic (Scandinavia) and conservative (Germany, Austria) model (Esping-Andersen, 1990, p. 55). Welfare states are not necessarily egalitarian in the sense that they distribute evenly or even redistribute, although that tends to be the effect at times, given that certain groups use welfare services more than others.

The Overconfident Public Health Community of the Early 20th Century

During World War I, a pandemic influenza (the 1918 influenza) raged Europe and the US, which had devastating consequences on the world. It lasted almost 3 years and infected over 500 million people across the globe. Estimates of deaths caused by the influenza range between 50 and 100 million. However, because of the war effort, we don't really know enough about what happened, even how many died from the disease. Tracking of the disease was lacking and media reporting was poor (arguably because journalists did not want to hinder the war effort of their respective countries).

During the early interwar era, the international public health community had gradually acquired confidence in its ability to alleviate human suffering by drastically reducing disease. In the UK, specialist clinics had been established which treated common illnesses and advised on nutrition and fitness. For the first time, there was growing confidence and (strikingly) near consensus about the etiology and epidemiology of many diseases and the physiological conditions and socio-economic factors contributing to human illness (Dubin & Weindling, 2009, pp. 56–80).

Particularly in the early years following the war, The Pasteur Institute, a private, non-profit foundation established already in 1897, whose mission is to help prevent and treat diseases, mainly those of infectious origin, through research, teaching, and public health initiatives, played an outsized international role, reflecting France's influence at the time, some of which continues today. Its current international network includes 32 institutes around the world, located in 25 countries on five continents (most notably across Europe, Africa, Asia, and South America), linked by missions of research, public health, and education. The first such overseas branch was established in 1891 in Ho Chi Minh City, then called Saigon, in Vietnam (Racine, 2014).

Founder Louis Pasteur's greatest breakthroughs in modern medicine at the time stemmed from his research on bacteria, his contributions to the germ theory of disease, and the methods he developed for sterilization aimed at reducing pathogens in food, a process eventually called pasteurization, as well as vaccines to control and treat anthrax and rabies.

The League of Nations—A First Effort to Manage International (Health) Relations

At the Paris Peace Conference of 1919, the Allies established the first-ever world organization, the League of Nations. The League would lay the foundations of our modern system of global healthcare control. The League mobilized international action that by 1921 had largely managed to contain the spread of the typhus epidemic which was ravaging countries in Central and Eastern Europe, through mass examinations, de-lousing and bathing and the imposition of quarantines.

The very first UK Ministry of Health was created through the Ministry of Health Act 1919, consolidating under a single authority the medical and public health functions of central government and culminated in the establishment of the National Health Service (NHS) in 1948, which seeks to provide free healthcare and medical services. In the UK, the NHS is readily considered to be one of the best in the world and, an institution that makes people proud to be British. In fact, the NHS beat the Armed Forces, the Royal Family, and the BBC in a 2013 popularity contest.

Rockefeller Foundation Takes to Disease Eradication in Latin America

As a result of two successful disease eradication efforts in Havana and Panama at the turn of the century, between 1918 and 1940 Latin America became a testing ground for an ambitious and controversial effort to eradicate disease. In reality, the support for this effort, led by the Rockefeller Foundation, was grounded in a budding fear of Latin America infecting or reinfecting the US. The additional effect was to shift the academic and technical center of influence from France to the US (Cueto & Weindling, 2009, pp. 222–243).

American Red Cross Shapes Post-WW II Health Focus in Europe

American influence in international health organizations was exercised through the powerful corporate philanthropic organizations of the American Red Cross and the Rockefeller Foundation. An offshoot of the former, The League of Red Cross Societies, known today as the International Federation of Red Cross and Red Crescent Societies (IFRC), was founded in 1919, the year after the end of

World War I, and won the Nobel Peace Prize in 1963. The League's aid work in countries where the populations had suffered most severely during the war was followed by extensive aid work in peacetime when flooding, droughts, and other natural disasters have led to hunger, need, and death (Nobel Media AB, 2020).

The Civilizing Process—And the Creation of a Hygiene Police

Norbert Elias' 1939 book *The Civilizing Process* (Elias, 2000) charts the social development of the state as a mental and political construct that profoundly changes human behavior. The implications for public health would be that the observable collective patterns, including the European psychic *habitus*, which begins to repress the bodily functions, and develop prudishness which, in turn, creates, the intimacy sphere, and a particular view of hygiene and manners connected to being a "civilized person" don't derive fully in any direct way from the individual intentions of the participants.

We may have come to call it "personal health", but its impetus is collective in nature, as a response to danger (and increased probability) of an early death, although it can equally be seen as a response to, and a reaction to, class struggles and inter-class distinctions (Douglas, 1966). These civilizing tendencies are, in Elias' mind, particularly European and become the motivation for specific versions of population health that value hygiene, sanitation, and cleanliness as the answer to eradicating disease (e.g. note the growing obsession with hand washing throughout the modern period). Arguably, this tendency also has to do with the rise of engineering and advances in the technology (Goudsblom, 1986). For sure, the internalization of medical materialism's strongly worded "advice" does have a significant effect on most people's behavior, rightly or wrongly so.

In Elias' mind, Western culture developed particularly sophisticated and rigid institutions apparent for instance in its decisive technological advances when compared to other cultures (Goudsblom, 1986). Interestingly, hygiene is typically what we assume separates the Middle Ages from the Modern Era (an interesting thing to ponder as coronavirus rages across the world and might institute a whole other hygienic regime that might, in Elias' line of thinking, again usher us into another era).

However, following Elias, as well as French contemporary sociologist Pierre Bourdieu, a "filthy" versus "clean" hygienic habitus, is equally what one historically, at least in France, and perhaps in the UK and elsewhere, would use to distinguish the working classes from the managerial and upper classes, as illustrated by the varying etiquette rules for eating, drinking, spitting, and sneezing that can still to this day to some extent be readily observed as variable across socio-economic groups or geography.

What that tendency does, however, is institute a level of control over human conduct that structures our lives into insiders and outsiders based on the hygienic practices we grew up with, given that these habits are learned early and stick with us long. What seemingly (outwardly) is self-compulsion is better explained as socially conduced and maintained through differential socialization.

The Beveridge Report Ushers the Modern Welfare State

With the outbreak of World War II, international health work came almost to a standstill. However, national efforts continued. In the UK, the 1942 Beveridge Report identified the five "giant evils" of "want, disease, ignorance, squalor and idleness", recommended universal insurance coverage, and a postwar Labor government codified the British welfare state partly as a result of that report, although it has little to say about medical care and nothing whatever to say about disease. Contrary to popular belief, Sir Beveridge argued the opposite of the Nanny state and said "the individual should recognise the duty to be well" (Musgrove, 2000).

The Creation of the WHO

The Constitution of the WHO, as a special agency of the United Nations (UN) was signed on July 22, 1946 by representatives of 51 Members of the UN and of ten other nations, and the organization came into force in 1948 (WHO, 2020). WHO fairly immediately starts to play an essential role in the global governance of health and disease; due to its core global functions of establishing, monitoring, and enforcing international norms and standards, and coordinating multiple actors toward common goals. For the most part, the organization has worked on a mix of communicable diseases like influenza and HIV, and non-communicable diseases like cancer and heart disease, often with confusing sets of priorities and mixed messages.

Its mandate and efforts are not without controversy. First off, it relies on the transparency of its member states—who tend to minimize the impact of pathogens when they appear. This happened during Ebola outbreaks and it happened curing coronavirus pandemic (Ravelo, 2020). The WHO has been accused of getting disease priorities wrong and has, at times, faced the same bureaucracy criticism as other parts of the UN system. Moreover, working with

194 member states, across six regions, and from more than 150 offices may not be the ideal structure if one wants to have a strong policy voice in Washington, in Brussels, or in Beijing as the coronavirus pandemic of 2020 shows. However, it is not incapable of change. The review of the West Africa Ebola outbreak recommended reforms, which led to the creation of WHO's health emergencies program. The current director general has also had a transformation agenda since he started in 2017.

Postwar Welfare States

Postwar industrialization is truly when public health became a central concern of government policy. In fact, public health flourished after World War II with the growth of modern welfare states and the development of social welfare systems in European countries and much later far beyond. Social medicine became a term in vogue (Sand, 1952). The narrative was one of progress, sanitation, and control (Porter, 1999).

The techno-economic innovation paradigms of economist E.F. Schumacher in the mid-1960s gained considerable prominence in the 1970s, after the publication of his 1973 treatise, *Small is Beautiful*. Schumacher argued that capitalism brought higher living standards at the cost of deteriorating culture. Instead, he was an advocate for people-centered technology, at times called "appropriate technology", creating a movement toward small-scale, locally affordable, decentralized, energy-efficient, and locally autonomous approaches (Morefield, 2019).

Schumacher's way was a novel model for technological development which gained favor among funding agencies in the 1980s and formed the techno-centric structure of the global health enterprise today. Those kinds of technology policies fit into and were enthusiastically adopted into neoliberal reforms underway in the 1970s agencies such as the US Agency for International Development (USAID) and others (Morefield, 2019).

For the latter part of this century, public health efforts have largely gone into efforts around vaccination to reduce epidemics, attempting to control infectious diseases, intervening in family planning (through encouraging and developing contraceptives), and monitoring and curbing tobacco use, mostly because of the strain it puts on the health system (Parker & Sommer, 2010). These efforts have largely (with some notable exceptions) been carried out with little concern for the cultural practices surrounding human choices. That approach, while, at times, effective in medical terms, has faced backlash in terms of social dynamics. There are signs that new approaches are needed, even to solve these classical problem sets, let alone to solve emerging challenges of even more far-reaching consequences.

There is another reason to be critical toward the notion of "appropriate technologies" and that is the issue of leapfrogging. Clearly, if we only deploy old technologies, the assumption is that each country and setting necessarily needs to go through the same stepwise evolution as Western societies, or similarly that poor urban neighborhoods in Western cities need to do the same. However, as the introduction of cell phones in Africa famously illustrates, there is no need to go via landlines. Hence, what is an appropriate technology for a specific setting might be a more complex question that requires knowledge of culturally specific practices on the ground—and partnerships that could yield even opportunities to truly innovate in relatively resource-poor settings.

The WHO's "Health for All by 2000" campaign starting in 1977 deployed technologies such as oral rehydration solutions, food supplements, antibiotics, vector control agents, water pumps, and latrines—known to be effective, and inexpensive in the Western world, or at least could be adapted and simplified for such exportation to the developing world. However, despite some early success, the "Health for All by 2000" campaign was largely a failure (Malkin, 2007). Similarly, the" tunnel vision focus" on AIDS of the early 2000s (Farmer & Garrett, 2007; Russell, 2013), for all its success in remedying that disease, might be similarly short sighted because it "drew attention away from other health problems of the poor, weakened public health systems, contributed to a brain drain, and failed to reach those most in need".

Contemporary Developments

Current public health topics are as diverse as the danger of arsenic in drinking water, asthma among children and adults, the re-emergence of cholera, increasing cancer rates and other chronic diseases, AIDS, malaria, and hepatitis, the crises faced by displaced or refugee populations to reproductive health and rights.

The role of globalization upon public health has also been profound in that the world's interconnectedness, characterized by increased population mobility, information technology advances, environmental change, and financial flows, and has profound impacts on health determinants and outcomes (Lee, 2015).

The role of private foundations, particularly the outsized role of the Gates Foundation is also something to watch. At the World Economic Forum in Davos, Switzerland in January 2003, Bill Gates Jr. announced a $200 million dollar grant partnership between the Gates Foundation and the US National Institutes for Health to address what he called the "Grand Challenges in Global Health".

The UN's Sustainable Development Goal 3 (SDG 3) targets, Technology and Global Public Health, formulated in 2015, aims "To ensure healthy lives and promote well-being for all at all ages".

Global health is currently being shaped by the development of remote-sensing technologies. Drones are beginning to be used for health surveillance and management. This monitoring at-a-distance introduces new challenges for jurisdictional control over a territory as well as opportunities to bypass territorial limitations at the same time. Similarly, health is also being reshaped by emerging cyberinfrastructures that enable (somewhat) secure sharing of health data and to some extent health transactions over the internet. Both drones and cyberinfrastructure impact health governance (Peckham & Sinha, 2019).

There is considerable tension within the donor community and policy circles internationally and domestically regarding the relative investment levels in population wide health initiatives (healthcare, water supply, and sanitation) versus new technologies and capacity-building in science and technology (Acharya, 2007). Broadband is another matter entirely because it enables telehealth which is part of that same discussion. Small devices (e.g. hand-held molecular diagnostic tools) could make a big difference in specific communities but might also become unsuccessful or downright detrimental unless tied to a larger healthcare system that can actually act on the diagnostics.

Evolving Disease Focus—And Moving beyond Diseases

Historically, the largest global public health efforts have been applied to infectious diseases such as HIV/AIDS, tuberculosis, malaria, childhood immunizations, cholera, Ebola, yellow fever, measles, polio, Zika, and pandemics. However, other notable foci are antibiotic resistance, prescription drug/opioid crisis, and access to fresh water. It is not immediately obvious how each of these topics rose in prominence, except to point out that although they linked to national public health and have risen and sunk in importance due to a host of other factors, such as lobbying by industry, social movements, political concerns, as well as technological developments.

It is far too easy to think of public health as the history of national health priorities. However, that would be revisionist history. Of key importance, although typically under-communicated, is the community health efforts (by doctors, nurses, educators, volunteers, organizations, and advocates).

How public health ties in with promoting good health, quality of life and longevity is another, more emerging story. There, again, historically, the state has had a lot to say about it, but these days, there is a wide-ranging awareness of the many choices that are becoming available—at least among the affluent. For that reason, I dedicate Chapter 6 to the natural wellness approach, which is increasingly a factor to bring into the public health discussion.

How Could COVID-19 Happen in Our Technologically Advanced World

Why did COVID happen? I am not alone in tracing this back to environmental degradation (which, in turn, heightens the probability of zoonotic diseases), poor pandemic preparedness in key countries around the world, and to cultural factors that slowed down traditional public health measures, although I was the first to publish a book to that effect (Undheim, 2020).

What later has emerged adds to the picture. It seems clear that China under-communicated the severity of the disease for months, which may have led to greater worldwide spread without containment. On the other hand, if China didn't manage to contain it, in a globalized world, what other nation would have been able to, even with flight mandates?

Public Health Stagnation over Last 100 Years

I am not sure there even is a discussion any more about whether public health innovation had stagnated, given that most public health measures are hundreds of years old (hand washing, containment, and even disinfection) and are not up with the latest know-how in behavioral psychology and culture (Undheim, 2020). What is happening to healthcare systems around the world as a result? What characterizes countries, cities, or communities with a good versus poor response? Will disparities continue to escalate? Where do we go from here? Will there be a new normal or a new reality? What role has health tech played in the COVID crisis so far and what role is it likely to play in the near and far future?

Wide Ranging Change Set in Motion by COVID

Perhaps the biggest changes from COVID are related to open science, international health cooperation, vaccine developments, and the future of work.

In terms of open science, COVID has spurred the most accelerated pace of sci-tech activity and publishing in decades perhaps in human history. It has also changed the speed of publication of research findings through pre-publications. Much has also been delivered as open science, meaning the licensing costs to view the content has been financed by the institutions themselves or covered by the publishers. The effect has been that scientists have been able to share research findings and potential cures at rapid speed.

International health cooperation is fickle. Much has been made of the failures of WHO. Despite those hiccups, never have nations cooperated more on health. There have not been new treaties signed (yet) but the scope and range of collaboration have increased. Moreover, the travel restrictions and somewhat uncoordinated national responses are likely to create an aftermath of multilateral cleanup and may lead to future treaties. Whether it was Trump's initial China or EU travel bans or the later mutual bans, or even the bans of travel from countries where variants have been discovered (UK, Brazil, South Africa, India and more), travel bans are controversial and of questionable effectiveness. Especially, since the disease has been so poorly monitored and genetically sequenced that no nation knows what variants are in their own countries at any given time.

Vaccine developments have accelerated drastically. Vaccines are likely to be the single most affected technology after the pandemic. While the emergency use authorizations (EUA) may not continue as long as the virus comes under control, the knowledge that vaccines could be developed much faster during a crisis will forever be part of the public consciousness. However, while the promise of vaccine platforms will ensure that the production of vaccines is transformed, there has not been a similar focus on global distribution platforms, the GAVI initiative being the exception.

The future of work is suddenly on everybody's mind and we have each been affected differently. The real question is what will happen once the pandemic is declared to be behind us. During the pandemic, the world's white collar workforce has largely been forced to and have been able to productively work from home. This is due to the advanced digitalization of work processes over the past decades. The same cannot be said for frontline workers although massive changes are underway here as well. Digital factories have been introduced in record time, 3D printing is advancing rapidly, and online shopping and ecommerce have advanced at breakneck speed even in countries where the public was initially hesitant.

Scenarios for the Future of Health Tech

The specific scenarios I see for health tech all involve accelerated innovation, but the degree of transformation will depend on many factors beyond the innovators' control.

In the medium range (5–7 years), COVID is likely to accelerate health tech innovation, specifically startups that innovate in areas adjacent to pandemic impacted fields (healthcare, manufacturing, travel, and remote work).

In the long term (10–25 years), the impact on health tech innovation is less clear. What seems certain is that the concept of telemedicine will go mainstream. Similarly, the notion of personalized medicine will rapidly gain ground as individualized therapies will multiply in numbers, decrease in cost, and

KEY TAKEAWAYS AND REFLECTIONS

1. How would you characterize the history of global public health innovation? Do you agree with the labels I attach (e.g. *colonial medicine* from the 19th century to the mid-20th century, *international health* in the post-World War II era, and *global health* from the late 20th century to the present day and then *individual (health &) wellness* starting to emerge as a parallel track over the past decade)? Are there other and better ways to delineate the history of public health that is more specific on the kinds of innovation taking place in each era?

   _____

2. In your own words, take a moment and reflect on where we are with public health at this moment. Jot down 2–3 sentences and ideally share notes with somebody to discuss, over coffee or just informally in conversation.

   _____

3. There are many answers to the question I'm asking next, but it is important because it leads to wildly diverging solutions: what are, in your mind, the (main) causes of disease? Try to think of the mix of epidemiological, social, and individual determinants of health and disease.

   _____

4. Next, think specifically about how humans have attempted to prevent disease. Think of it at the societal level, then at community level, and finally at the individual level. What are the major successes? Try to boil it down to only three things.

   1. _____

   2. _____

   3. _____

5. The real question everyone grapples with is this: why is public health (innovation) so complicated to get right? I want you to push yourself to make a succinct, one sentence answer.

   _____

6. What are the two major health challenges the globe is facing right now? Next try to pick the one that you personally are the most fascinated by (or perhaps have the most ideas around).

   Note that it is important to have your own answer to that question because it will direct where you put the emphasis in your own innovation work. The deeper and more insightful approach you can come up with, the more impact you will have. No book can answer this question for you as the answer will change depending on the context you find yourself in, and the resources you have available.

---

7. How has technology entered the picture and what are its limitations? Think of one historical technology that had massive impact and then try to think of a contemporary technology which is poised to have a similar (or larger) scale of impact.

---

8. What about social innovation? Name one such innovation you know of. Where do we go from here? How will social innovation scale in this specific case? What are the major barriers?

---

9. The last challenge I want to throw at you is this: I happen to believe that many of the most inspiring and impactful solutions to global public health innovation (which often are local innovations) will come from non-health professionals. Or, at least, they will come from individuals (or groups) who are not traditionally educated in the health field (they are not "professionals"—although they may be community health workers, or they could be former patients, startup founders, students, or even policy makers). As you ponder that question, what would this mean if I'm right? What are the implications for health professionals? What are the knowledge needs for such would-be innovators?

---

will be sought after. Behavioral apps and technologies to monitor diseases will benefit from a growing number of inexpensive sensors that will become pervasive throughout society and in the home, and on our bodies (wearables and implantables).

Conclusion

Historically, the largest global public health efforts have been applied to hygiene, initially fueled by colonialism, and to infectious diseases (from cholera to coronavirus), fueled by the pharma industry. Over the past a few decades, there has been an increasing focus on poverty alleviation, fueled by advances in the scientific understanding of nutrition and a burgeoning supplements industry eager to get in on the game. Given the experimental approaches, we are now seeing in (a) public health education, the beginning focus on (b) innovation within governmental healthcare, and (c) emerging insights on scaling bottom-up local and social innovation, we are likely to see a novel set of issues, approaches, and solutions emerge.

Without a doubt, the current models for innovation are not inclusive enough and the systems not flexible enough to make use even of the greatest ideas and concepts, unless they get help from established players in the healthcare system. This "starter help" is likely a panacea because we all know that the system itself is part of the problem. However, in my assessment, looking at health tech progress over centuries, attempting to bypass the system will only work in liminal cases, and while the breakthroughs might initially seem exciting, they are unlikely to be sustainable over time as there will be system backlash. That's why I believe in a reboot—not trying to cancel the system out but instead resetting and recentering the system as new features are implemented to ensure the features are fully integrated.

In the next chapter, I cover digital health tech: AI, wearables, digital therapeutics, social media, and telemedicine.

References

Acharya, T. (2007) 'Science and technology for wealth and health in developing countries', *Global Public Health*, 2:1, 53–63, Available at: DOI: 10.1080/17441690600673833 (Accessed 18 November 2020).

Brown, T.M. and Cueto, M. (2010) 'The World Health Organization and the World of Global Health', *Routledge Handbook of Global Public Health*, edited by R. Parker and M. Sommer, 18–30. London: Routledge. Available at: https://www.routledge-handbooks.com/doi/10.4324/9780203832721 (Accessed 18 November 2020).

Cueto, M. 1995. 'The Cycles Of Eradication: The Rockefeller Foundation and Latin American Public Health, 1918–1940', *International Health Organisations and Movements, 1918–1939*, P. Weindling (Author), Cambridge Studies in the History of Medicine, 222–243. Cambridge: Cambridge University Press. doi:10.1017/CBO9780511599606.013

Detels, R., Gulliford, M., Karim, Q.A., and Chuan, C. (2015) *Oxford Textbook of Global Public Health*, 6th edn. Oxford: Oxford University Press. Available at: https://oxfordmedicine.com/view/10.1093/med/9780199661756.001.0001/med-9780199661756-chapter-1 (Accessed 18 November 2020).

Douglas, M. (1966) *Purity and Danger: An Analysis of Concepts of Pollution and Taboo.* London: Routledge.

Dubin, M.J. and Weindling, P. (2009) 'The League of Nations Health Organisation'. *International Health Organisations and Movements, 1918–1939*, edited by P. Weindling, 56–80. Cambridge: Cambridge University Press [Online]. Available at: https://www.cambridge.org/core/books/international-health-organisations-and-movements-19181939/91BC233A29984EFCA34A53B3B3DA10F7 (Accessed 18 November 2020)

Elias, N. (2000) *The Civilizing Process. Sociogenetic and Psychogenetic Investigations.* [Orig. 1939]. Rev. ed. Oxford: Blackwell.

Esping-Andersen, G. (1990) *The Three Worlds of Welfare Capitalism.* Cambridge: Polity Press.

Fidler, D.P. (2001) 'The globalization of public health: The first 100 years of international health diplomacy', *Bulletin of the World Health Organization*, 79, 842–849, Available at: https://www.who.int/bulletin/archives/79(9)842.pdf (Accessed 16 November 2020).

Farmer, P. and Garrett, L. (2007, March/April) 'From "Marvelous Momentum" to health care for all: Success is possible with the right programs', Foreign Affairs. Available at: https://www.foreignaffairs.com/articles/2007-03-01/marvelous-momentum-health-care-all-success-possible-right-programs (Accessed 18 November 2020).

Goudsblom, J. (1986) 'Public health and the civilizing process', *The Milbank Quarterly*, 64:2, 160–188, Available at: http://norberteliasfoundation.nl/docs/pdf/Goudsblom-PublicHealth&CP.pdf (Accessed 18 November 2020).

Howard-Jones, N. (1975) 'The scientific background of the International Sanitary Conferences', 1851–1938, *History of International Public Health*, (1), 1–110, Available at: https://apps.who.int/iris/handle/10665/62873 (Accessed 16 November 2020).

Keller, Richard C. 2007. *Colonial Madness: Psychiatry in French North Africa.* University of Chicago Press.

Kuhnle, Stein and Sander, Anne. 2010. 'The Emergence of the Welfare State', *The Oxford Handbook of the Welfare State*, edited by Francis C. Castles, Stephan Leibfried, Jane Lewis, Herbert Obinger, and Christopher Pierson, 61–80. Oxford: Oxford University Press.

Lee, K. (2015) 'Globalization', *Oxford Textbook of Global Public Health*, edited by R. Detels, M. Gulliford, Q.A. Karim, and C. Chuan, 6th edn. Oxford: Oxford University Press. Available at: https://oxfordmedicine.com/view/10.1093/med/9780199661756.001.0001/med-9780199661756-chapter-5 (Accessed 18 November 2020).

Malkin, R. (2007) 'Design of health care technologies for the developing world', *Annual Review of Biomedical Engineering*, 9, 567–587.

Morefield, H. (2017) 'Technology and global health syllabus', Johns Hopkins University. Available at: https://static1.squarespace.com/static/5aba17a97e3c3ac20ca7c78c/t/5b6f1d2b0e2e72e145a37300/1534008622379/Morefield--Tech+and+Global+Health+Syllabus+Fall+2017.pdf (Accessed 18 November 2020).

Morefield, H. (2019) *Developing to Scale: Appropriate Technology and the Making of Global Health*. PhD Dissertation, Johns Hopkins University. Available at: https://jscholarship.library.jhu.edu/handle/1774.2/61972 (Accessed 18 November 2020).

Musgrove, P. (2000) 'Health insurance: The influence of the Beveridge Report', *Bulletin of the World Health Organization*, 78:6, 845, Available at: https://www.who.int/bulletin/archives/78(6)845.pdf (Accessed 18 November 2020).

Nobel Media AB (2020) 'League of Red Cross Societies – Facts', *NobelPrize.org*. Available at: https://www.nobelprize.org/prizes/peace/1963/red-cross-league/facts/ (Accessed 18 November 2020).

Peckham, R. and Sinha, R. (2019) 'Anarchitectures of health: Futures for the biomedical drone', *Global Public Health*, 14:8, 1204–1219, Available at: DOI: 10.1080/17441692.2018.1546335 (Accessed 17 November 2020).

Perdiguero, E., Bernabeu, J., Huertas, R., et al. (2001) 'History of health, a valuable tool in public health', *Journal of Epidemiology & Community Health*, 55, 667–673, Available at: https://jech.bmj.com/content/55/9/667.info (Accessed 18 November 2020).

Porter, D. (1999b) *Health, Civilization, and the State: A History of Public Health from Ancient to Modern Times*. London: Routledge.

Racine, V. (2014) 'The Pasteur Institute (1887-)', Embryo Project Encyclopedia. Available at: http://embryo.asu.edu/handle/10776/8151 (Accessed 18 November 2020).

Ravelo, J.L. (2020) 'Battered with criticism, what's next for WHO?', Devex.com [Online], 18 May 2020. Available at: https://www.devex.com/news/battered-with-criticism-what-s-next-for-who-97257 (Accessed 18 November 2020).

Russell, B.S. (2013) 'The history of medical innovation in global health interventions', Final Term Paper. Introduction to Global Medicine, Harvard Medical School. Available at: http://www.brandon-russell.com/innovation.shtml (Accessed 19 November 2020).

Sand, R. (1952) *The Advance to Social Medicine*. London: Staples Press.

Schumacher, E.F. (2000) *Small Is Beautiful* [Orig 1973]. New York: Harper Collins.

Undheim, Trond Arne (2020). *Pandemic Aftermath: How Coronavirus Changes Global Society*. Austin, TX: Atmosphere Press. Available at: https://www.amazon.com/Pandemic-Aftermath-Coronavirus-Changes-Society/dp/1648261906

Van Kersbergen, K. (2016) 'The Welfare State in Europe', BBVA Open Mind. Available at: https://www.bbvaopenmind.com/en/articles/the-welfare-state-in-europe/ (Accessed 18 November 2020).

WHO (2020) 'Origin and development of health cooperation', Global Health Histories, WHO. Available at: https://www.who.int/global_health_histories/background/en/ (Accessed 18 November 2020).

Chapter 2

Digital Health Tech— Telemedicine and AI, Wearables, Social Media, Digital Therapeutics

As recently as 2012, an estimated 63% of physicians were still using the fax machine as a primary means of communication (Reisman, 2017). Anywhere but in the health sector, this is a striking, embarrassing statistic. I thought this was an appropriate start to a chapter about revolutionary health tech because it should remind us that progress may not be as swift as we think—and also that the wide diffusion of one tech platform might slow down the emergence of another (Figure 2.1).

Interlinked Digital Health Technologies

There are a multitude of sci-tech health candidates that may transform health in the coming decades: more effective intervention, monitoring, communication, support, and healing, drone delivery of medical supplies, AI that's better than medical experts at spotting tumors, pocket-sized ultrasound devices that cost multiples times less than the machines in hospitals and connect to your

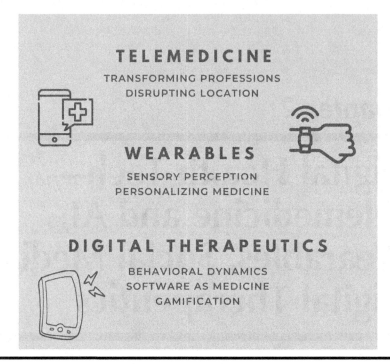

Figure 2.1 Digital health tech.

smartphone, virtual reality that speeds recovery in rehab, the opportunities are near endless (Remes et al., 2020; Time, 2019).

The COVID-19 response itself brought more advanced population surveillance, case identification, contact tracing, evaluation of mobility data, leveraging smartphones, large online data sets, and advances in machine learning (Budd et al., 2020).

Telemedicine's Impact on Health

Telemedicine (also called telehealth) is the digital provision of healthcare services in situations where the health professional and the patient (or two health professionals) are not in the same location, and includes a wide variety of services, including consultation, monitoring, and surgery (Cox, 2016). It typically involves secure transmission of medical data and information, through text, sound, images, or other forms needed for the prevention, diagnosis, treatment, and follow-up of patients (Raposo, 2016). The promise is an always on, connected health experience (Kvedar, Colman, & Cella, 2015).

Telemedicine started in ancient times by patients receiving medical advice using representatives and evolved through the invention of electricity and radio that allowed doctors and patients to communicate remotely in the 19th century to the development of TV and the internet in the 20th century, transmitting medical images, and eventually conducting full-fledged medical consultations through broadband-enabled streaming. The main use cases throughout the EU in 2014 were related to radiology, dermatology, stroke, diabetes, and chronic heart failure. Innovative examples as of today include use of drones to reach patients for emergencies such as heart attacks which is quicker than an ambulance. However, in 2015, only 1% of 930 million doctor's visits in the US were e-visits even though the American Medical Association (AMA) states that 75% of all doctors are either unnecessary or could be handled via telemedicine (PWC, 2018).

The uptake of information technologies is, historically, the main accelerator for telemedicine. Having said that, a single (and unfolding) event, the coronavirus pandemic, has had a tremendous impact on its acceleration. Even before the pandemic, the EU (2020) stated the market potential was strong and expected to grow at 14%. In fact, there is significant evidence that the higher the share of telemedicine—the more cost-effective wide-scale deployment becomes. Furthermore, an increasing share of telemedicine decreases the total cost of the patient journey, total consultation time, distance travelled, quality of life, patient survival and mortality rates, while increasing quality-adjusted life-year (QALY) gains (PWC, 2018).

The main barriers to uptake include cultural resistance, regulatory and policy limitations (notably data privacy), social security, industrial and technical, a lack of knowledge among medical practitioners (about the existence of readily available approaches), financial and market-related (such as cumbersome or non-existent reimbursement procedures). In the EU, a study noted that only consumer models are successful so far because institutional players cannot pay for such services or are not reimbursed for telemedicine tools and services (PWC, 2018).

Telemedicine utilization has remained surprisingly low in the US over the last decade. Only 33% of inpatient hospitals and 45% of outpatient facilities offered telehealth services to their patients because of concerns with fraud, data security, lack of coverage over Medicaid until 2018, as well as cost of implementation and training. It was only with COVID-19 that the uptick happened. Now, 75% of US hospitals are using it, with Zoom as the biggest vendor with 1,032 installations over Cisco's 489 (Waldron, 2019a).

Benefits of telemedicine include improving rural care (a massive problem exists with hospital deserts), potentially greater patient satisfaction (given the reduced wait times and lower care costs). There are also challenges, including

Figure 2.2 The impact of AI on health.

fraud concerns, compliance issues, and insurance coverage (Moriarty, 2020) (Figure 2.2).

AI's Emerging Impact on Health

Today, artificial intelligence (AI), which as I define it is the ability of a computer program or a machine to learn and solve problems is capable of domain-specific analytics. For medicine, let's take radiology, this means that AI is able to analyze radiology charts for the most part, better than humans, and provide an initial analysis useful to the radiologist, who, of course, has to make much more than a technical analysis and also develop a clinical treatment recommendation or make judgments on what a finding means in the larger picture of disease.

However, note that if we were to define radiology strictly as *classifying* as opposed to *interpreting* the meaning of digital X-ray charts, we would not need very many radiologists any longer. For the profession of radiology, AI is highly challenging, but on the positive side, it frees up radiologists to redevelop radiology expert-informed AI to improve the profession's accuracy and save lives.

The use case of radiology is unique because it specifically has to do with image recognition, a stronghold of AI. If we were to take, literally, any other medical specialty, AI would not fare that well today.

Moving on to the evolution of AI in health, there are numerous emerging use cases, such as detection, diagnosis, precision surgery, drug discovery, literature review, and population health (Waldron, 2019a,b). In each of these areas, AI is starting to make huge inroads, is already becoming clinically relevant and will, over time, start to dominate these fields. It will not happen overnight. In the next chapter, I will look at a few startups who are innovating in these fields.

For now, suffice to note that the technology in question would have to move from the current neural net paradigm into some even more experimental types of algorithmic approaches, before true progress would be made. There is also, notably, a potential for backlash in the form of a (highly justifiable) movement toward transparency, fairness, and explainability of AI. Currently, much of AI is a black box, even to its practitioners. This poses ethical as well as practical challenges to making rapid progress. Change will also not happen overnight.

If we look at where AI can be applied to health 3–5 years from now, a distinct picture starts to emerge. For the most part, the advances we are looking at are somewhat incremental, in that they will contribute to summarizing a huge collection of data about human DNA, about social dynamics that may or may not be highly applicable and actionable toward bettering health, as well as a few X factors which include a step change in the discovery of drugs that can start to impact some of the smaller disease areas (smaller in that they affect a so small number of people that it is not going to be worth it for thousands of human experts to look sufficiently into the detailed picture that they would make progress on the disease in the short term). The promise of AI in that time frame is mostly in these niche disease areas.

AI cannot, at this point, outgun a huge team or collections of human teams, say in lung cancer or brain cancer research. What it can do, however, is apply itself to much more specific diseases or problem sets such as identifying interesting correlations, navigating huge data sets, and specifically identifying patterns in images. This is, in and of itself, a huge breakthrough. It is not, however, a step change in the overall picture. For that, we will have to wait a decade or more, until several more platform technologies are more fully baked (notably nanotech, quantum tech, and synthetic biology).

There is one other barrier which may or may not be broken in the 3–5 year period, which is that of the lacking interoperability of key databases needed for AI (or humans) to calculate interrelationships and interpret complex data sets jointly. Currently, even though there are data standards that help the situation, there is not one truth in terms of what the appropriate data format should be. As a result, both AI and humans are, at times, even at crucial points, literally comparing Apples and Oranges. What it would take to fix this problem is painstaking standard work and compromise among the world's leading data vendors, pharmaceutical companies, and academic hospitals. Right now, the incentives are not sufficiently aligned for a unified set of data to emerge.

Having looked at AI as a solution, it is almost tragic to observe the day-to-day cognitive overload of clinicians which is hampered by a lack of even basic tools for processing, documenting, and communicating care activities (Waldron, 2019a).

Wearables' Emerging Impact on Health

Only 1,800 US hospitals use mobile applications, which equates to less than 25% of all US hospitals (Waldron, 2019b). Health trackers and remote monitoring devices are only projected to make up $20 billion of the 2023 market. The other $40 billion is predicted to be earned by assistive hearables. This is a very diverse market, with devices ranging from wireless earbuds to hearing aids (Moriarty, 2019).

Despite that, the wearable space is at an inflection point where consumer devices are about to become powerful medical devices. This is partly due to the advances in sensors and partly due to the advances in AI. For example, in 2018 MIT spinout Empatica's AI-based smart watch was cleared by the Food and Drug Administration (FDA) in neurology for monitoring seizure. Another product, Google Glass Enterprise has been used by various experimental groups.

Augmedix is a tech-enabled service making use of wearable technology (powered by Google Glass and smartphone devices) connecting its clinic with a charting service that allows doctors to focus on patient care, still look at you, the patient, and now away at the screen, and avoid the annoying medical scribes we saw in the examination room over the past few years. At present, it is highly experimental, uses a highly manual process (essentially replacing doctor time with medical scribe time instead of the automatic AI transcription one might initially expect) and the data sets it can make use of are highly limited (Landi, 2020). It is still also quite cumbersome, and its service is only rolled out to a small set of doctors, although the company went public in 2020 with great ambitions.

The buzzword is "digital phenotyping" (or personal sensing), which refers to the fact that smartphone enabled, wearable sensors provide moment-by-moment data streams (far better than the episodic testing conducted at a hospital lab). The data is generated passively and requires no effort by the user (or patient). A wide variety of conditions could theoretically be monitored (e.g. youth mental health, opioid overdose detection, harmful alcohol drinking behaviors, and suicide risk). The successful development of digital phenotyping is of specific relevance to the future, effective care of young people with psychological distress (Huckvale, Venkatesh, & Christensen, 2019).

The promise of smart wearables is in the advancement in sensors as well as in the increased sophistication of the algorithms used to interpret the sensory data. After a few years, perhaps 3–5 years, the accumulation of data will also make a difference.

However, the big struggle with all hardware-dependent products, no matter how advanced the algorithms or the software itself, is to get the form factor right. It has to be appealing to its users, it has to be available at the right price point, and it has to have the magical "it" factor of a consumer device. Without those elements, it cannot scale. This is a tall order.

Wearables will perhaps start to outshine cell phones already toward the end of the decade (Undheim, 2021, p. 223). They will not all be medical devices, of course, but they can increasingly perform functions that are synergistic with personalized medicine, meaning they can start to collect medically relevant data that impacts disease and, definitely, wellness. What follows wearables will likely be implantables, including brain implants, which we will take a brief look at in the next chapter.

One of the true challenges with health relevant data streams from wearable sensors is that somebody (or some algorithm) needs to interpret all of the data. This is not always the case right now and may not become the case in the future either. We will have to prioritize it. For example, I personally suffer from sleep apnea and have a Philips Respironics Dreamstation auto CPAP machine at my bedside at all times. I use it 8 hours a night every night, even when I'm traveling. The device records a number of parameters such as water pressure (cmH_2O), Apnea-Hypopnea Index (AHI), and sleep report (defined as usage in hours/night), and saves it to an SD card on the device. Every morning, the device uploads my data to the cloud. According to the provider, in my case Regional Health Care, my data is shared with my doctor, but I have never—never—discussed the sleep data with my doctor during my annual visits. One would wonder if the data gets there. I would guess it perhaps is theoretically accessible to him if he calls up the regional provider. I have not seen the data in my online health record in the Partners Gateway system at Massachusetts General Hospital, where I get my healthcare from. This, even though that app has gotten progressively more advanced.

All of this simply to say that while it is marginally useful for me to occasionally look at my daily or monthly stats which are available in the machine, although I know basic thresholds, I do not have sufficient knowledge to judge whether the levels are worrisome in any way over time—partly because the device does not seem to keep my data over time. That data, presumably, is still in the cloud somewhere, accessed by nobody. The only thing that for sure does get monitored by external parties is the hours of usage and not for my health benefits, purely because my insurance company wants to ensure that I am worth spending money on.

From a personal angle, the prices I get through my provider are so high that I have resorted to buying my CPAP supplies through online platforms instead of getting through my health provider. As an aside, I found a video online where a hacker has found a method to "fool the insurance company into thinking you are using it". Not my cup of tea, but it shows you that this era of health data sharing has its discontents. It also shows that it is not just about what data is being measured but how cleverly that data is being used to benefit a patients' health.

Social Media's Emerging Impact on Health

Public health advertising campaigns are well known in public health since the 1960s (WHO, 2009). It has been deployed to combat cancer and other diseases, as well as to boost vaccination rates. Such campaigns have been successfully employed but is not without its risks (and its critics) (e.g. health consequences of smoking campaigns and warnings).

Social media today is capable of overturning elections, creating lasting psychological damage, but also of mass engagement and social mobilization at unprecedented scale. The social movements of the past few years are almost unthinkable without social media. Movements ignite faster, scale bigger, and get instant coverage, by citizen journalists who cover events on their cell phones and stream directly to social media like YouTube, TikTok, and Instagram.

Healthcare is an area that has seen the influx of social media, too. I'll cover digital therapeutics in a separate section to follow but suffice to say that it is now becoming clinically relevant.

However, the significance of social media became apparent way before focused digital therapeutics apps, mostly as mobilization tools for patient engagement. It also has served as a major instrument for health promotion, both in the west and in development countries.

Chat groups about health have existed since the beginning of digital communication over the world wide web. In fact, it was touted as one of the killer applications early on. No longer did you have to be embarrassed about your condition (acne, homosexual desires, weight problems, sensitive diseases such as Sexually transmitted diseases (STDs), Acquired immunodeficiency syndrome (AIDS), and the like), there was always a chatroom to explore and get advice from others in the same situation, perhaps a little further along.

These chatrooms have evolved. They have turned into advocacy communities, organizations, pressure groups, and they have mushroomed in size, variety, and duration. They have gone from text-based to visual. There is some evidence that mindful use of social media among non-profit organizations can significantly enhance their health promotion efforts (Vedel, Ramaprasad, & Lapointe, 2020). It seems pretty clear that public health organizations (and anybody else) can take advantage of social media to deliver fully automated, targeted, and cost-effective behavior change interventions at scale, but those efforts may also backlash and be perceived as a threat to autonomy (Dunn, Mandl, & Coiera, 2018).

Social media can also be used for health monitoring at a global scale. John Brownstein, a professor at Harvard Medical School and CIO at Boston Children's Hospital, together with a team of software developers built a real-time public health surveillance system (aka digital epidemiology) called HealthMap. The system mines internet data like news stories, blogs, government websites, and social data to monitor disease outbreaks. In 2014, HealthMap picked up on the deadly Ebola outbreak in West Africa a week before an official announcement was made. John Brownstein and Sachin H. Jain, CEO of CareMore Health, coined the term digital phenotype in 2015 (Venkatesan, 2019).

Online health information is now a major component of the web. The challenge is to verify that information.

For professional communities, health publications have also mushroomed. I have listed the core publications you should consider tracking in the appendix. The challenge is now to wade through all the science and find the most relevant data at the right moment in time without wasting valuable resources searching for information and experiencing information overload.

Opportunities and Challenges for Social Media in Health

The opportunity is for scalable public health campaigns where partnerships between governments, non-profits, corporations, and big tech—using uniform messages that are co-developed, vetted, and agreed—efficiently not only spread messages but continuously take in feedback, adjust, and improve based on public feedback. By the way, we have not seen many such moments in history, perhaps apart from the no smoking campaigns (Yale University Library, 2021).

Second, the opportunity to find high-quality information online for any given topic is there. With that comes the potential for patient empowerment. However, with misinformation and information overload, quickly finding the right information, being able to assess it and put it to use, is a growing challenge, especially since all information gets mediated by social media, meaning it flows through filters, recommendations, opinions, influencers, and manipulation by nefarious actors or governments.

Assessing Social Media

A recent systematic review of social media in public health (Giustini et al., 2018) was inconclusive, which indicates deeper science is needed to answer the ultimate question of whether its effects are largely positive or negative. On the other hand, it's entirely possible that that question is irrelevant because it all depends on the context. Also, by the time we find out, social media will have evolved.

Today, social media is at its apex and nobody knows where it will go next. My prediction would be that it morphs into something less distinguishable as social media, into separate niches which begin to become somewhat less generic, and, hopefully, more focused, useful, and life changing in a positive way.

Digital Therapeutics' Emerging Impact on Health

What is digital therapeutics? According to the Digital Therapeutics Alliance (2020), digital therapeutics (DTx) deliver "evidence-based therapeutic interventions to patients that are driven by high quality software programs to prevent, manage, or treat a broad spectrum of physical, mental, and behavioral conditions". Estimations of the total investment in digital therapeutics vary wildly. By one estimation, it topped $600 million already back in 2018 (Crunchbase, 2018). By another it would have reached $2.88 billion in 2019 (McCourier, 2020).

Most commonly, at this stage, we find individual apps for specific conditions, generally chronic diseases (e.g. diabetes, dementia, Alzheimer, chronic pain, and insomnia) or neurological disorders, such as anxiety, depression, insomnia, for pain management in general, as well as for cardio metabolic conditions or lifestyle diseases (obesity, eating disorders, smoking cessation) and wellness (e.g. nutrition). Such apps have also been used to optimize medication adherence as well as other areas such as addiction. However, the market is moving toward innovators with more significant claims toward handling multiple diseases and disorders, which presents some interesting challenges and opportunities.

In short, first, this is about online apps that treat patients remotely. Second, to use these services typically need a prescription, e.g. the process is facilitated by a doctor, and the keyword is "evidence-based". Third, the assumption is that this kind of effort helps patients modify their behavior and lifestyle to achieve a positive clinical outcome.

There is also still a completely unregulated set of digital therapeutics or disease management apps that may have peer-reviewed studies and may be reimbursable by payers but lack the clinical rigor imposed by regulatory scrutiny (Goad, 2020). These typically fall into the category of Internet-based Cognitive Behavioral Therapy (iCBT).

In 2016, the first meta-analysis in the novel research field of ICBT for children and adolescents with psychiatric or somatic disorders found only 25 studies, covering a range of 11 psychiatric and somatic conditions, with anxiety and pain as the most commonly targeted problems. The benefits included decreased therapist time overall and better treatment adherence. The greatest effect was found for psychiatric problems compared to somatic conditions (Vigerland et al., 2016).

Either way, digital therapeutics have a strong behavioral focus, using the smartphone as the vehicle both to capture (through sensors) or input (through user or patient input) information and (to some extent) to analyze the data and transmit medical interventions in the form of text messages, emails, and alerts.

The smartphone mechanisms used to collect patient data include the screen, the accelerometer, and the microphone, and the output mechanisms include the screen, chat, and notifications ("go to sleep", "remember to adhere to your diet", "you haven't exercised today", etc.). Arguably, using these apps, DTx can be used to replace or augment treatments such as counseling, medical devices, or drugs (Goad, 2020).

Even though many of these apps are built as standalone, innovators also typically seek integration with providers, e.g. anyone who provides care: primary care doctors, pediatricians, gynecologists, chiropractors, clinical psychologists, optometrists, nurses, nurse practitioners, dentists, clinical social workers, or even with associated product and service providers, such as pharmacists. The provider group is hard to convince for the myriad of reasons that got healthcare into the mess it is in the first place. They are overworked, unconvinced about tech as a panacea, have had bad experiences with any electronic medical record (EMR) system, and don't want to have to check and copy over data from yet another app for patient updates, no matter how many percentage points the patients will improve.

Less ambitiously, many app innovators seek integration with payers, which either means insurance companies or government health authorities. This group is slightly easier to convince because insurance workers and executives work remotely to a higher degree than care professions and understand that modality.

The FDA launched a Digital Health Center of Excellence in fall 2020. The fact that FDA-approved therapies recognize the domain itself has proven to be a game changer. Due to COVID-19, for the first time in history, an FDA Emergency Use Authorization (EUA) has included digital health tools, otherwise known as Software as a Medical Device (SaMD).

In a process they began to explore in 2015, another US regulatory agency, the Centers for Disease and Prevention (CDC) recognized digital therapeutics under its diabetes prevention program in 2018, enabling it to become reimbursable as a medical benefit under Medicare (Cohen, 2018). The advantages and challenges of digital therapeutics in the next 3–5 years depend on where you sit—as a patient or caregiver, as a healthcare provider or as a payer.

Main Advantages for Digital Therapeutics Next 3–5 Years

A major advantage of digital therapeutics is that it offers the physicians an option to provide treatment anywhere and anytime, transcending the physical borders of a clinic or a hospital, potentially providing a one-to-many scenario enabling one provider to scale their practice substantially. The opportunity for personalized treatment without huge investments is also a positive intervention, and likewise, the potential of monitoring medication or desired behavior adherence. Furthermore, one can monitor or offer treatment for diseases associated with stigma that may affect patient willingness to interact with healthcare providers.

Similarly, the ability to monitor chronic conditions that are not so easily checked during infrequent provider visits (Dang, Arora, & Rane, 2020) is another opportunity. Chronic conditions typically need frequent, high-touch therapeutic interventions, which is impractical with traditional care. Lastly, there may be the potential for a clinical feedback loop either by the clinician or in combination with AI (Palanica et al., 2020). All in all, the promise lies in both developing a more holistic picture and in scalability, and lack of travel costs (in time, inconvenience, and money).

Top Challenges for Digital Therapeutics Next 3–5 Years

What are the main challenges for digital therapeutics in the next 3–5 years? In short, difficulty in distinguishing these apps from general health and well-being apps in the market, uneven incentives (demanding changes in healthcare provider workflows, thus increasing physician burden), and patient retention (Dang, Arora, & Rane, 2020).

January of each year is a common time for surges in mental health app downloads related to new year resolutions, but that surge is usually transient (Rosner, 2020).

In the same way that consumer applications experience a massive fall-off immediately after signup, the same can be said for therapeutic apps—unless—there is sufficient incentive to log in over time. However, drug adherence is similarly tricky. Approximately 50% of patients do not take their medications as prescribed (Brown & Bussell, 2011). Studies have consistently shown that 20%–30% of medication prescriptions are never filled (Viswanathan et al., 2012). It should also be said that digital therapeutics often targets conditions that are poorly addressed by the healthcare system including chronic diseases or neurological disorders (Dang, Arora, & Rane, 2020).

Finally, as digital therapeutics increasingly works in conjunction with a drug regimen to address more complex conditions, like asthma or cancer treatment, extending that type of interaction, and watching how and when the pharma industry at large will partner in this charge (or not), will be crucial.

In the appendix, you can find shortlists of (a) who you should track (scientists, innovators, and startup founders), (b) what you should read (publications), and (c) what tech conferences you should attend (virtual or in person), to have any inkling about where it truly is evolving day-by-day, year-by-year for each of these emerging technologies.

Technologies That Are Still Highly Experimental

Here are some technologies that I find still too experimental to yield immediate benefits beyond clinical trials and small-scale experimentation in clinical settings.

Virtual Therapeutics

In a recent book, *How Virtual Therapeutics Will Revolutionize Medicine*, Brennan Spiegel who directs one of the largest and most widely cited therapeutic virtual reality programs in the world, Cedars-Sinai Medical Center in Los Angeles, outlines how VR can already do wonders for patient care when it comes to pain, anxiety, and depression, and even to specific conditions such as burn injuries, stroke, Acquired immunodeficiency syndrome (AIDS), or even schizophrenia. The effect seems to come from manipulating perception and our senses to process our pain differently. The treatment effects he describes seem similar to those that can be achieved with digital play therapy (Stone, 2020), digital art therapy (Malchiodi, 2018), movie making therapy, and a whole host of visually fanciful treatment options that undoubtedly will become part of the future medical repertoire. However, just to take VR, the devices are not yet good enough, or inexpensive enough, to deploy at grand scale across hospitals across the world. We may get there this decade, but some further tweaking both of the hardware formfactor, efficiency, and the treatment protocols seem to be needed. Having said that, it is a welcome change from overmedication.

Population Health

Population health is another emerging area with great future promise but few existing proof points that indicate it will reach maturity in the next 3–5 years. The coronavirus pandemic, for one, kicked such a notion off the table. Having said that, there are studies harnessing wearable data (from 200,000 Fitbits) to improve real-time surveillance of influenza (Radin et al., 2020). Future wearables might include sensors to "prospectively track blood pressure, temperature, electrocardiogram, and cough analysis, which could be used to further characterise an individual's baseline and identify abnormalities" (Radin et al., 2020).

Interoperable Electronic Medical Records (iEMRs)

There simply are no interoperable electronic medical records systems across primary care doctors, hospitals, provider networks, states, or countries that are efficient or even remotely working well today. It will likely take some time. With privacy regulations in place and strengthening (for good reasons), it will take even longer. It is not a technology challenge at this time but a coordination challenge and a process in need of a business model.

Conclusion

Four technology platforms will have an outsized impact on the next 3–5 years: AI, wearables, social media, and digital therapeutics. What is the common denominator? Each of these technologies is highly software enabled, tied to a set of business models, and exemplified by a few highly visible lowcode or nocode interfaces: Alexa (AI), Fitbit (wearables), Facebook (social media), and Pear (digital therapeutics). Moreover, they have the potential to increasingly interact in life-changing ways. At the end of the day, the question is not so much which technologies are inherently the most advanced, but which combination of tech, products, solutions, and business models can solve common problems if they achieve mass usage, yet can look and feel tailored for each region, country, city, and local setting, perhaps, even for each individual, health practitioner, intermediary, or patient.

The outspoken rule in global health is that an "appropriate" technology always is a simple technology, a frugal technology (Howitt et al., 2012), an old technology, or even a proven technology. It is true that nothing is proven until it is tried out in the setting one wishes to apply it. On the other hand, many newer, nocode technologies are so easy to apply that they triumph legacy technologies.

There are no quick fixes to how technology should best be applied to health. Even though there is emerging best practice, it is always situated, meaning it came out of one specific context and cannot easily be generalized to other situations. The best advice for any complex of healthcare actors implementing health tech is to invest in wisdom. Take the time to study examples of how technology works and especially when it has not worked in the past. Ensure you experiment at a smaller scale before you implement something bigger. Learn from your mistakes. Bring in outsiders to assess your performance. Keep iterating. Set big goals

KEY TAKEAWAYS AND REFLECTIONS

1. What digital health tech are you exposed to on a daily basis?

_____

2. Thinking specifically about AI, wearables, digital therapeutics, social media, and telemedicine, which areas do you feel will impact the next two decades the most and why?

_____

3. What health technologies are on the horizon? What would it take to develop these?

_____

but realize that progress goes in growth spurts. Innovation in health is both step-by-step, incremental, and also, at times, exponential. There is not always a way to identify which is likely to be which and we might have to live with that. It certainly makes it more interesting.

In the next chapter, I discuss the innovation actors of the next decade: industry turnarounds, startups, and patients.

References

Brown, M.T. and Bussell, J.K. (2011) 'Medication adherence: WHO cares?', *Mayo Clinic Proceedings*, 86(4), 304–314. Available at: DOI: 10.4065/mcp.2010.0575 (Accessed 20 November 2020).

Budd, J., Miller, B.S., Manning, E.M. et al. (2020) 'Digital technologies in the public-health response to COVID-19', *Nature Medicine*, 26, 1183–1192. Available at: DOI: 10.1038/s41591-020-1011-4 (Accessed 3 January 2021).

Cohen, J.K. (2018) 'CDC recognizes "digital therapeutics" provider Omada Health under its diabetes prevention program', Becker's Hospital Review [Online], 4 June 2018. Available at: https://www.beckershospitalreview.com/care-coordination/cdc-recognizes-digital-therapeutics-provider-omada-health-under-its-diabetes-prevention-program.html (Accessed 22 November 2020)

Crunchbase (2018) Crunchbase Analyst Reports, May 2018. Available at: http://www.crunchbase.com (Accessed 21 November 2020)

Cox, A. (2016) 'Legal landscape struggles to keep pace with the rise of telemedicine', Lexology.com [Online]. Available at: https://www.lexology.com/library/detail.aspx?g=d5a7ff25-a0d9-4d11-993e-eba98c96da33 (Accessed 20 November 2020).

Dang, A., Arora, D., and Rane, P. (2020) 'Role of digital therapeutics and the changing future of healthcare', *Journal of Family Medicine and Primary Care*, 9(5), 2207–2213. Available at: DOI: 10.4103/jfmpc.jfmpc_105_20 (Accessed 20 November 2020).

Digital Therapeutics Alliance (2020) 'Digital Therapeutics Alliance' [Online]. Available at: https://dtxalliance.org/ (Accessed 21 November 2020).

Dunn, A.G., Mandl, K.D., and Coiera, E. (2018) 'Social media interventions for precision public health: promises and risks'. *npj Digital Medicine*, 1, 47. Available at: DOI: 10.1038/s41746-018-0054-0 (Accessed 20 November 2020).

EU (2020) 'European Economic Forecast: Autumn 2020. Institutional Paper 136, November 2020. Available at: https://ec.europa.eu/info/sites/default/files/autumn_20_forecast.pdf (Accessed 6 July 2021)

Giustini, D., Ali, S.M., Fraser, M., and Kamel Boulos, M.N. (2018) 'Effective uses of social media in public health and medicine: a systematic review of systematic reviews', *Online Journal of Public Health Informatics*, 10(2), e215. Available at: DOI: 10.5210/ojphi.v10i2.8270 (Accessed 21 November 2020).

Goad, M. (2020) 'Prescription digital therapeutics (PDTx): an investor's guide', Omers Ventures [Online], 19 February 2020. Available at: https://medium.com/omers-ventures/prescription-digital-therapeutics-pdtx-an-investors-guide-2f5ddc258896 (Accessed 20 November 2020).

Howitt, P. et al. (2012) 'Technologies for global health', *Te Lancet* 380, 507–535. https://pubmed.ncbi.nlm.nih.gov/22857974/

Huckvale, K., Venkatesh, S., and Christensen, H. (2019) 'Toward clinical digital phenotyping: a timely opportunity to consider purpose, quality, and safety', *npj Digital Medicine*, 2, 88. Available at: DOI: 10.1038/s41746-019-0166-1 (Accessed 20 November 2020).

Kvedar, J.C, Colman, C., and Cella, G. (2015) *The Internet of Healthy Things*. Boston: Partners Connected Health.

Landi, H. (2020) 'Google Glass-powered medical scribe service going public as part of reverse merger deal', Fierce Healthcare, 22 October 2020. Available at: https://www.fiercehealthcare.com/tech/google-glass-powered-medical-scribe-service-going-public-as-part-spac-deal (Accessed 27 February 2021).

Malchiodi, C.A. (2018) *The Handbook of Art Therapy and Digital Technology*. London: Jessica Kingsley Publishers.

McCourier (2020) 'Digital Therapeutics Market 2020–2026', The Courier, McCourier, 20 November 2020. Available at: https://www.mccourier.com/digital-therapeutics-market-2020-2026-size-share-and-growth-analysis-research-report-global-players-livongo-health-medtronic-omada-health-pear-therapeutics/ (Accessed 21 November 2020).

Moriarty, A. (2019) 'Breaking down the healthcare wearables market', The Definitive Blog, 29 May 2019. Available at: https://blog.definitivehc.com/breaking-down-healthcare-wearables-market (Accessed 27 November 2020).

Moriarty, A. (2020) '4 impacts of telemedicine adoption', The Definitive Blog, 15 September 2020. Available at: https://blog.definitivehc.com/ways-telemedicine-changing-healthcare (Accessed 27 November 2020)

Palanica, A., Docktor, M. J., Lieberman, M., & Fossat, Y. (2020) 'The need for artificial intelligence in digital therapeutics', *Digital Biomarkers*, 4(1), 21–25. Available at: DOI: 10.1159/000506861 (Accessed 20 November 2020).

PWC (2018) 'Market study on telemedicine', PWC [Online]. Available at: https://ec.europa.eu/health/sites/health/files/ehealth/docs/2018_provision_marketstudy_telemedicine_en.pdf (Accessed 20 November 2020).

Radin, J.M., Wineinger, N.E., Topol, E.J., and Steinhubl, S.R. (2020) 'Harnessing wearable device data to improve state-level real-time surveillance of influenza-like illness in the USA: a population-based study', *The Lancet Digital Health*, 2:2, e85–e93. Available at: DOI: 10.1016/S2589-7500(19)30222-5 (Accessed 20 November 2020).

Raposo, V.L. (2016) 'Telemedicine: the legal framework (or the lack of it) in Europe', *GMS Health Technology Assessment*, 12, Doc03. Available at: DOI: 10.3205/hta000126 (Accessed 20 November 2020).

Reisman, M. (2017) 'EHRs: The Challenge of Making Electronic Data Usable and Interoperable', *P & T: A Peer-Reviewed Journal for Formulary Management*, 42:9, 572–575.

Remes, J.H., Linzer, K., Singhal, S., Dewhurst, M., Dash, P., Woentzel, J., Smit, S., Evers, M., Wilson, M., Rutter, K-A., and Ramdorai, A. (2020) 'Ten innovations that can improve global health', McKinsey Global Institute, 15 July 2020. Available at: https://www.mckinsey.com/industries/healthcare-systems-and-services/our-insights/ten-innovations-that-can-improve-global-health (Accessed 3 January 2021).

Rosner, B. (2020) 'You may speed now. The FDA's changing digital health speed limits during a pandemic', Node Health, 17 August 2020. Available at: https://nodehealth.org/2020/08/17/fdas-digital-health-speed-limits-during-a-pandemic-autobahn-or-the-interstate/.

Spiegel, B. (2020) *BrVRx: How Virtual Therapeutics Will Revolutionize Medicine*. New York: Basic Books.

Stone, J. (2020) *Digital Play Therapy*. London: Routledge.

Time (2019) '12 innovations that will change health care and medicine in the 2020s', Time Magazine [Online]. Available at: https://time.com/5710295/top-health-innovations/ (Accessed 3 January 2021).

Undheim, T.A. (2021) *Future Tech*. London: Kogan Page.

Vedel, I., Ramaprasad, J., and Lapointe, L. (2020) 'Social media strategies for health promotion by nonprofit organizations: multiple case study design', *Journal of Medical Internet Research*, 22:4, e15586. Available at: https://www.jmir.org/2020/4/e15586; DOI: 10.2196/15586 (Accessed 20 November 2020).

Venkatesan, P. (2019) 'Digital phenotyping: a revolution or a privacy breach?', MedCityNews, 14 January 2019. Available at: https://medcitynews.com/2019/01/digital-phenotyping-a-revolution-or-a-privacy-breach/?rf=1 (Accessed 20 November 2020).

Vigerland, S., Lenhard, F., Bonnert, M., Lalouni, M., Hedman, E., Ahlen, J., Olén, O., Serlachius, E., and Ljótsson, B. (2016) 'Internet-delivered cognitive behavior therapy for children and adolescents: a systematic review and meta-analysis', *Clinical Psychology Review*, 50, 1–10. Available at: DOI: 10.1016/j.cpr.2016.09.005 (Accessed 20 November 2020).

Viswanathan, M., Golin, C.E., Jones, C.D., Ashok, M., Blalock, S.J., Wines, R.C., Coker-Schwimmer, E.J., Rosen, D.L., Sista, P., and Lohr, K.N. (2012) 'Interventions to improve adherence to self-administered medications for chronic diseases in the United States: a systematic review', *Annals of Internal Medicine*, 157:11, 785–795. Available at: DOI: 10.7326/0003-4819-157-11-201212040-00538 (Accessed 20 November 2020).

Waldron, T. (2019a) 'Cognitive overload in healthcare: how to ease the pain', The Definitive Blog, 7 May 2019. Available at: https://blog.definitivehc.com/healthcare-cognitive-overload (Accessed: 27 November 2020).

Waldron, T. (2019b) '3 surprising ways healthcare is using AI', The Definitive Blog, 10 October 2019. Available at: https://blog.definitivehc.com/ways-healthcare-using-ai (Accessed: 27 November 2020).

WHO (2009) 'Public health campaigns: getting the message across', WHO. Available at: https://www.who.int/about/history/publications/9789240560277/en/ (Accessed: 27 February 2021).

Yale University Library (2021) 'Selling smoke: Tobacco advertising and anti-smoking campaigns'. Available at: https://onlineexhibits.library.yale.edu/s/sellingsmoke/page/antismoking (Accessed: 28 February 2021).

Chapter 3

Innovation Actors of the Next Decade— Industry Turnarounds, Startups, and Patients

The coronavirus pandemic, rising healthcare costs, an aging population, stifling regulations, and the complexity of present-day technological offerings make the trillion-dollar healthcare industry ripe for disruption (Buhr, 2020). Overwhelming, right? The questions, though, are many: who will truly innovate (as opposed to merely attempt it), when will each innovation ripen, and what will be the systemic consequences (and in what time frame)?

On my run this morning, I tried a new health app: Asics Runkeeper (for the benefit of this book). Nine minutes into my run, I was interrupted by a voice saying I had run a mile, at a pace of 9 minutes and 15 seconds. I like to think on these morning runs, about what has happened over the past few days, about my marriage, why my teenager often is mad at me, and about my plans for the day. This morning I was reminded of how short we have come on the path toward personalized health and medicine. I was using an app unconnected to my health records, giving me random cues that are only useful if I want to run faster, consume more calories, or perhaps compare yourself against others. I don't want another voice telling me what to do. Quite the contrary, my runs are my Zen time. That is, unless I'm running for a specific goal, for example this year I'm training for the Boston Marathon.

DOI: 10.4324/9781003178071-3

As I reflect on using this app, I have some thoughts on what would change my mind, what would make me feel that this app, or another one, is an instrumental part of my life. What if the app was connected to my health record—not just my personal health record—but to my primary care doctor and the hospital I am connected to, the mighty Massachusetts General Hospital. What if the app could detect if I was unusually slow and would prompt me to check in with my primary care doctor, or more likely the nurse, to see if something was wrong? What if the app went one step further and actually asked me some prompting questions about the last week's activities? What if the app could predict an impending heart attack—and stop it by recommending pre-emptive actions based on my surroundings? However, I went a bit further. I thought about the fact that the real value of these runs is not just improving my health, it is improving my mind. My mind matters a lot to me, I write books, I try to support startup innovation through my work as a venture capitalist, I am also a futurist looking into complex sci-tech and societal developments.

What I need is an app that tells me how to get to a state where my neurons are spiking or at least alert me immediately before it is about to happen, so I can prepare. Does this sound fanciful? I don't think so.

Where we are with digital health trackers right now is at a turning point. They can delve further into consumer hell with audio cues that encourage social media interaction during the run, or myopic sports analytics stats, or we can morph into a world where we find that wearables enable us to be our best self. We are—seemingly—heading in both directions at the same time. However, without interoperability and standardization, apps and devices will not be talking to each other, will be largely duplicative, and will likely lock us into proprietary data ecosystems that are costly, siloed, and full of advertising you cannot get rid of which slots your brain and makes you less independent, creative, and—less healthy.

My vision, the central thought guiding this book, is that we need healthcare at the edge, that is we need not just the right sensors where we are at any given moment, but we need to be in control of that information, it needs to make us better people, healthwise, ethically, and professionally. My metaphor of the "edge" is not chosen at random. Innovation happens at the edges, this is not some toothless reality where wearables or medical professionals, or healthcare companies (likely another iteration of big tech) control my every move. I want to be free, untethered, yet connected when it matters. I want to send my health data to the cloud for protection, for analysis, but I also want to own my data. I want to have it back for safekeeping if I feel like it. I want to be able to cut off the cord.

Most importantly, I want my data to serve my own best, not the best of some health corporation—regardless whether they are using my data to lower everybody's health insurance premiums, to improve population health, or to develop the next vaccine or even to remedy a rare disease. Yes, I do want to contribute to all that, but I want to make active choices every time. Do I want to enroll in a trial? Maybe yes, maybe now.

Why do I think health apps are so central to the future of innovation in digital health and in healthcare and health tech? I don't think they are relevant at all, but they are precursors to something bigger. Augmented reality interfaces will have many different form factors, but some version—phones, watches, glasses, implants, artificial limbs—will be the future delivery agent of medicine—or poison. The ancient Greek word "pharmakon" is paradoxical and can be translated as "drug", even in English, which means both "remedy" and "poison". I want to ensure that those devices lead to a better future, not George Orwell's dystopian one (Figure 3.1).

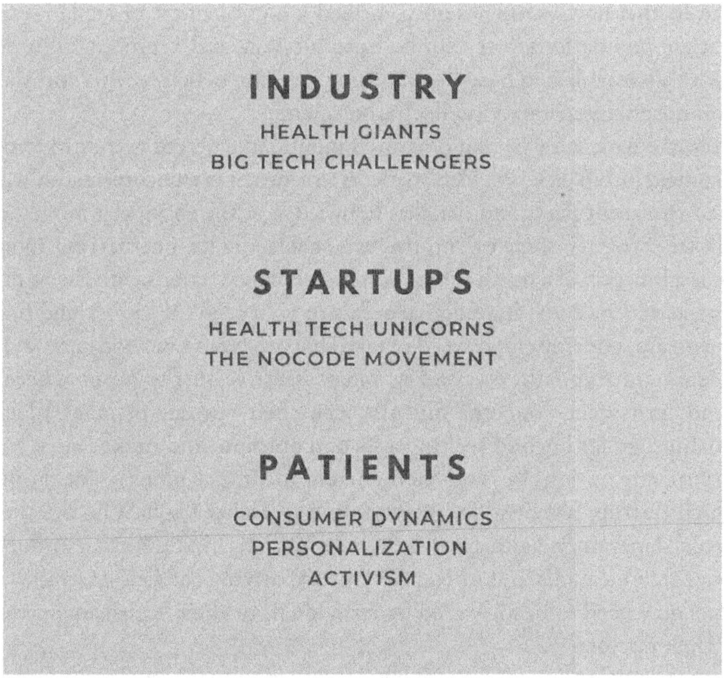

INDUSTRY

HEALTH GIANTS
BIG TECH CHALLENGERS

STARTUPS

HEALTH TECH UNICORNS
THE NOCODE MOVEMENT

PATIENTS

CONSUMER DYNAMICS
PERSONALIZATION
ACTIVISM

Figure 3.1 Innovation actors in the next decade.

Movers and Shakers of the Future

In the current healthcare system, the established professions (doctors, nurses) and institutions (hospitals, insurers, pharma industry) rule the scene. However, in the emerging healthcare landscape, a new set of actors emerge as reformers, innovators, and game changers.

First off, once the frustrations with the existing system becomes too hard to bear, intrapreneurs start to emerge on the scene, challenging status quo and suggesting ideas, concepts and even technologies to remedy or even gradually transform healthcare from the inside.

Startups are starting to truly chip at healthcare, not from one angle but from literally hundreds of angles, everything from the ways certain procedures are carried out, to the relationship between various providers, to the patient relationship itself. To some extent, startups partner with industry, whether pharma, medical device, or other types of service providers in the health field.

Academic research hospitals have become playgrounds for change, given that they stand at the intersection of the hospital world and the innovation spinout activity of engineering and medical labs. However, not all of them are able to compete in this new world where you need a combination of stellar research, huge patient populations to try out new products on, and a spinout culture combined with an established based of venture capitalists who readily fund startups based on hospital-generated intellectual property.

Lately, the patient, or patient organized input, has emerged as a third force. No longer content just to pick providers, patients to a greater extent come with their own suggested treatment plans and detailed knowledge of the entire chain of events in a healthcare career. To some extent, this was enabled by the internet, but more and more, it is a function of a much more complex set of interactions with the healthcare providers itself. Once you have digital access to your medical history and ongoing testing, you are suddenly empowered to take charge of your own body and wellness.

Patients are rightfully becoming more assertive to the point where they might not just voice concerns but also exit their current primary physician relationships, go far beyond seeking a second opinion, and make use of supplementary private options beyond their current insurance plans or local options.

Which startups are breaking new ground in technology? Who are the tech influencers, emerging scientists, and experts? Which think tanks are influential? What research hospitals and university labs are driving the field forward? These questions now need to be answered by individuals or their health advocates, not just by their doctors.

Health Systems

In many countries, the healthcare system is nationalized, and the largest healthcare systems are national. Most famously, the National Health Service (NHS) in the UK which is the largest employer in England and includes 1.2 million staff spread on 1,600 hospitals. In China, hospitals can be public or private, nonprofit or for-profit, and there are 12,000 public hospitals and 21,000 private hospitals (The Commonwealth Fund, 2020).

In the US, the system is privatized, and the largest players are private health system conglomerates. Collectively, the largest health systems manage more than 1,300 hospitals—nearly 20% of active hospitals in the US (Moriarty, 2020a).

The top 10 US health systems by net patient revenue include HCA Healthcare (by a large margin at $42 billion), Kaiser Permanente, CommonSpirit Health, Ascension Health, Providence St. Joseph Health, Kaiser Permanente Northern California, Tenet Healthcare, Kaiser Permanente Southern California, Trinity Health, University of California Health (Moriarty, 2020a,b).

Top 10 largest health systems [or integrated delivery networks (IDNs)] in the US by member hospitals include HCA Healthcare (211), Universal Health Services (179), Department of Veterans Affairs (162), Encompass Health Corporation (135), Ascension Health (124), Select Medical Corporation (115), Community Health Systems (109), Tenet Healthcare (84), LifePoint Health (88), and Kindred Healthcare (81) (Moriarty, 2020b). However, size does not indicate quality or sci-tech focus. In the US, as well as around the world, that distinction typically goes to academic medical centers (AMCs), which I will feature next.

The hospitals that are the most technologically advanced in the world include El Camino Hospital, California, Fortis Memorial Research Institute, India, Bumrungrad International Hospital, Thailand, Gleneagles Medical Center, Singapore, Asklepios Klinik Barmbek, Germany, Guy's and St. Thomas', UK, Wooridul Spine Hospital, Seoul, and Upper River Valley Hospital, Canada (HCI, 2020). In fact, there are hundreds of healthcare organizations around the world who have achieved the Gold Seal of Approval from Joint Commission International (JCL) as accredited entities (https://www.jointcommissioninternational.org/).

Academic Medical Centers—In Need of New Business Models?

An AMC is a tertiary care hospital (e.g. specialized on in-depth disease knowledge as opposed to primary care) that is organizationally and administratively integrated with a medical school. There are about 1,100 teaching hospitals in the US. Hospitals in Texas, Massachusetts, and Pennsylvania are among the 50 best major teaching hospitals in the US based on patient outcomes, civic leadership, and value of care, according to a ranking released by *Washington Monthly Magazine*, in partnership with nonpartisan healthcare think tank the Lown Institute (Gooch, 2020).

Texas Medical Center (TMC) is the largest medical city in the world. Johns Hopkins Medicine is another notable center in the US. AMCs serve a crucial role in the healthcare industry. The organizations account for $562 billion in healthcare spending and treat some of the sickest and most vulnerable patients in the country.

Internationally, leading centers include six in the UK (King's Health Partners, Cambridge University Health Partners, Imperial College Academic Health Science Centre, Manchester Academic Health Science Centre, Oxford Academic Health Science Centre, and UCL Partners), each linked to the top universities in England. In the Nordics, the most famous one is Karolinska Institutet in Sweden.

The challenges the AMC's face is to stay abreast of sci-tech innovation across the competition as specialty care becomes globalized, becoming more nimble (to respond to consumer whims), plus the fact that, arguably, new entrants to the healthcare industry (new hospitals, telemedicine, digital health apps) are "skimming the cream", resulting in AMCs seeing sicker and costlier patients (LaPointe, 2019).

Big Company Innovators in Healthcare

There are 30 large public healthcare companies in the world (including pharma) on the Forbes Global 500 (Fortune, 2020), including United Health Group, Johnson & Johnson, CVS Health, Pfizer, Cigna, Novartis, Roche, GlaxoSmithKline, Bayer, Anthem, Sanofi, AbbVie, Medtronic, Walgreens Boots Alliance, Bristol-Myers Squibb, Abbot, Thermo Fisher Scientific, Gilead Sciences, Ely Lilly, HCA Healthcare, Humana, AstraZeneca, Fresenius, Novo Nordisk, Becton Dickinson, Stryker, Biogen, Boston Scientific, Philips, and Takeda. It does not take a wizard to predict that not all of these will be on this list a decade from now. Big tech would have entered healthcare (and pharma) in a massive way and, at minimum, the healthcare revenue of these seven companies [e.g. Amazon, Alphabet (Google), Salesforce, Apple, Microsoft, IBM (Watson), and Tencent] will have surpassed at least half of them. I would also bet on a few new (health) tech companies entering the scene up from startup status.

Many of the companies appearing on BCG's most innovative companies ranking over time are likely to be contenders for healthcare leadership in the next decade, even based purely on survival instinct. In fact, it is not likely to find many top 10 companies a decade from now who are not world leaders in health-care. The reason is that healthcare is just a small part of the even more relevant longevity industry (e.g. a novel type of preventive medicine based on biomark-ers, precision health, and personalization). Longevity, at $17 trillion is, arguably, the biggest industry there is, and the most complex, because it encompasses the synthesis of advanced biomedicine, data science and artificial intelligence (AI), finance and investment, governance and policy, and a myriad of socioeconomic domains (Kaminskiy & Colangelo, 2020, p. 18).

If we look at Forbes most innovative companies (right now), we find an entirely different set of companies on top. Among the contender for healthcare leadership are perhaps Salesforce (#3), Amazon (#5), Illumina (#20), and Tencent (#25), or even Intuitive Surgical (#44) which provides robotic-assisted technologies, tools, and services for surgery, or Baidu (#45), which has an AI-based Clinical Decision Support System (Forbes, 2020).

The fact that BCG's most innovative companies ranking (for 2020) has an entirely different set of companies, again, perhaps goes to show that innovation is hard to measure. On BCG's list, Apple (#1), Alphabet (#2), Amazon (#3), Microsoft (#4), and Siemens (#21) rank highly and Philips is ranked as the world's most innovative medtech company (BCG, 2020). It will be interesting to watch both Siemens, founded in Berlin in 1847, and Philips, founded in the Netherlands in 1891, as well as General Electric, founded in 1892 in the US, as they battle for survival and world dominance among contemporary tech—and it will likely be either or.

Why a fight for survival? This is simple. Healthcare is a massive market and will indeed (hopefully) hold a few competitors. It will, however, not support an unlimited number of huge conglomerates. Even as large as the longevity industry might become, there is no space for all historical giants together with all big tech giants—even if we don't assume the emergence of more than one tech giant per decade (which is immensely conservative, all things considered).

Right now, big tech is seeking to emerge as leaders in healthcare, leveraging their current strengths. To take a few examples, Google is capitalizing on data from their search engine, Apple is leveraging their immensely popular consumer devices, notably the iPhone, Amazon is leveraging its online–retail prowess as the world's biggest marketplace, and Microsoft is still milking its former Windows monopoly in operating systems, with some recent cloud computing advances, to emerge as a trusted leader in healthcare IT (Turea, 2019).

Over the next few decades, some of the current big tech players will likely morph into healthcare corporations focused on the longevity opportunity and will approach $10 trillion market caps, which represents roughly a 10× growth from today for each of them (Kaminskiy & Colangelo, 2020, p. 24).

Google's Health Efforts

Google is applying its AI capabilities in the areas of disease detection, data interoperability, health insurance, and population health (the latter makes sense given its data trove in search data which have been found to be valuable to things like predicting influenza trends). Google AI was folded into DeepMind soon after Google's 2014 acquisition, but Google Health is now a 500-employee strong operation. About 7% of its daily searches are health related, that is around 1 billion health questions every day. Google currently has a portfolio of 57 health tech startups, the biggest in the world, which represent about half of GV's investments (Dyrda, 2020).

Verily, Alphabet's life science research was a division of Google X until 2015 but is now an independent subsidiary. Alphabet is serious about securing a stronghold in the healthcare industry, filing 186 health-related patents between 2013 and 2017. Android is supporting a big third-party health app ecosystem.

In November 2017, Apple partnered with Stanford Medicine to conduct the Apple Heart Study, f Apple using its products to track diseases. And is of course supporting a massive third-party health app ecosystem. Apple Pay is also streamlining healthcare payments.

Amazon's Health Efforts

In 2014, Amazon first entered the medical supplies business with a deal through Cardinal Health and as a result, is now licensed to distribute medical supplies to providers in 43 states. Apple Pharmacy was launched in late November 2020, based on its 2018 MIT Startup PillPack acquisition.

Haven Healthcare, the JV between Amazon, JPMorgan Chase, and Berkshire Hathaway to bring together the resources and capabilities of the three companies to create better outcomes, greater satisfaction, and lower costs for their US employees and families by pursuing "common-sense fixes", for "US-based employees and families from Amazon, Berkshire Hathaway, and JPMorgan Chase", and, importantly "free from profit-making incentives and constraints". The venture failed less than three years after it started, struggling to find its identity (Toussaint 2021).

Microsoft's Health Efforts

Microsoft—longstanding role in healthcare, with Windows as the go-to hospital operating system which puts the Azure IT infrastructure product in the prime position to its ability to manage data security and HIPAA compliance in the cloud. Microsoft filed for 73 healthcare-related patents between 2013 and 2017 largely related to AI and telehealth. Twenty-two companies are part of the Microsoft AI in Health Partner Alliance (Turea, 2019).

Other Innovative Players Regionally

Interestingly, if we look at a regional ranking for the same year, entirely other companies come out on top. On AFR BOSS Most Innovative Companies list recognizes the most innovative organizations in Australia and New Zealand, as judged by the expert panel assembled by The Australian Financial Review and Inventium, companies judged to have the top health innovations include Arriba Group for their Digital Wellness Platform with programs and tools for people to manage their mental health, Medtronic for their Carelink 360 tool to simplify the data produced by pacemakers and defibrillators implanted into patients, as well as a curiosity, Bodycare Workplace Solutions with its COVID-19 Daily Health Check, a questionnaire giving employers confidence that only people who are healthy are going to work, Webstercare, with its Pharmacist Shared Medicine List, as well as My Emergency Doctor, which gives rural and regional patients access to medical specialists from their local hospital or medical facility so that they do not have to travel for appointments with senior doctors or specialists (Cain, 2020).

I include this regional list to indicate that I believe none of these companies are likely to appear even in a regional list a decade from now, that is, unless they also appear in a global list. In short, the market will globalize, and winning ecosystems will take it all.

The Healthcare Business Models of the Future

However, why does this matter? It matters to my discussion because it begins a discussion about the business models of the future. As I pointed out in an earlier chapter, there are many contenders, although platform or ecosystem models are in vogue. What it quite likely will *not* be is alliances in the traditional sense, based on companies providing the same services (e.g. an airline alliance). Rather, they might be open ecosystems that provide a myriad of services that interoperate. I get support in this view from McKinsey, who is a believer in healthcare ecosystems, e.g.

> ecosystem as a set of capabilities and services that integrate value chain participants (customers, suppliers, and platform and service providers) through a common commercial model and virtual data backbone (enabled by seamless data capture, management, and exchange) to create improved and efficient consumer and stakeholder experiences, and to solve significant pain points or inefficiencies.
>
> *Singhal et al. (2020*

which they say is better suited as healthcare moves from episodic care in the post WWII era to continuous care more suited for chronic conditions.

In McKinsey's view, the big players will not need to choose to operate at only one level (engagement, intelligence, or infrastructure) but can deliver products and services across these layers, and to some extent are already. For example, Amazon's AWS platform is a backbone of digital infrastructure across the board (not just in health) and now they are also operating an online pharmacy (through their acquisition of MIT startup PillPack). This may be true but is also where big tech needs to be careful. Healthcare is a different ball game than other digitalizing industries. If they play too hard, they will be regulated into oblivion. Taking a role across each layer will become pretty obvious to regulators as well as to consumers. Amazon, for one, is already on everybody's mind as a player that is getting a too big piece of the pie. Can this continue? Likely not for very long, and Bezos knows it.

Emerging Social and Business Dynamics

The Philips Future Health Index (2020) aims to provide insights into the next generation of healthcare professionals all under age 40, a group that will form the majority of healthcare workforce over the next 20 years. The survey reveals massive skills and knowledge gaps and that they are overwhelmed by digital patient data and feel the biggest change needed is to fix problems that impair digital health, notably interoperability, data accuracy, and security. Not surprisingly, they want smarter, more flexible work environments, and emphasize the importance of workplace culture, having the latest technology, working for a reputable employer, and having work/life balance.

Samsung's Health Tech Efforts

Samsung is sailing up as a big player in healthcare and notably in telehealth. Samsung Medical Center (SMC) opened in 1994 and currently has 1,200 doctors and 2,300 nurses, 40 departments, 10 specialist centers, 120 special clinics, and 1,306 beds and 800 specialists (Wikipedia, 2020). International Healthcare Center (IHC) which opened in 1995 is a center dedicated solely to the care of patients at SMC, one of South Korea's leading hospitals. IHC opened in September 1995 and is the premier medical clinic for resident expatriates and patients in Korea. However, the hospital received widespread criticism because of the spread of MERS in 2015 and Lee Kun-hee, head of South Korea's largest family-run conglomerate, or chaebol, had to apologize (Reuters, 2015).

Tencent—Big Tech Healthcare from China

In 2017, the Chinese government designated Tencent to advance intelligent healthcare. Tencent Trusted Doctor, a leading non-public online-to-offline healthcare company in China, revealed four sets of new AI-powered products to facilitate medical visits and health checkup in Q1 2019 (Moran, 2019).

Medical Device Industry

The medical device industry, a much older industry than the digital space created with the internet, has not grown at the same pace as digital health but is also digitalizing as medical devices go online and increasingly become part of the digital hospital landscape (MDDI, 2020). Top medical device companies include Medtronic, Johnson & Johnson, Cardinal Health, Abbott Laboratories, Siemens, Stryker, General Electric, Baxter, 3M, Boston Scientific and Becton, and Dickinson and Company (University Lab Partners, 2020). Boston Scientific ranked #1 on Forbes' 2019 list of America's Best Large Employers in the Healthcare Equipment and Services industry. The Marlborough-based company employs 2,300 people locally and 32,000 worldwide (Boston Scientific, 2020). As medical devices increasingly become connected to Internet of Things (IoT) devices, the sector would reasonably be expected to catch up with overall IT sector growth. The caveat would be that regulations, in some jurisdictions such as the EU, are so concerned about protecting consumers that it threatens to cripple innovation.

Healthcare Unicorns

If we consider the next decade as a timeframe for healthcare innovation, there is no way to ignore current healthcare unicorns, e.g. healthcare startups currently valued at $1B+ in market capitalization.

Globally, there are 46 healthcare unicorns, valued in aggregate at $117 billion, with over $45 billion of cumulative value in digital health unicorns alone, with initial public offering (IPO) of several multibillion-dollar digital health companies over the last few years, including Teladoc Health, Livongo, American Well, and GoodRx, which currently have a combined market value of more than $55 billion, according to a SEC filing by HAAC (Landi, 2020a,b).

According to CB Insights (2020a,b), the US can claim 21 healthcare unicorns—nearly half of the global total. Asia comes in second, with ten healthcare unicorns, all of which are in China except South Korea's biopharmaceutical firm Aprogen. Europe is home to nine healthcare unicorns, five of which are based in the UK (CB Insights, 2020a). The 2020 Digital Health 150 startups have raised over $20B in total funding across 600+ deals from 900+ unique investors (as of 8/10/2020). That list includes 12 unicorns (companies valued at $1B+) focused on a diverse range of digital health solutions (CB Insights, 2020b).

Digital Health Startups

There must be tens of thousands of startups innovating in digital health at the moment, though that figure is hard to track. Many of them will obviously disappear into oblivion. Right now, the top 10 countries for medical startups are the US, UK, Israel, India, Canada, Germany, France, China, Singapore, and Australia (Medical Startups, 2020), but that country composition could change as digital health trickles through the world's innovation hubs. Having said that, it is likely to find digital health leadership on each continent for some time to come, even as the industry globalizes.

What about the investors? In the digital health space, Khosla Ventures remains the most active investor, followed by Lux Capital, Oak HC/FT Partners, Casdin Capital, and UnityPoint Health Ventures. I define digital health to include companies in the healthcare space that use technology and software as a key differentiator (CB Insights, 2020c).

However, some that have won prizes or otherwise are worthy of mention because of the services they provide—as an indicator of future, broader healthcare offerings, that will be available more widely, include the following (where companies are listed by emergent category—and only top innovators are considered). Babylon Health, SilverCloud Health, One Medical, and Butterfly Network are already growth players.

For clarity, analysts (and journalists) tend to divide digital health startups into broad categories: AI/ML platforms, Digital therapeutics, Emerging & Nascent categories or markets, MedTech, Telemedicine, Traditional specialties being disrupted, and Wellness (CIO Review, 2020; Fast Company, 2020; Johnston, 2019; Global Digital Health 100, 2020; Ku, 2019; Lastovetska, 2020; Licholai, 2020a; Medical Futurist, 2020; MobiHealthNews, 2020; Paavola, 2020; Somers, 2020; Sullivan, 2020; Walrath, 2020). More extensive company lists are included in the appendix.

Scaling Up Digital Health Consumerization

Health assurance (https://www.healthassurance.ai/) is an "emerging category of consumer-centric, data-driven healthcare services that are designed to bend the cost curve of care and help us stay well. Built on the principles of open technology standards, these services employ empathetic user design and responsible AI" (Taneja, 2020b; Taneja, Klasko, & Maney, 2020). Arguably, this is the future of your health experience, or it is clearly a powerful vision. I find the open standards aspect is important because it has the potential to unlock interoperability, which is the holy grail of true progress on health tech. In the US alone, there are 18 different vendors of electronic health record (EHR) systems, with market leaders (e.g. dominant players) being Epic Systems Corporations followed by Cerner (Waldron, 2019a,b). Only 44% of hospitals using a vendor outside of the top 10 market share vendors which are Epic, Cerner, SAP, Oracle, Meditech, Change Healthcare, Allscripts, Infor Healthcare, and CPSI (Waldron, 2019a,b).

Hemant Taneja is a small, bearded man with five degrees from MIT who once wanted to become an academic. His family moved to Boston from India when he was in high school. He was born in Delhi, India and, groomed in systems thinking from MIT, and he grew up to be a venture capitalist (Downey, 2018). Through General Catalyst, the Cambridge, MA, based VC firm founded in 2000 which he joined in 2002, he invested in 371 companies, perhaps most notably AirBnB, Hubspot, Livongo, Snap, Stripe, and Warby Parker, each household names in their category.

Health Assurance Acquisition Corp. is a new blank check company which went public on NASDAQ on November 13, 2020, formed by Hemant Taneja, Glen Tullman, Stephen K. Klasko MD, MBA, Quentin Clark, Jennifer Schneider, MD, Anita V. Pramoda, and Evan Sotiriou, to execute its part in a broad mission of enabling the digital transformation of care, bringing disruptive innovation to the healthcare system through technology (Renaissance Capital, 2020). Health Assurance Acquisition priced its initial public offering of 50M securities at a price of $10.00, valuing itself at $500 million.

"Over the next decade, we think that 10 to 20 new businesses will have the opportunity to become very large platforms that shape parts of our emergent health assurance system in society", thinks healthcare VC Taneja (2020), who wants to "fundamentally shift the way the industry thinks about backing its most innovative, impactful founders" and "meaningfully reduce the overall healthcare GDP". What this means, we will find out, but the blank check instrument has historically been used to quickly enable startups to get to IPO.

In *UnHealthcare*, Taneja et al. want to usher in a new age of digital of mobile consumerism, merging the worlds of healthcare and technology innovation, transforming our fragmented, expensive, and inequitable healthcare system into something which would (somehow) result in very little sick "care". To do so, they feel we need to disrupt insurers and pharma, removing the current alignment between who decides, who pays, and who benefits, and moving beyond traditional vendor–customer relationships (Race To Value podcast, 2020). It also has something to do with consumerizing healthcare altogether and moving from a logic of scarcity to a logic of abundance (Damassa & Holt, 2020).

Health assurance is about creating partnerships between technologists and providers, applying data, recentering healthcare toward individuals, evolving the payer-patient-provider system, aligning incentives, and scaling healthcare while still allowing it to dynamically accommodate scope and demand changes (Taneja, 2020b; Taneja, Klasko, and Maney, 2020).

A blank check company is a development stage company that has no specific business plan or purpose or has indicated its business plan is to engage in a merger or acquisition with an unidentified company or companies, other entity, or person (Butler, 2020). It seems Taneja and his backers have something additional up their sleeve, and do not know, but I conjecture it will reshape health tech.

Some of it has to do with the interoperable health tech innovation platform, Commure, which will arguably play a large and vital role in this new system. "EHR vendors grew on the back of a closed system mentality. Given that their economics are tied to a lack of interoperability, EHRs vehemently fight regulation that would create a more open system", writes Taneja in his launch note for Commure (Taneja, 2020c). Commure is building a federation of data sources for healthcare systems across medical, financial, operational, and third-party applications like Livongo, Color, and Ro (Taneja, 2020b).

There has been an increasing number of technology-focused blank check companies issued in recent months, including SOC Telemed, Hims & Hers, and Augmedix (Landi, 2020a). $9.4 billion raised by 31 blank check companies in 2017 alone (BulldogInvestors, 2020).

Platforms of Telehealth

Diabetes alone costs the US Healthcare system and employers $245 billion every year (Echo, 2020). For the longest time, standard of care was blood testing strips that were expensive and entirely dependent on self-directed patient action (Kleiner Perkins, 2020). Instead, people stayed connected to Livongo, a digital health startup founded in 2014, through its blood glucose meter as well with certified coaches on an app and has, arguably, changed the entire diabetes management system. By March of 2019, it had 164,000 customers. Livongo had intended to expand from a single disease to create a broader platform addressing hypertension, behavioral health, diabetes prevention, and obesity (Kleiner Perkins, 2020). Their 2019 IPO market an industry at the threshold of transformation (Melton, 2019). By "prioritizing consumer experience and aligning incentives, we could build significant technology-enabled healthcare businesses that enjoy great customer love and economic fundamentals", writes Hemant Taneja, one of the authors of *UnHealthcare* (Taneja, 2020c; Taneja, Klasko, and Maney, 2020).

The merger of Diabetes coaching company Livongo with telehealth provider Teladoc (founded in 2002) is a sign of things to come in the digital health industry. Niche disease players will merge with platform players, or vice versa, in order to achieve scale, in an ongoing market consolidation (Cooney, 2020). This $18.5B merger ensure they together cover the span, a person's entire health journey (Reuter, 2020a,b; Teladoc, 2020).

Teladoc provides on-demand remote medical care connecting patients able to board-certified, state-licensed physicians within minutes. Teladoc was one of the first telehealth providers in the US and has grown by acquiring companies such as BetterHelp in 2015, Best Doctors in 2017, and Advance Medical in 2018. It is now a US$553 million (2019) revenue publicly traded company active in 130 countries, serving 27 million members (Globe Newswire, 2019).

Prescription Digital Therapeutics

Pear Therapeutics, founded by Stephen Kennedy Smith, William Greene, and Corey McCann in 2013, is a Boston-based software-based digital therapeutics platform designed to treat disease and enhance the efficacy of pharmaceuticals (Matter, 2018). Their first product targeted substance use disorder, and it received landmark approval as the first software as a medical device (SoMD) (Licholai, 2020b). Pear also has an opioid use disorder app (Hale, 2019).

Their prescription smartphone app for insomnia treats chronic insomnia by cognitive behavioral therapy in a set of 6–9 weeks' sessions based on restricting sleep to a specific schedule and aiming to improve sleep over time. In clinical studies of more than 1,400 adults, the app reduced the amount of time it took to fall asleep and cut the time awake, and lowered insomnia symptoms (Hale, 2020). Their insomnia app was previously marketed through a Novartis partnership with addiction treatment specialists but is now marketing it directly to patients /consumers. There is an estimated 30 million people suffering from chronic insomnia in the US. Pear has raised $134 million so far. At the time of writing, late June 2020, Pear had just announced its intention to go public through a SPAC associated with the Pritzker Vlock Family Office.

Gamification in Healthcare

If you ever needed a reason to let your kids play video games, Akili has it for you. Akili Interactive, is a Boston-based digital therapeutics startup founded in 2011 pioneering prescription digital treatments with direct therapeutic activity, delivered through an action video game experience. Currently in Series C-funding with a total of $13m raised so far, their pipeline of programs treats cognitive deficiency, and a variety of neurological and psychiatric conditions, including ADHD, MDD, ASD, and various inflammatory diseases. Sustained attention, selective attention, and goal management—it's all being worked on through a computer game.

On top of the June 15, 2020 FDA approval, which was based on five clinical studies involving 600 ADHD patients, where a game-like interface was used 25 minutes a day, 5 days a week, for 4 weeks, Akili has now also received a CE

Mark for EndeavorRx, which opens a pathway to advance their treatment for ADHD into Europe (UCSF, 2020). EndeavorRx is a prescription therapeutic gaming device designed to improve inattention or combined-type ADHD in youths between the ages of 8 and 12 and is intended for clinical use in concert with therapy, pharmaceutical treatment, and patient education (Martin, 2020). At the time of writing, Akili had just launched a consumer campaign, "Made for the Mind You Love" on Instagram, Facebook and TikTok, with a value proposition of treating ADHD in 96 days at $450, except that people without insurance would have access below $100/month. This literally changes the game for medical treatment campaigns in the US market.

The Digitalization of Pathology

For 150 years, pathologists have been looking through microscopes at tissue samples from patients. They make the determination: is this a pathology or not? Is it cancer? However, studies have shown that pathologists are only 67% consistent (with themselves) only 6 months apart, in short, the error rate is high, perhaps 3%–9% of cases (Dougherty, 2018). A pathologist looks at hundreds of million cells a day in order to identify individual cancer cells—which is what a machine is good at.

PathAI, which was co-founded by Andrew Beck and Aditya Khosla in 2015 out of MIT and Harvard Medical School, does screening and diagnostics using AI. PathAI's mission is to improve patient outcomes with AI-powered pathology and has so far raised a total of $75 million (2019). Task one is to distinguish normal cells from cancer. The promise is not only to improve accuracy and reproducibility of disease diagnosis but also to support the development of new medicines to treat those diseases (Wiggers, 2019). Could there be hidden patterns in digital pathology scans from which one can detect clues to the evolution of a disease which eludes even the human eye of a domain-trained pathologist at a top hospital with 20 years of experience? Even more, can these machine models quantify cell types (cancer cells and immune cells) so as to identify personalized treatments that have a higher success rate given the specific cell composition? Could it predict the probability of surviving 5 years? This is hard to do for humans (Dougherty, 2018).

The technology allows advances toward sensitive and accurate tumor biomarker quantification, its deep learning and machine learning models (particularly image recognition) automatically identify tumor regions and quantified specific gene expression on tumor and immune cells, with potential clinical use (DPA, 2020).

At the end of the day, as with many other types of professional man–machine interactions, the magic is not in having machines take over for humans but in producing informational overlays that augment human experts, adding value that way.

Women's Health Clinics

There are several pathblazing startups active in women's health, including Babyscripts, Maven, Ovia Health, Pacify, and Wildflower Health (Chamberlain, 2018). Maven, the world's largest virtual clinic for women's and family health was founded in 2014 by Katherine Ryder who is also the current CEO. Maven was built on the idea that access to better care before, during, and after pregnancies was a win-win for patients and employers. The services have now expanded. Women can access gynecological care, mental health resources, lactation consultants, postpartum therapists, fertility experts, and the resources they need to improve their maternal outcome, from their smartphone. Maven also provides fertility benefits such as egg freezing, IVF, and genetic counseling—even an app to assist patients in managing payment and reimbursement of such services (Bonebright, 2020; Reader, 2020).

Maven raised $45M in February 2020. What distinguishes this telehealth service from other such online services is that there is a dedicated health advocate that can be messaged at any time, providing continuity of care, a set of proactive interventions (symptom lookouts, etc.), as well as personalized content curated for each member. Maven Clinic is fee-for-service and not covered by insurance. However, rates are affordable to increase access to care for women. For example, a 10-minute video appointment with a nurse practitioner like myself is just $18—less than most peoples' copay.

Maven has been recognized as Fast Company's #1 Most Innovative Health Company. Maven has supported over 5 million women and families and raised $90 million in funding from leading investors like Sequoia Capital, Oak HC/FT Partners, Icon Ventures, and Female Founders Fund (Pallarito, 2020). Before the pandemic, only one in ten Americans had tried telemedicine. During the pandemic, Maven's marketing shifted from B2B to B2C and started offering free appointments. On the other side of the pandemic, their goal is that people will think of telemedicine as normal (Hercher, 2020).

Why Health Tech Fails

Healthcare is complicated. Startups are complex. There are a myriad of reasons why health tech ventures fail (Cole, 2020; Herzlinger, 2006). Herzlinger notes that there are six exogenous forces on new ventures attempting to innovate in healthcare: structure, financing, public policy, consumers, accountability, and technology, all of which can become barriers to innovation.

In Figure 3.2, I have classified the top reasons healthcare innovation fails using the forces of disruption framework. *Tech disruption* is a two-fold challenge: legacy technology blocks and overoptimism about novel tech creates unrealistic

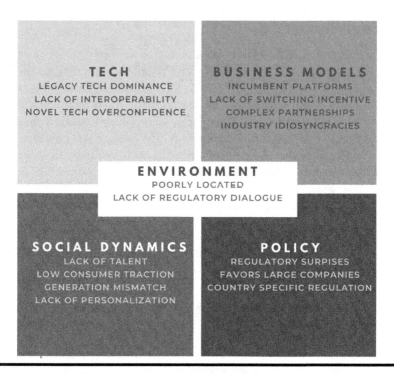

Figure 3.2 Why health tech fails.

expectations that cannot be met. *Business model disruption* happens (or more often does not happen) as incumbent platforms are entrenched, and because stifling, existing, and crisscrossing partnerships are near totalitarian in their alignment of incentive to keep the status quo. *Policy disruption* occurs when existing ways are implicitly supported by existing regulation, yet policy fails to propose or get through new measures that open the market. Stasis is still aptly called disruption because the normal way policy operates is as an adaptive tool where widespread stakeholder consultation keeps dynamism in the markets at all times. *Social dynamics disruption* takes place if consumerization fails, new generations fail to get on board, and services do not get personalized to a sufficient degree. Environmental disruption takes place if human institutions are not properly located, properly in dialogue with other actors (regulators in a country's capital or away from the industrial nexus of its own market), encroach on nature to the degree that the interaction of those ecosystems causes zoonotic spillovers of infectious diseases from animals to humans.

My functional explanation is that health tech fails if any of these five factors fail individually or in combination. They are all related. Each has to interact before one builds up too much pressure that has to be relieved onto the neighboring set of concerns.

Conclusion

With a little luck, the movers and shakers in the healthcare system of the future will, as a general rule, and with some exceptions, not at all be similar to those that have succeeded in the past and who have the largest current footprint, such as payers (governments and insurers) or providers (particularly academic hospitals, specialist, and primary care doctors).

The emergence of startups, intrapreneurs, engineers, patients, and service providers is quite apparent although their influence has not even scratched the surface of what will happen next. The writing is on the wall. Having said that, no other industry will change as much as healthcare over the next decade and beyond, but the emphasis might be on beyond—this could take 20 years to shake up, not just a few years. Implementing interoperability does have a cost because it changes who is kingmaker from the insurers and big pharma. It shifts the advantage toward any nimble actor, big or small.

In this chapter, I focused on the emerging future by ways of identifying individual changemakers, institutional innovators, pathbreaking startups, and even nonprofits that already are making a difference. To have any inkling of the trajectory you need to follow them, that part is obvious, but the scale is impressive and hard to track meaningfully since it is evolving in real time. That is why the appendix contains a comprehensive guide to the innovation landscape and to information sources as well as influencers who you can use to follow trends.

In the next chapter, I will look at the disruption of healthcare.

KEY TAKEAWAYS AND REFLECTIONS

1. What digital health tech are you exposed to on a daily basis?

   _____

2. Thinking specifically about AI, wearables, digital therapeutics, social media, and telemedicine, which areas do you feel will impact the next two decades the most and why?

   _____

3. What health technologies are on the horizon? What would it take to develop these?

   _____

References

BCG (2020) "The most innovative companies 2020: The serial innovation imperative', BCG. Available at: https://image-src.bcg.com/Images/BCG-Most-Innovative-Companies-2020-Jun-2020-R-4_tcm9-251007.pdf (Accessed 26 November 2020).

Bonebright, A. (2020) 'Maven Clinic and the reimagination of contemporary medicine', Michigan College of Engineering Center for Entrepreneurship. Available at: https://cfe.umich.edu/maven-clinic-and-the-reimagination-of-contemporary-medicine/ (Accessed 27 November 2020).

Boston Scientific (2020) 'Boston scientific recognized on Forbes America's best large employers list', Boston Scientific, Press Release. Available at: https://news.bostonscientific.com/forbes-americas-best-employers-2019# (Accessed 26 November 2020).

Buhr, S. (2020) 'Where top VCs are investing in healthcare B2B and infrastructure'. Available at: https://techcrunch.com/2020/05/12/where-top-vcs-are-investing-in-healthcare-b2b-and-infrastructure/ (Accessed 26 November 2020).

BulldogInvestors (2020) 'Blank check companies', BulldogInvestors. Available at: https://bulldoginvestors.com/services/#Blank-Check-Companies (Accessed 26 November 2020).

Butler, D. (2020) '"Blank Check" IPOs: What investors need to know', The Motley Fool, 24 July 2020. Available at: https://www.fool.com/investing/2020/07/24/blank-check-ipo-what-investors-need-to-know.aspx (Accessed 26 November 2020).

Cain, A. (2020) 'The 10 most innovative health companies', Financial Review, 9 October 2020. Available at: https://www.afr.com/companies/healthcare-and-fitness/the-10-most-innovative-health-companies-20200930-p560ly (Accessed 26 November 2020).

CB Insights (2020a) 'Mapping healthcare unicorns around the world', CB Insights, 28 May 2020. Available at: https://www.cbinsights.com/research/healthcare-unicorns-q1-20/#:~:text=The%20US%20boasts%2021%20healthcare,are%20based%20in%20the%20UK (Accessed 26 November 2020).

CB Insights (2020b). 'Digital health 150: The digital health startups transforming the future of healthcare', CB Insights. Available at: https://www.cbinsights.com/research/report/digital-health-startups-redefining-healthcare/ (Accessed 26 November 2020).

CB Insights (2020c). 'Here are Q1's most active healthcare investors', CB Insights. Available at: https://www.cbinsights.com/research/most-active-healthcare-vcs-q1-20/#:~:text=In%20the%20digital%20health%20space,software%20as%20a%20key%20differentiator (Accessed 26 November 2020).

Chamberlain, G. (2018) 'Deconstructing the telehealth industry: Part II: Improving the access points of healthcare delivery', White Paper, *Ziegler*. Available at: https://www.ziegler.com/z-media/3828/ziegler_telehealth_whitepaper_fnl_nogutter-spreads.pdf (Accessed 27 November 2020).

CIO Review (2020) 'Top 50 healthcare solution companies', CIO Review. Available at: https://healthcare.cioreview.com/vendors/top-healthcare-solution-companies.html (Accessed 26 November 2020).

Cole, E. (2020) 'Top challenges of founding a healthcare startup in 2020', MyTechMag [Online]. Available at: https://healthcare.mytechmag.com/top-challenges-of-founding-a-healthcare-startup-in-2020-1557.html (Accessed on 27 November 2020).

Cooney, E. (2020) 'As health tech flourished, Teladoc and Livongo saw an opportunity to 'accelerate,' executives say', Stat+, 10 September 2020. Available at: https://www.statnews.com/2020/09/10/teladoc-and-livongo-opportunity-to-accelerate/ (Accessed on 27 November 2020).

Damassa, J. and Holt, M. (2020) 'THCB's Bookclub, August 2020 – UnHealthcare: A Manifesto for Health Assurance', The Health Care Blog [Blog post & Video], 19 August 2020. Available at: https://thehealthcareblog.com/blog/2020/08/19/thcbs-bookclub-august-2020-unhealthcare-a-manifesto-for-health-assurance/ (Accessed on 27 November 2020).

Dougherty, E. (2018) 'Artificial intelligence decodes cancer pathology images', Novartis, 12 November 2018. Available at: https://www.novartis.com/stories/discovery/artificial-intelligence-decodes-cancer-pathology-images (Accessed on 27 November 2020).

Downey, K. (2018) 'Education meets innovation', Spectrum, MIT. Available at: https://spectrum.mit.edu/winter-2018/education-meets-innovation/ (Accessed on 28 November 2020).

DPA (2020) 'PV20 Vendor Showcase: PathAI', Digital Pathology Association (DPA). Available at: https://digitalpathologyassociation.org/pathai-showcase (Accessed on 27 November 2020).

Dyrda, L. (2020) '18 things to know about Google in healthcare for 2020', Becker's Health IT, 7 January 2020. Available at: https://www.beckershospitalreview.com/healthcare-information-technology/18-things-to-know-about-google-in-healthcare-for-2020.html (Accessed 26 November 2020).

Echo (2020) 'Developing high-value relationships to improve consumer health', Echo Health Ventures. Available at: https://echohealthventures.com/sites/default/files/2019-05/Livongo-Echo-Health-Ventures-Case-Study.pdf (Accessed 27 November 2020).

Fast Company (2020) 'The 10 most innovative health companies of 2020', Fast Company, 10 March 2020. Available at: https://www.fastcompany.com/90457848/health-most-innovative-companies-2020 (Accessed 27 November 2020).

Forbes (2020) 'The world's most innovative companies', Forbes. Available at: https://www.forbes.com/innovative-companies/list/#tab:rank (Accessed 26 November 2020).

Fortune (2020) 'Fortune 2000'. Available at: https://www.forbes.com/global2000/#3fbd773a335d (Accessed 26 November 2020).

Global Digital Health 100 (2020). 'Global Digital Health 100', The Journal of mHealth, 24 November 2020. Available at: https://thejournalofmhealth.com/digital-health-100/ (Accessed 26 November 2020).

Globe Newswire (2019) 'Teladoc health reports first quarter 2019 results', Globe Newswire, 30 April 2019. Available at: https://www.globenewswire.com/news-release/2019/04/30/1813070/0/en/Teladoc-Health-Reports-First-Quarter-2019-Results.html (Accessed on 27 November 2020).

Gooch, K. (2020) '50 top teaching hospitals in the US, ranked by Washington Monthly Magazine', Becker's Hospital Review, 1 October 2020. Available at: https://www.beckershospitalreview.com/rankings-and-ratings/50-top-teaching-hospitals-in-the-us-ranked-by-washington-monthly-magazine.html (Accessed 27 November 2020).

Hale, C. (2019) 'Pear Therapeutics raises $64M, launches prescription app for opioid use disorder', Fierce Biotech, 9 January 2019. Available at: https://www.fiercebiotech.com/medtech/pear-therapeutics-raises-64m-launches-prescription-app-for-opioid-use-disorder (Accessed on 27 November 2020).

Hale, C. (2020) 'Pear Therapeutics launches digital insomnia app through direct-to-patient telehealth model', Fierce Biotech, 18 November 2020. Available at: https://www.fiercebiotech.com/medtech/pear-therapeutics-launches-digital-insomnia-app-through-direct-to-patient-telehealth-model (Accessed on 27 November 2020).

HCI (2020) '8 of the most advanced hospitals in the world', Healthcare International Blog [Online]. Available at: https://www.healthcareinternational.com/blog/article/8-of-the-foremost-advanced-hospitals-in-the-world (Accessed 27 November 2020).

Hercher, J. (2020) 'Telemedicine startup Maven Clinic's marketing plan shifts from B2B To B2C, due to the pandemic', Ad Exchanger [Online], 9 April 2020. Available at: https://www.adexchanger.com/online-advertising/telemedicine-startup-maven-clinics-marketing-plan-shifts-from-b2b-to-b2c-due-to-the-pandemic/ (Accessed on 27 November 2020).

Herzlinger, R.E. (2006) 'Why innovation in health care is so hard', *Harvard Business Review*, May. Available at: https://www.hse.ie/eng/about/who/healthbusinessservices/hbs-news-and-events/why-innovation-in-health-care-is-so-hard.pdf (Accessed 22 November 2020).

Johnston, M. (2019) '9 digital health startups that could join the IPO wave', Investopedia, 15 July 2019. Available at: https://www.investopedia.com/9-digital-health-startups-that-could-join-the-ipo-wave-4692853 (Accessed 26 November 2020).

Kaminskiy, D. and Colangelo, M. (2020) *Longevity Industry 1.0: Defining the Biggest and Most Complex Industry in Human History*. London: Deep Knowledge Group.

Kleiner Perkins (2020) 'Improving the lives of people with chronic disease: Founder: Glen Tullman', Kleiner Perkins. Available at: https://www.kleinerperkins.com/case-study/livongo/# (Accessed on 27 November 2020).

Ku, L. (2019) '9 leading AI healthcare companies in 2020', Plug and Play, 17 December 2019. Available at: https://www.plugandplaytechcenter.com/resources/7-leading-ai-healthcare-companies-2020/ (Accessed 26 November 2020).

Landi, H. (2020a) 'Former Livongo execs start new company and prepare for $500M IPO', Fierce Healthcare, 28 October 2020. Available at: https://www.fiercehealthcare.com/tech/former-livongo-execs-form-blank-check-company-and-prepare-for-500m-ipo (Accessed 26 November 2020).

Landi, H. (2020b) 'How Teladoc's blockbuster deal could impact the entire virtual care landscape', Fierce Healthcare, 10 August 2020. Available at: https://www.fiercehealthcare.com/tech/here-are-key-takeaways-teladoc-livongo-deal-from-analysts-and-digital-health-leaders (Accessed on 27 November 2020).

Lapointe, J. (2019) 'Academic medical centers adapting with new business models', Practice Management News, Rev Cycle Intelligence, 6 May 2019. Available at: https://revcycleintelligence.com/news/academic-medical-centers-adapting-with-new-business-models (Accessed on 27 November 2020).

Lastovetska, A. (2020) '10 digital health startups you need to watch in 2020', Legal Reader, 22 April 2020. Available at: https://www.legalreader.com/10-digital-health-startups-you-need-to-watch-in-2020/ (Accessed 26 November 2020).

Licholai, G. (2020a) 'Digital healthcare growth drivers in 2020', Forbes, 14 January 2020. Available at: https://www.forbes.com/sites/greglicholai/2020/01/14/digital-healthcare-growth-drivers-in-2020/?sh=4d02254d511d (Accessed 26 November 2020).

Licholai, G. (2020b) 'Digital therapeutics leaders focus on reimbursement', Forbes, 23 February 2020. Available at: https://www.forbes.com/sites/greglicholai/2020/02/23/digital-therapeutics-leaders-focus-on-reimbursement/?sh=6f4aa1324d0f (Accessed on 27 November 2020).

Martin, L. (2020) 'The Video Game Will See You Now', Psychiatric Times, 22 June 2020. Available at: https://www.psychiatrictimes.com/view/video-game-will-see-you-now (Accessed 27 November 2020).

Matter (2018) 'Tales from the trenches: Corey McCann, Founder of PEAR Therapeutics', Matter [Video], 25 April 2020. Available at: https://www.youtube.com/watch?v=VxKcDz2CKBA (Accessed 27 November 2020).

MDDI (2020) 'Medical device and diagnostic industry'. Available at: https://www.mddionline.com/ (Accessed 26 November 2020).

Medical Futurist (2020) 'The top 100 digital health companies: an infographic', The Medical Futurist, 10 September 2020. Available at: https://medicalfuturist.com/the-top-100-digital-health-companies-an-infographic/ (Accessed 26 November 2020).

Medical Startups (2020) 'Medical Startups.org' [Online]. Available at: https://www.medicalstartups.org/ (Accessed 26 November 2020).

Melton, E. (2019) 'Livongo—An evolution from digital health startup to market leader', Threshold Ventures, 25 July 2019. Available at: https://medium.com/threshold-ventures/livongo-an-evolution-from-digital-health-startup-to-market-leader-82aa597fea6b (Accessed 27 November 2020).

MobiHealthNews (2020) 'Digital health funding is off to a roaring start in 2020', MobiHealthNews, 3 April 2020. Available at: https://www.mobihealthnews.com/news/digital-health-funding-roaring-start-2020 (Accessed 26 November 2020).

Moran, J. (2019) 'Could China upend American healthcare', MedCity News, 29 July 2019. Available at: https://medcitynews.com/2019/07/could-china-upend-american-healthcare/ (Accessed 26 November 2020).

Moriarty, A. (2020a) 'Top 10 largest health systems in the U.S.', *The Definitive Blog*, 23 July 2020. Available at: https://blog.definitivehc.com/top-10-largest-health-systems (Accessed 27 November 2020).

Moriarty, A. (2020b) 'Effects of IDN & GPO consolidation on the healthcare supply chain', The Definitive Blog, 15 October 2020. Available at: https://blog.definitivehc.com/idn-gpo-consolidation-healthcare-supply-chain (Accessed 27 November 2020).

Paavola, A. (2020) '5 of healthcare's next billion-dollar startups from 2020 Forbes list', Becker's Hospital Review, 28 May 2020. Available at: https://www.beckershospit-alreview.com/rankings-and-ratings/5-of-healthcare-s-next-billion-dollar-startups-from-2020-forbes-list.html (Accessed on 27 November 2020).

Pallarito, K. (2020) '"Femtech" is busting taboos around women's health and wellness—But what is it exactly?', Health.com [Online]. Available at: https://www.health.com/mind-body/femtech-womens-health (Accessed 27 November 2020).

Philips Future Health Index (2020) 'Philips future health index' [Online]. Available at: https://www.philips.com/a-w/about/news/future-health-index (Accessed 26 November 2020).

Race to Value podcast (2020) 'UnHealthcare: A manifesto for health assurance (Part I), with Dr. Stephen Klasko', The Race to Value podcast, 9 November 2020. Available at: https://www.racetovalue.org/2020/11/09/unhealthcare-a-manifesto-for-health-assurance-part-i-with-dr-stephen-klasko/ (Accessed 27 November 2020).

Reader, R. (2020) 'This innovative telemedicine network wants companies to think beyond maternity leave', Fast Company, 10 March 2020. Available at: https://www.fastcompany.com/90457553/maven-clinic-most-innovative-companies-2020 (Accessed 27 November 2020).

Renaissance Capital (2020) 'General Catalyst's SPAC Health Assurance Acquisition files for a $500 million IPO', Renaissance Capital, 26 October 2020. Available at: https://www.renaissancecapital.com/IPO-Center/News/72692/Health-technology-SPAC-Health-Assurance-Acquisition-files-for-a-$500-millio(Accessed26November 2020).

Reuter, E. (2020a) 'Livongo's top leaders to depart after Teladoc merger', MedCityNews, 26 October 2020. Available at: https://medcitynews.com/2020/10/livongos-top-leaders-to-depart-after-teladoc-merger/ (Accessed 26 November 2020).

Reuter, E. (2020b) 'Teladoc, Livongo finalize $18.5B merger', MedCityNews, 30 October 2020. Available at: https://medcitynews.com/2020/10/teladoc-livongo-finalize-18-5b-merger/ (Accessed 26 November 2020).

Reuters (2015) 'Samsung scion apologizes for MERS spread at group hospital', Reuters.com [Online]. Available at: https://www.reuters.com/article/us-health-mers-southkorea-outbreak/samsung-scion-apologizes-for-mers-spread-at-group-hospital-idUSKBN0P300920150623 (Accessed 26 November 2020).

Singhal, S., Kayyali, B., Levin, B., and Greenberg, Z. (2020) 'The next wave of health-care innovation: The evolution of ecosystems', McKinsey, 23 June 2020. Available at: https://www.mckinsey.com/industries/healthcare-systems-and-services/our-insights/the-next-wave-of-healthcare-innovation-the-evolution-of-ecosystems (Accessed 25 November 2020).

Somers, M. (2020) '15 MIT startups to watch', MIT Sloan, Ideas made to matter, 21 September 2020. Available at: https://mitsloan.mit.edu/ideas-made-to-matter/15-mit-startups-to-watch.

Sullivan, M. (2020) 'Could these 50 hot tech startups be tomorrow's unicorns?', Fast Company, 10 June 2020. Available at: https://www.fastcompany.com/90509585/could-these-50-hot-tech-startups-be-tomorrows-unicorns (Accessed 26 November 2020).

Taneja, H. (2020a) 'Announcing commure: a system of innovation for healthcare', Commure blog, 5 February 2020. Available at: https://blog.commure.com/ announcingcommure/ (Accessed 28 November 2020).

Taneja, H. (2020b) 'Announcing UnHealthcare', Medium. [Online], 15 July 2020. Available at: https://medium.com/health-assurance/announcing-unhealthcare-8d6fb147d774 (Accessed 27 November 2020).

Taneja, H. (2020c) 'Introducing the health assurance acquisition corp.', General Catalyst, 17 November 2020. Available at: https://www.generalcatalyst.com/ gcamplified/introducing-haac/ (Accessed 27 November 2020).

Taneja, H., Klasko, S., and Maney, K. (2020) *UnHealthcare: A Manifesto for Health Assurance*, Morrisville, NC: Lulu Press.

Teladoc (2020) 'Creating a new standard in the global delivery, access and experience of healthcare', Press Release, Teladoc. Available at: http://go.teladochealth.com/ livongo/ (Accessed 26 November 2020).

The Commonwealth Fund (2020) 'International health care system profiles', The Commonwealth Fund. Available at: https://www.commonwealthfund.org/interna tional-health-policy-center/system-profiles (Accessed 27 November 2020).

Toussaint, J.S. (2021) 'Why Haven Healthcare Failed', Harvard Business Review, Jan 06, 2021. Available at: https://hbr.org/2021/01/why-haven-healthcare-failed

Turea, M. (2019) 'How the "Big 4" tech companies are leading healthcare innovation', Healthcare Weekly, 27 February 2019. Available at: https://healthcareweekly.com/ how-the-big-4-tech-companies-are-leading-healthcare-innovation/ (Accessed 26 November 2020).

UCSF (2020) 'Digital health tool makes history with recent commercialization', UCSF Innovation Ventures. Available at: https://innovation.ucsf.edu/digital-health-tool-makes-history-recent-commercialization (Accessed on 27 November 2020).

University Lab Partners (2020). '11 leading medical device companies in 2020', University Lab Partners, 26 November 2020. Available at: https://www.univer-sitylabpartners.org/blog/leading-medical-device-companies-2020 (Accessed 26 November 2020).

Waldron, T. (2019a) 'HIMSS19 recap: The future of analytics technologies', The Definitive Blog, 7 March 2019. Available at: https://blog.definitivehc.com/ himss19-recap-the-analytics-revolution (Accessed on 27 November 2020).

Waldron, T. (2019b) 'Top 8 healthcare trends in 2019', The Definitive Blog, 19 March 2019. Available at: https://blog.definitivehc.com/top-8-healthcare-trends-2019 (Accessed 27 November 2020).

Walrath, R. (2020) 'Agtech, health tech dominated the 2020 MIT $100K challenge', BostInno, 22 May 2020. Available at: https://www.bizjournals.com/boston/inno/ stories/news/2020/05/22/agtech-health-tech-dominated-the-2020-mit-100k.html (Accessed 26 November 2020).

Wiggers, K. (2019) 'PathAI raises $60 million for AI pathology and diagnostic tools', Venture Beat, 17 April 2020. Available at: https://venturebeat.com/2019/04/17/ pathai-raises-60-million-for-ai-pathology-and-diagnostic-tools/ (Accessed 27 November 2020).

Wikipedia (2020) 'Samsung Medical Center'. Available at: https://www.wikiwand.com/ en/Samsung_Medical_Center (Accessed 26 November 2020).

Chapter 4

The Disruption of Healthcare

The global healthcare system faces a cerberus-like trifecta of problems: untenable economics, a disparity in access, and highly variable quality. The technologies fueling this system are both crumbling themselves and stifling innovation at the same time.

Just in the US, healthcare accounted for 18% of the 2017 GDP and will likely reach nearly 20% by 2025, while hospital-induced deaths have skyrocketed, and tens of millions of people remain uninsured (Herzlinger, 2021).

To understand disruption, in my recent book, *Future Tech*, I tailored various existing threads into a strategic framework that streamlines my thinking around five specific forces of disruption: technology, policy, business models, social forces, and the environmental context that surrounds them (Undheim, 2021).

What that means is that whoever uses this lens on the world is equipped to do five things. One, track changes in emerging technologies based on deep exploration of sci-tech R&D. Two, understand who are trying to enact policy changes or predict relevant regulatory changes. Three, deeply understand how organizations deploy various business models—and even develop new ones. Four, ponder social dynamics, such as the emergence and impact of social movements, as well as consumer activism, which can help you determine which priorities to chase, which interrelationships to be aware of, and what gaps to fill. Five, become aware of the location-based dynamics that shape the appropriation of a technology or project. The forces of disruption framework can be applied

DOI: 10.4324/9781003178071-4

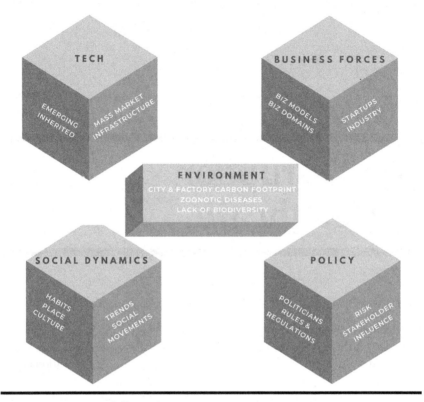

Figure 4.1 Forces of disruption.

both as an internal strategy tool for an organization, as a tool to assess external risk, and as a product-specific scenario tool (Figure 4.1).

Six Forces Complicating Healthcare Innovation

Herzlinger notes that there are six exogenous forces on new ventures attempting to innovate in healthcare: structure, financing, public policy, consumers, accountability, and technology. *Structure* refers to the players that constitute the existing institutional framework of healthcare. *Financing* is not as straightforward as it may seem because the process of generating and acquiring capital in healthcare differs from most industries. *Public policy* which refers both to policy development and advocacy, and especially to regulations, pervade the healthcare industry because incompetent or fraudulent suppliers can do irreversible human damage. *Consumers* are becoming so engaged in their own healthcare that the term "patients" (at times) seems outdated. *Accountability* stems from the demand from both consumers and payers that healthcare products be safe, effective, and cost-effective. *Technology* is the foundation for advances in treatment as well as for more efficient and convenient delivery (Herzlinger, 2006, 2013, 2021).

Creating the innovations in healthcare that can meet these needs is not only a priority, and an opportunity, but also it is a necessity. Luckily, many are those who question the status quo in healthcare. I have faith that many would be willing to experiment with implementing new solutions that lower costs while increasing both quality and access. The challenge is how to do it but also how to understand the changes that are already underway.

It is in this light that disruption in healthcare needs to be seen in a particularly positive light, even if you are among the incumbent actors who have benefited from the current system. Luckily, not only can health tech be applied to a myriad of conditions, including diabetes (Klonoff, Kerr, & Mulvaney, 2020), health tech is also chipping away at the overall system, disrupting it slowly but surely, and—at times—invisibly, yet quicker than many realize.

The Pivotal Role of Technology

To some extent, there has always been technology involved in healthcare delivery, so its evolution cannot be viewed fully isolated from existing approaches. Nowhere is that truer than in the field of medical devices, which has tended to be viewed separately from digital health, even though medical devices have increasingly come online, either simply providing local electronic measurements or even more powerfully, we have seen such devices get connected with hospital systems or even online medical records accessible to doctors or patients wherever they reside, provided they have the right access.

The Explosion of Digital Health Apps

At the same time, digital health app space, as an emerging subfield of health tech, has recently exploded. The myriad of apps that have mushroomed represent a veritable startup boom that is starting to match other online innovation paradigms seen in the early days of the internet. This is no surprise, given the tremendous stakes, enormous potential economic bounties in the healthcare market, as well as the promises of increased efficiency and effectiveness using online approaches.

Why Is Healthcare Disruption Happening Now?

I have been tracking the field of digital health since 2005 when I was asked to build the European Commission's best practice exchange framework for e-government, e-inclusion, and e-health. Back then, e-health meant back-office improvements as well as health information. True transactional services were few and far between. Interoperability problems hampered many projects, and there was a great emphasis on resolving such issues because the potential was well known and reality available for everyone to see. Yet, many years passed before true breakthroughs happened. Why? Healthcare is not an area where governments are particularly well positioned to act. The field is contentious, multi-faceted, tech-intensive, and over-regulated. Where governments aim to protect, they end up disenfranchizing their own citizens, slowing down industry, and complicating life for startups trying to disrupt. This largely happens because governments become beholden to special interests but also because the full picture is too complicated to comprehend and difficult to improve with broad stroke measures at their disposal.

In these 15 years, the progress has been steep but not exponential. That is, until about 2 years ago, when the field began a steep increase in adoption, innovation, and investment. Part of the reason, I would like to think, is that best practice has, by now, been exchanged for long enough that the core lessons about what works are widely available to innovators both in public and private sector.

The enormous advances in sensor technology, which I tackle in the next chapter in my discussion of wearables, although sensors are not necessarily wearable, have had a huge impact on the healthcare device space. The ubiquity of sensors, the variety of sensor formfactors, capabilities, and the drastically lowered price points due to the scaling-up of production capacity in Asia, notably in Shenzhen, China over the past decade, have changed the ball game. The main impetus of that phenomenon is the growth of the cell phone platform, which has created a sea of suppliers. With that kind of hardware extension being made available to innovators, there is almost no end to the new functionalities that can be added to health innovations, whether they choose the cell phone, emerging wearable formfactors or even traditional medical devices as their form factor.

Digital health tools, which were a game changer as well, began hitting the market in the early 2000s, followed by the explosion of direct-to-consumer health apps available via online app stores such as Apple's App Store and Google Play. As a consequence, the lines between medical applications and consumer health applications began to blur (Digital Healthcare Timeline, 2020).

Digital Healthcare Is Suddenly Growing Exponentially

Healthcare has arguably been slower than other industries to absorb technology and capture the tailwinds of digitalization. Well-meaning regulation must take some of the blame for making the system rigid. The winner takes all characteristics of services that are available to the masses is another factor. The relative success of the pharma industry's quick fix drug technologies throughout the 20th century is a third. The US Centers for Medicare and Medicaid Services (CMS) estimates that in 2019, $360.3 billion will be spent on retail prescription drugs in the US alone (ASPE, 2020). If only a fraction of that will start to move toward the digital space, that's interesting for investors and could make a difference to patients taking far too many drugs contemporaneously and with huge potential for adverse drug interactions.

According to Mercom Capital Group, global VC funding for Digital Health companies in the first half of 2020 shattered all previous funding records, bringing in $6.3 billion. Funding activity was up by 24% (Bryant, 2020). Digital healthcare, arguably, moved slowly for 30 years and then, suddenly, it has started to move. Why?

It would be tempting to attribute the rise to the coronavirus pandemic, but, in fact, the rise started a few months before. Something else is also going on. What? Licholai (2020) claims:

> the key drivers are expanded patient engagement as well as institutional investment with the ultimate goal of reducing costs. Big pharma, payers and insurance companies have recognized the business benefits of patient empowerment. Digital applications are helping patients become better decision makers for their own health by providing personalized insights.

The pivotal role of business models, in addition to technology, regulation, and social dynamics, is often hidden until they kick in and start to dominate. Clever business models are what give everything else legs.

Tech Maturity

Certain health tech measures, tools (basic medical devices gradually being upgraded and digitally enhanced), processes, and innovations are already working well, and others are in their infancy (AI, wearables, robotics, sensors, and digital therapeutics).

How Technology Forces Impact Health

Many of us have observed the current lag in adoption of technology into healthcare. It would be easy to consider that as the natural state of affairs. I am here to tell you that it isn't necessarily so, though changing this dynamic won't be easy. The degree to which science and technology is embedded in society varies. I see them as breaking down into the following categories: emerging, infrastructure, common, mass market, and legacy (or inherited), listed after degree of future orientation (Undheim, 2021, p. 48). Each impacts health in a different way.

Emerging tech, e.g. technology that still has an adoption curve into the future, and is aspirational, complicated, even unproven (Undheim, 2021, p. 48), is mostly what I am concerned with in this chapter. However, infrastructure technologies vary between different countries and settings and cannot be assumed not to be a challenge to reckon with. Many developmental aid projects in global health have stranded on that issue because they either clash with national infrastructures or threaten to uproot them, and gets shut down. Similarly, common technologies, such as laptops (as a form factor) are not common in all places, and may serve a different function, have different ownership, trajectory or importance, but the good thing is that it largely is not so deeply embedded that its relative absence or presence matters very much because it can be substituted, for example, by desktops or cell phones.

Mass market technologies, are, largely, not a huge concern, in that they are readily available usually at acceptable cost levels. The decision to deploy them to a greater extent can still have significant impact or cost (e.g. broadband). Arguably, broadband, is the great lever both in work and health because it enables remote work and telehealth. Luckily, it can be implemented in numerous ways (fiber, copper, cell towers, satellite, etc.), which makes a patchwork model feasible.

Legacy technology is, on the other hand, a huge problem in health because they typically have poor interoperability—they cannot communicate easily with newer systems. The lack of health interoperability can render many innovative health efforts useless over the long haul. Examples of such challenges include medical devices that cannot share data, mobile or wearable devices with poor batteries and insufficient data-transfer capability to work seamlessly with other systems, as well as older, centralized databases, and computer systems that contain health data that can no longer be read or utilized for diagnostics. State-of-the art investments can turn into legacy tech quite rapidly, which can render archives useless only after a few years. There are too many examples to count.

How Business Forces Impact Health Tech

To understand health disruption (and innovation), we need to consider how new business models, often put forward by startups, reshape industry and business functions. Business models, in particular, have become a major instrument of innovation because novel business models can reshape (some) industries almost instantly (Undheim, 2021, p. 13). Business models could be connected to an entirely new tech platform, a new way to charge for something, or simply a good idea that nobody has thought of charging for before in that same way. Healthcare, being so entrenched for so long, is full of such opportunities.

However, the healthcare industry is among the most complex industries there is, partly because it is so much more than an industry, it is a set of cultural expectations, an area of high public sector concern (and spending). It is sometimes difficult to know which angle is the best one to come at it from. Healthcare organizations include patient groups, health plans, providers, employers, universities, hospitals, business organizations, and the pharmaceutical, biotechnology, and medical device industries.

Business models have traditionally stayed the same over long spans of time in the healthcare field. Countries have each had their own models. The American model has emphasized private payers, employers working in consort with insurance companies, and the European model has, largely, emphasized public healthcare although private healthcare has entered at the top end of the market, catapulting the wealthy out of wait times and giving them the ability to choose higher end providers, cross-border if needed.

Traditional and Emerging Healthcare Business Models

If we look more closely, a small set of business models have been at play for a long time. The four traditional business models: manufacturer, distributor, retailer, and franchise (Undheim, 2021, p. 93), all come into play somewhere along the healthcare chain, as medically relevant goods and services need to be produced, distributed, sold, and delivered across vast territories.

Emerging business models in healthcare include platform-based models (often based on technology or some other feature that delivers scale, such as a partnership or peer-to-peer interaction), subscription, digital content, micropayments, multisided marketplaces, or indeed other ways to leverage network effects.

Particular attention should be given to healthcare at the "base of the pyramid" poverty scenario, which is prevalent in many parts of the world, indeed there are segments of the population with these characteristics in nearly every country, meaning communities that cannot pay (much) for care, has led to business models that emphasize the co-creation of patient needs, community engagement, continuous involvement of customers, innovative medical technology, focus on human resources for health, strategic partnerships, economies of scale, and cross-subsidization. They may include bottom-up assessments of what such patients (or their spokespersons or donors) know, want, trust, and are willing to pay for (Angeli & Jaiswal, 2016).

Business model (for-profit, hybrid, B2B, and peer-to-peer) might become more important than which industry sector the service operates (IFTF, 2007). As Amazon moves into healthcare with the purchase of MIT startup Pillpack and rolls out online pharmacy services in the fall of 2020, the drug delivery model changes drastically for existing players such as CVS. The web suddenly, and overnight, becomes a mainstream distribution channel for prescription drugs for existing Amazon Prime customers.

Similarly, retail and health are coming together in other ways as CVS MinuteClinic as well as other concepts (QuickHealth, Farmacia Remedios, and RediClinic) roll out across the world.

Another emerging model is the subscription model for primary car, healthcare as a service (HaaS), aligns incentives between the patient and provider (Shah, 2018).

The once unthinkable unbundling or disaggregation of healthcare (which simply means being able to procure individual pieces of care without necessarily buying it all from one source) is increasingly happening, at least at the fringes of healthcare, all around the world. In the US, the Affordable Care Act expanded healthcare to some 22 million US consumers who don't have healthcare through their employer (or have pre-existing conditions) by requiring them to buy health insurance. With the Food & Drug Administration (FDA)'s 2013 Mobile Medical Applications guidance which was subsequently revised in 2019, retail and app-based care solutions have exploded and have the opportunities for online review of health practitioners, providers, and hospital services (Williams, 2019). Home-based genetic testing services (e.g. 23andMe the startup which went public in June 2021) are also slowly eroding the once monolithic system. Telemedicine (Teladoc and Doctor on Demand— see Chapter 3) are similarly chipping at the system. Asynchronous communication (chat, messaging) also changes the dynamic.

Pricing transparency has not come very far but some initiatives, such as the Surgery Center of Oklahoma's web-based tool (https://surgerycenterok.com/), are embryonic improvements. Until I browsed that tool, I had no idea that my tennis elbow surgery cost about $3200, or my 3D image sinus surgery $11,900, for instance. Admittedly, it is easier to provide a-la-carte pricing for "routine" surgery which is a somewhat commoditized part of healthcare (Shah, 2018) although people still feel strongly about which particular doctor or hospital should be trusted with their surgeries.

When health is disaggregated and moves toward value-based care (a buzzword), collaboration and partnerships become essential, for all parts of the healthcare chain. For pharma companies this has also mean an increase in what's been called "pill+" initiatives, e.g. efforts to engage with patients and stakeholders beyond providing them a drug. One way is "pill plus skill" where you attract customers through knowledge.

Voice assistants such as Alexa, Siri, and Cortana are increasingly used to fetch medical information. Amazon Alexa has an invite-only HIPAA-compliant app dev program. Value-based care ties payments to real-world outcomes, clinical (e.g. cancer is in remission) and corollary (e.g. elevated blood pressure has been alleviated). Interest is high, but information on its prevalence and how it works is scarce since nearly all such arrangements are confidential. They are increasingly becoming a tool in the toolbox for innovative healthcare providers who want to negotiate fair terms. Other barriers include operational complexity and regulatory constraints (e.g. anti-kickback statute enforcement and Medicaid best price reporting) (NEHI, 2020).

Open Health Business Models

User-led innovation will also become more important. Distributed knowledge creation pools are already making themselves relevant in the chronic disease space (IFTF, 2007). For example, La Familia Medical Center in New Mexico is a patient-to-patient self-management center for diabetes. That model follows known paths taken by Alcoholics Anonymous and Weight Watchers and is, of course now exploited by online apps as well trying to build patient communities with group behavioral incentives. Innocentive runs online platforms for solving scientific questions including in the health field, the Tropical Disease Wiki at Duke University is a platform for collaboration on neglected diseases.

Within social movements, biocitizenship, the affinity, and shared identity between individuals with shared biological make-up begin to coordinate and make demands (e.g., Chernobyl survivors, AIDS activists, could also be thought of as a business model because they could conceivably set prices almost like a trade union would operate). The anti-vaxxer community could also be seen in this light, particularly as it aligns itself with the nutritional supplements industry.

Before the pandemic, globalization as well as the internet's challenge to information asymmetry was about to create a global healthcare market. Services such as BestDoctors.com or Preferred GlobalHealth will assist to find the best providers regardless of geographical location. However, the ability to use such services either assume telehealth or the economics and convenience of mobility, which also is brought into question by the pandemic. Will we continue to travel for medical care? Is it even safe?

Emerging healthcare business models tend to show up with new opportunities. Cannabis is one such example as it represents a panoply of wellness-related use cases and addresses pain points of many different market segments, from chronic pain, to entertainment, to nutrition, and beyond.

Luna DNA charges research institutions and pharmaceutical companies a fee each time they request patient data. Project Baseline charges pharmaceutical companies for data analysis and monitoring capabilities relevant for clinical tri-als. Both are examples of Patient-data-as-a-service (PdaaS) businesses. Generally, subscription models are moving into healthcare (Shah, 2018).

The startup Pager offers 24/7 access to its call center where patients can obtain a free medical screening via chat, voice, or video. With the help of AI tools, Pager's nurses suggest patients the appropriate next steps (virtual consulta-tion, physical visit, and hospital), essentially disintermediating healthcare.

In some communities, people are willing to pay to support others' health-care. Medishare, Sedera, and Liberty HealthShare are examples (Shah, 2018). However, there are clear barriers to new healthcare business models. Current modes of paying for healthcare frequently do not support provision of more dis-tributed care, and new payment models would be needed to support it (Dentzer, 2018, p. 9).

How Government Forces Impact Public Health

Government clearly must take a myriad of roles in healthcare—risk taker, inno-vator, and protector—and that is at minimum (Undheim, 2021, pp. 69–70). Government typically runs a core set of health services or facilities, or at the very least is, ultimately, the overseer, no matter how privatized a system has become.

In healthcare, when faced with disruption and innovation, governments typically apply strong legal protections as a countermeasure. For innovators, this means that the regulatory emphasis must be correspondingly strong in order to prevail.

Public Health in the EU—And the EU's Role in Global Health

The EU is an interesting jurisdiction for health in that health services are excluded from the application of the Directive on Services in the Internal Market (Directive 2006/123/EC of 12 December 2006); yet the Commission has enacted many impactful rules related to healthcare, including a European framework for e-health (Callens, 2010, p. 462).

The EU has paid attention to e-health since the e-Europe initiative in 1999, which included the Health Online Action adopted an eHealth Acton plan in 2004 (e.g. SEC(2004)539} / COM/2004/0356 final) another one in 2012 and will presumably adopt one in 2021. In response to COVID-19, the EU launched EU4Health 2021–2027—a vision for a healthier European Union (EU). With an R&D investment of €5.1 billion, this is the largest health program ever in mon-etary terms. EU4Health will provide funding to EU countries, health organiza-tions, and NGOs, focusing on creating reserves of medical supplies, healthcare staff, and increased surveillance of health threats. Commission priorities such as the fight against cancer, reducing the number of antimicrobial-resistant infections, and improving vaccination rates are also boosted (European Commission, 2020b).

However, the EU4Health is a bit of a stopgap measure. The EU eHealth Action Plan 2012–2020 will presumably soon be replaced by its successor, a new Action Plan, following the next Multiannual Financial Framework 2021–2027, which is more comprehensive in nature. Arguably, EU4Health, ESF+, InvestEU, HorizonEurope, Next Generation EU, and the Green Deal initiatives, all fall short of ambition (EuroHealthNet, 2020).

The EU is a regional trade organization but also a global actor. Its role in global health is, in many ways, more substantial than the EU's work on public health within its own borders. The reason is that there are no regulatory constraints on its cross-border mandate (Emmerling & Kickbusch, 2016). Global Health came to prominence on the European agenda with the EU's first health strategy and policy framework in 2007. The Commission adopted a Communication on the "EU Role in Global Health" on March 31, 2010, accompanied by three Commission staff working papers focusing on specific areas of that Communication (European Commission, 2020c). Shortly thereafter, the Council, in response, adopted ambitious Conclusions on Global Health. Arguably this was not followed up with actions (Berner-Rodoreda et al., 2019). However, given COVID-19, the emphasis on global health will only be strengthened in the coming years.

How Social Dynamics Impact Public Health

Social dynamics are extremely sensitive in the area of public health, partly because they may be so consequential compared to medical factors, particularly on who becomes sick or injured in the first place (Braveman & Gottlieb, 2014).

Healthcare depends on the habits specific groups of the population have as regards hygiene, nutrition, doctor's visits, and their view and trust in government, expertise, hospitals, professions, doctors, nurses, and their employers. When something goes wrong with healthcare, it typically does not just affect individuals (although that happens as well) but huge social groups. Chronic patients tend to turn to patient advocacy groups which, at times, become veritable social movements and sometimes morph into associations that work in a more structured manner.

There is a whole emerging area connected to what has become termed the "social determinants of health", meaning the economic and social conditions that influence (and at times explain) individual and group differences in health status. They include factors like socioeconomic status, education, neighborhood and physical environment, employment, and social support networks, as well as access to healthcare (Artiga & Hinton, 2018). Taken altogether, social determinants refers to all of the factors apart from medical care that can be influenced by social policies, or social dynamics unaffected or yet difficult to alter through policy, yet which may shape health in powerful ways. Many of these social dynamics are so ingrained, deeply cultural, or steeped in specific trajectories or living conditions that are enormously difficult to impact one way or another.

To summarize all these factors as "income, wealth, and education" (which is often done) is far too simplistic because which type of employment, and what the working conditions are, is also hugely important, as well as a host of environmental factors that I'll get to in a bit. Lastly, it is often, to some observers somewhat mysteriously, to others even naturally, highly dependent on ethnicity.

Arguably, over the past decade, there has been a broader system movement toward, first, "care integration", presumably the idea that providers speak together and/or at least share information, tests, and perhaps, one day, health records. Second, there is an embryonic focus on "whole-person" delivery models, aiming to address patients' physical, mental, and social needs. Finally, there is at least a discussion, if not yet a shift toward payments tied to value, quality, or outcomes (Artiga & Hinton, 2018).

The challenge for the healthcare profession(s) is that social determinants are traditionally, by definition, outside the realm of standard medical care. It is also not something they necessarily know much about. Social dynamics is definitely not an area they typically are educated to handle. Despite this, it seems the profession typically speaks in big words with an authoritative voice whenever they do address the topic and, arguably, without sufficient humility.

If it is the case that social dynamics are becoming increasingly important to healthcare, at what point do we have to consider physicians and nurses more like engineers than have traditionally been considered by the profession, as critical, yet ancillary elements of a much bigger picture? In my view, the time will come within this decade to make that call. What that will mean for healthcare is an open question, but it will, in and of itself, radically change the premise. Peer-to-peer medicine has been advanced and should perhaps be seriously looked at as a systemic fix for physician shortages, particularly in rural and disadvantaged areas.

How Environmental Factors Impact Public Health

The way the environment comes into play mostly depends on three things: where you live (and breathe), where you work, and where you spend your leisure life. People living in urban demographics theoretically have greater access to healthcare, should they be able to afford it, but also face greater competition for the services that do exist. People living in rural demographics may well be living in de facto hospital deserts, far away from high-quality or full-service healthcare, and should there be spikes in demand, the size and condition of the kinds of facilities available rapidly escalate into trying conditions, even in western, developed societies (partly because they have remote areas that are not particularly developed).

The tense and fraught relationship between humans and nature cause zoonotic spillover on a regular basis which causes infectious disease and all kinds of hygiene issues. Humans also increasingly live in conditions of pollution which drastically impacts their quality of life and healthspan, as well as potentially their lifespan.

Gradual improvements do not require much more than budget upgrades to invest in and track, but each field of medicine is moving faster and faster and the end result is not easy to account for, whether you are a hospital administrator or a patient wanting the latest and (still safe) treatment. However, more radical improvements are happening in previously slow-moving fields, which complicates things. To what extent is health tech the solution?

Transformational innovation is underway both due to hardware and software upgrades and mostly their interaction. Operating this new equipment and managing new workflows are complex. Realizing what the opportunities are is important. Evaluating the healthcare you are being given to see if it really is the best there on the market is also becoming an important patient and caregiver skill, at times professionalized to family healthcare consultants. However, not all can afford to hire such a function or would want to outsource such a key competency.

The chapter provides a way to navigate the emerging technologies and make the best choices, looking at what startups and corporate providers have available now and in the next few years, across a plethora of disease areas and domains of healthcare, including primary care, surgery and non-acute care, including elderly care (Figure 4.2).

Digital Health—A Pivotal Area

If there is one area which is poised to transform healthcare as we know it, it is digital health. The reason is not that it is so much more important than anything else, but rather the fact that its defining characteristic may be said to be its ability to be transformative yet work within the current financial paradigms of healthcare, which is severely entrenched. There are set of reasons why this is the case, although like anything, it is a truth with modifications.

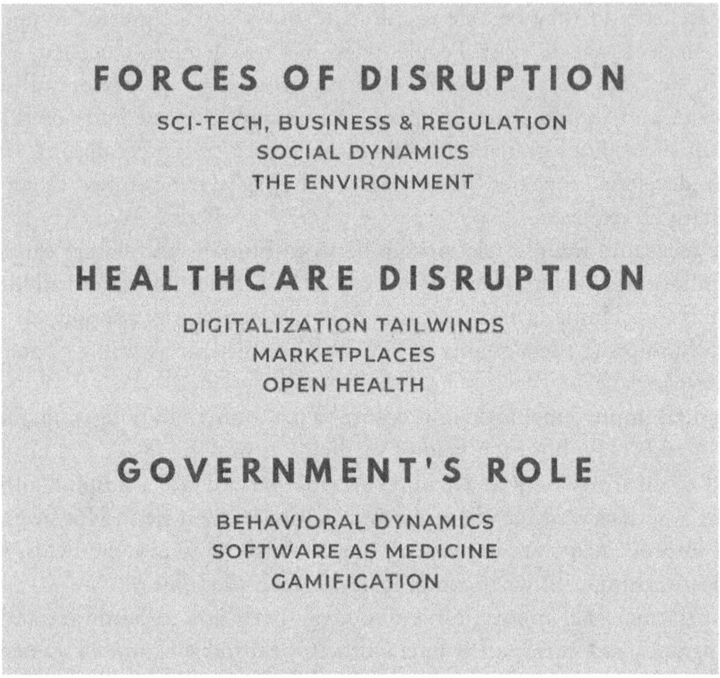

FORCES OF DISRUPTION

SCI-TECH, BUSINESS & REGULATION
SOCIAL DYNAMICS
THE ENVIRONMENT

HEALTHCARE DISRUPTION

DIGITALIZATION TAILWINDS
MARKETPLACES
OPEN HEALTH

GOVERNMENT'S ROLE

BEHAVIORAL DYNAMICS
SOFTWARE AS MEDICINE
GAMIFICATION

Figure 4.2 The disruption of healthcare.

Benefits of Digital Health

I will start by first looking at the benefits of digital health, which are many (when executed well). Some of these benefits are well known, and have become truisms, without an exact meaning. Digital health is not a panacea.

The FDA (2020a) lists five main benefits of digital health: (a) reduce inefficiencies, (b) improve access, (c) reduce costs, (d) increase quality, and (e) make medicine more personalized for patients.

However, there are tremendous barrier to adoption, including a lack of awareness and trust in digital health tools and services (among patients as well as citizens and healthcare professionals). Additionally, the high startup costs involved in setting up digital health systems, inadequate or fragmented legal frameworks (for example, a lack of reimbursement schemes), and lack of interoperability between systems. Privacy concerns are a tremendous concern. The EU General Data Protection Regulation (GDPR), which became applicable on May 25, 2018 and which provides a uniform set of data protection rules across the EU, is also a significant barrier to adoption of digital health (Spontoni, Pecsteen, & Skouteli, 2018).

FDA's Role in Digital Health

The US FDA defines digital health broadly to include categories such as mobile health (mHealth), health information technology (IT), wearable devices, telehealth and telemedicine, and personalized medicine (FDA, 2020a). As such it includes technologies intended for use "as a medical product, in a medical product, as companion diagnostics, or as an adjunct to other medical products (devices, drugs, and biologics)", or in order to "develop or study medical products".

A substantial number of mobile medical applications come under the FDA's enforcement discretion, including apps helping patients organize and track their health information, providing easy access to information related to conditions or treatments, or helping patients self-manage their disease or condition (e.g. wellness applications) without providing specific treatment (Dang, Arora, & Rane, 2020). There are also gray areas.

However, many innovators in the space do apply for either a rigorous De Novo approval (new devices, Class I or Class II) or 510(k) approval (similar solutions exist, e.g. "substantial equivalence") from the FDA (2020c). If submitted for 510(k), the FDA applies a risk analysis to figure out if the submission raises different questions of safety and effectiveness than with other approved devices.

Why does the FDA care so much? My guess is that the explosion in digital innovation meant that a plethora of consumer devices started to appear on the market without the FDA's approval. To some extent, this is the case because these initiatives (startups and other efforts) likely started as a pure consumer service and were hoping to operate under the radar.

According to the study mHealth Economics 2017—Current Status and Future Trends in Mobile Health, 325,000 healthcare applications were available on smartphones, which equates to an expected 3.7 billion mobile health application downloads that year by smartphone users worldwide, with users including healthcare professionals, consumers, and patients (Research 2 Guidance, 2017).

As a result of such studies by 2017, it eventually became apparent to the FDA that software solutions were starting to take a role in giving medical advice, or in fact were morphing into medical devices of sorts or at least needed to be categorized as such (for lack of other terminology) and also that traditional medical devices increasingly were starting to communicate with each other and to some extent with the public. In 2017, the FDA formed the Software Precertification (Pre-Cert) Pilot Program to help develop a framework for a future regulatory model for software-based medical devices. The FDA's software categories were updated in 2019.

The FDA now either puts digital health software functions that use "light, vibrations, camera, or other similar sources to perform medical device functions" in moderate-risk (Class II) or high-risk (Class III) devices in order to assure safety and effectiveness. Another obvious case to regulate includes software functions that "control the operation or function (e.g., changes settings) of an implantable or body worn medical device" or software functions that are used in "active patient monitoring to analyze patient-specific medical device data" (FDA, 2020b).

As of 2020, the FDA has this to say: "Many medical devices now have the ability to connect to and communicate with other devices or systems. Devices that are already FDA approved, authorized, or cleared are being updated to add digital features".

> If you are developing a mobile health app that collects, creates, or shares consumer information, use the tool on the Federal Trade Commission's website to find out when the FDA, Federal Trade Commission (FTC), or Office of Civil Rights (OCR) laws apply.
>
> *FDA (2020b)*

However, due to the pandemic, the FDA has issued multiple Emergency Use Authorizations (EUAs) in the digital mental health space.

EU's Regulation of Medical Devices

The EU, which considers itself the global leader in the medical devices sector, has found that there are 500,000 types of medical devices and in vitro diagnostic (IVD) medical devices on the EU market providing functions to "diagnosis, prevention, monitoring, prediction, prognosis, treatment or alleviation of disease" (European Commission, 2020a).

To sell medical devices in the EU, you must undergo a conformity assessment and obtain or apply CE (Conformité Européenne) Marking for your product. CE Marking indicates that your medical device complies with the applicable EU regulations and enables the commercialization of your products in 32 European countries (EMA, 2020).

The EU's state goal for public health systems overall is to "overcome inequalities and look after an ageing society". The provisions on the 2017 legislation which were due to come into force in 2020 were postponed and will now apply from May 26, 2021 (European Commission, 2020b).

In the EU, telemedicine is regulated through Directive 2011/24/EU patients' rights in cross-border healthcare and Article 3.d. clearly defines that healthcare is considered to be provided in the Member State where the healthcare provider is established and Article 7.7 re-asserts the rights to the free movement of patients, services, or goods.

The EU interoperability gateway went live on October 19, 2020, attempting to link up coronavirus contact tracing and warning apps.

Conclusion

The growth of the space of health disruption either shows that the system is broken or that the innovations have matured so much that they have become easier to implement than it is to keep the existing system. Either way, the *forces of disruption* (sci-tech, business models, policy & regulation, social dynamics, and the environment) are what makes change happen, or what stalls progress. Several highly promising innovative technologies and treatment approaches based on technology are still 7–15 years out before they can have sweeping effects on the healthcare system, including VR, population health, and interoperable electronic medical records. However, the reason they will take time has less to do with the maturity of the technology and more to do with the ingrained shortcomings of the current system across all disruptive forces.

In the next chapter, I will investigate the so-called grand health challenges of our time: pandemics, aging, and preventive healthcare, look at how these get such elevated status at any given time and what the consequences are.

KEY TAKEAWAYS AND REFLECTIONS

1. Reflect briefly on the disruptive factors in health tech. Which ones have been the most cumbersome in the field you think the most about on a daily basis?

_____

2. If you were investing in health tech this year, where would you place your bets?

_____

3. Name three areas ripe for government regulation in the health space?

_____

References

Angeli, F. and Jaiswal, A. K. (2016) 'Business model innovation for inclusive health care delivery at the bottom of the pyramid', *Organization & Environment*, 29:4, 486–507, Available at: DOI: 10.1177/1086026616647174 (Accessed 22 November 2020).

Artiga, S. and Hinton, E. (2018) 'Beyond health care: the role of social determinants in promoting health and health equity', KFF Issue Brief, KFF [Online], 10 May 2018. Available at: https://www.kff.org/racial-equity-and-health-policy/issue-brief/beyond-health-care-the-role-of-social-determinants-in-promoting-health-and-health-equity/ (Accessed 20 November 2020).

ASPE (2020) 'Prescription drugs market', The Office of the Assistant Secretary for Planning and Evaluation (ASPE). Available at: https://aspe.hhs.gov/prescription-drugs (Accessed 20 November 2020).

Berner-Rodoreda, A., Rehfuess, E.A., Klipstein-Grobusch, K., Cobelens, F., Raviglione, M., Flahaut, A., Casamitjana, N., Fröschl, G., Skordis-Worral, J., Abubakar, I., Ashrafian, H., Agardh, A., Visser, L., Schultsz, C., Plasència, A., Jahn, A., Norton, R., van Leeuwen, R., Hagander, L., and Bärnighausen, T. (2019). 'Where is the "global" in the European Union's health research and innovation agenda?', *BMJ Global Health*, 4:5, e001559, Available at: DOI: 10.1136/bmjgh-2019-001559 (Accessed 22 November 2020).

Braveman, P., and Gottlieb, L. (2014). 'The social determinants of health: it's time to consider the causes of the causes', *Public Health Reports (Washington, D.C.: 1974)*, 129(Suppl 2), 19–31, Available at: DOI: 10.1177/00333549141291S206 (Accessed 20 November 2020).

Bryant, M. (2020) 'Digital health funding hits new high with $6.3B in H1 2020', BioWorld, 17 July 2020. Available at: https://www.bioworld.com/articles/455848-digital-health-funding-hits-new-high-with-63b-in-h1-2020?v=preview (Accessed 19 November 2020).

Callens, S. (2010) 'The EU Legal Framework on e-Health', *Health Systems Governance in Europe: The Role of European Union Law and Policy* (Health Economics, Policy and Management), edited by E. Mossialos, G. Permanand, R. Baeten, and T. Hervey, 561–588. Cambridge: Cambridge University Press. Available at: doi: 10.1017/CBO9780511750496.014 (Accessed 20 November 2020).

Dang, A., Arora, D., and Rane, P. (2020) 'Role of digital therapeutics and the changing future of healthcare', *Journal of Family Medicine and Primary Care*, 9:5), 2207–2213, Available at: DOI: 10.4103/jfmpc.jfmpc_105_20 (Accessed 20 November 2020).

Dentzer, S. (Ed.). (2018) 'Health care without walls: a roadmap for reinventing U.S. health care (executive summary)', Network for Excellence in Health Innovation (NEHI). Available at: https://www.nehi.net/writable/publication_files/file/nehi_health_care_without_walls_executive_summary.pdf (Accessed 21 November 2020).

Digital Healthcare Timeline (2020) 'Digital Healthcare Timeline [online]'. Available at: http://digitalhealthcaretimeline.com/digital-healthcare-timeline/#1990s (Accessed 21 November 2020).

EMA (2020) 'Medical devices', European Medicines Agency [Online]. Available at: https://www.ema.europa.eu/en/human-regulatory/overview/medical-devices (Accessed 22 November 2020).

Emmerling, T. and Kickbusch, I. (2016) *The European Union as a Global Health Actor* (Global Health Diplomacy, Vol. 4). Singapore: World Scientific. Available at: DOI: 10.1142/9714 (Accessed 22 November 2020).

EuroHealthNet (2020) 'Health and wellbeing must be better integrated into future EU budgets and recovery measures', EuroHealthNet. Available at: https://eurohealthnet.eu/media/news-releases/health-and-wellbeing-must-be-better-integrated-future-eu-budgets-and-recovery.

European Commission (2020a) 'Medical devices – sector', European Commission [Online]. Available at: https://ec.europa.eu/health/md_sector/overview_en (Accessed 20 November 2020).

European Commission (2020b) 'EU4Health 2021–2027 – a vision for a healthier European Union', European Commission [Online]. Available at: https://ec.europa.eu/health/funding/eu4health_en (Accessed 20 November 2020).

European Commission (2020c) 'Global health [Online]'. Available at: https://ec.europa.eu/health/international_cooperation/global_health_en (Accessed 22 November 2020).

FDA (2020a) 'What is digital health?', U.S. Food & Drug Administration [Online]. Available at: https://www.fda.gov/medical-devices/digital-health-center-excellence/what-digital-health (Accessed 19 November 2020).

FDA (2020b) 'Examples of device software functions the FDA regulates', U.S. Food & Drug Administration [Online]. Available at: https://www.fda.gov/medical-devices/device-software-functions-including-mobile-medical-applications/examples-device-software-functions-fda-regulates (Accessed 19 November 2020).

FDA (2020c) 'De novo classification request', U.S. Food & Drug Administration [Online]. Available at: https://www.fda.gov/medical-devices/premarket-submissions/de-novo-classification-request (Accessed 20 November 2020).

Herzlinger, R.E. (2006) 'Why innovation in health care is so hard', Harvard Business Review, May. Available at: https://www.hse.ie/eng/about/who/healthbusinessservices/hbs-news-and-events/why-innovation-in-health-care-is-so-hard.pdf (Accessed 22 November 2020).

Herzlinger, R.E. (2013) 'Innovating in health care-framework', Case Study, Harvard Business Review, May. Available at: https://store.hbr.org/product/innovating-in-health-care-framework/314017?sku=314017-PDF-ENG (Accessed 22 November 2020).

Herzlinger, R.E. (2021) *Innovating in Healthcare: Creating Breakthrough Services, Products, and Business Models*, New York: Wiley.

IFTF (2007) 'Rethinking business models: In the global health economy: A toolkit for innovation', Institute for the Future. Available at: https://www.iftf.org/uploads/media/SR-1038_Rethinking_Business_Models_01.pdf (Accessed 21 November 2020).

Klonoff, D.C., Kerr, D., and Mulvaney, S.A. (Eds.). (2020) *Diabetes Digital Health*, Amsterdam: Elsevier.

Licholai, G. (2020) 'Digital healthcare growth drivers in 2020', Forbes [Online], 14 January 2020. Available at: https://www.forbes.com/sites/greglicholai/2020/01/14/digital-healthcare-growth-drivers-in-2020/?sh=28af0f2e511d (Accessed 19 November 2020).

NEHI (2020) 'Takeaways from Oct. 27 next generation value-based arrangements briefing'. NEHI, 28 October 2020. Available at: https://www.nehi.net/news/588-takeaways-from-oct-27-next-generation-value-based-arrangements-briefing/view (Accessed 21 November 2020).

Research 2 Guidance (2017) 'mHealth Economics 2017 – Current Status and Future Trends in Mobile Health', *Research 2 Guidance* [online]. Available at: https://research2guidance.com/product/mhealth-economics-2017-current-status-and-future-trends-in-mobile-health/ (Accessed 19 November 2020).

Shah, N. (2018) 'Business model innovation in healthcare', USV.com [Online]. Available at: https://www.usv.com/writing/2018/10/business-model-innovation-in-healthcare/ (Accessed 21 November 2020).

Spontoni, C, Pecsteen, E., and Skouteli, K. (2018) 'A new era for eHealth in the EU', Expert Briefing. Sector Analysis. Financier Worldwide. Available at: https://www.financierworldwide.com/a-new-era-for-ehealth-in-the-eu#.X7mDw2hKiUk (Accessed 20 November 2020).

Undheim, T.A. (2021) *Future Tech*. London: Kogan Page.

Williams, B. (2019) 'Disaggregation of healthcare: the great unbundling proceeds', Digitally Cognizant, Cognizant, 3 December 2019. Available at: https://digitally.cognizant.com/disaggregation-of-healthcare-the-great-unbundling-proceeds-codex5241/ (Accessed 21 November 2020).

Chapter 5

The Grand Health Challenges of Our Time—Pandemics, Aging, and Preventive Healthcare

Every year, embattled WHO comes out with a list of what they see as the top global health issues to track. In 2021, what made the list were priorities as nebulous as solidarity toward global health security, speeding up access to COVID-19 tests, medicines and vaccines, focusing on health for all, tackling health inequities, revitalizing the efforts to tackle communicable diseases such as polio, HIV, tuberculosis, and malaria, combating drug resistance, treating noncommunicable diseases (cancer, diabetes, and heart disease), improving people's mental health, building back greener and better, and global solidarity (WHO, 2020). Did you note that this almost covers all ills plaguing the world population? It is hardly a list of priorities, more a laundry list of all the issues on the table.

DOI: 10.4324/9781003178071-5

The Welfare State as a Paradoxical Obstacle

The national welfare state sounded like a great idea at the time. After all, it was invented at a time where European nations were flush with cash, were rebuilding after the World War II, got fueled by American Marshall Aid, and subsequently influenced by a friendly socialist wave, quite unlike the militantly antagonistic one facing America at the moment. It was a time of common quest and belief in progress for the many, but it was also an alignment of interest of workers, employers, and governments (Gough & Therborn, 2010).

The build-up of healthcare systems meant creating national solutions. Rights and responsibilities were tied to citizenship. Only in the past few decades has this become somewhat problematic as the EU increasingly has observed how citizens moving across country borders are faced with radically different rules and face many challenges. The global economy is even further reason to do a rethink (Filgueira et al., 2018).

In the welfare state, health is, largely, seen as a common good. The notion is that the more of the population that is healthy, the better for employment, culture, and even for business because workers are healthy and (presumably) motivated to work. Only, there were some adverse consequences. In countries with a large influx of immigrants, the entitlements were not earned, and felt like an opportunistic gift, and an opportunity for enrichment. This was not taken well by the citizens who had indeed spent years boosting government sponsored healthcare through their paycheck (Figure 5.1).

Pandemics

The existence of infectious diseases, and the huge outbreaks that from time to time sweep the earth, has always motivated public health efforts. First it was cholera, then it was polio, and subsequently a whole host of diseases, from HIV/AIDS to, influenza, and now, coronavirus.

The COVID-19 challenge fits in the picture of grand public health challenges, except that it seems to challenge a *broader* spectrum of society's institutions than previous—or current—grand challenges. In so doing, it has unlocked opportunity for change. It was, essentially, the first reboot, or many needed reboots. What that means is the need for increased collaboration across borders, as well as trade-offs between economic efficiency in the short term versus effectiveness over the long term. Beyond that, at the level COVID-19 is currently affecting our societies, it cannot be compared to any other disease in history, apart from the Black Death and the Great Influenza of 1918 (Undheim, 2020).

If I now consider the health tech challenges of COVID-19, an interesting picture emerges. The phenomenon has already—after only 2 years and

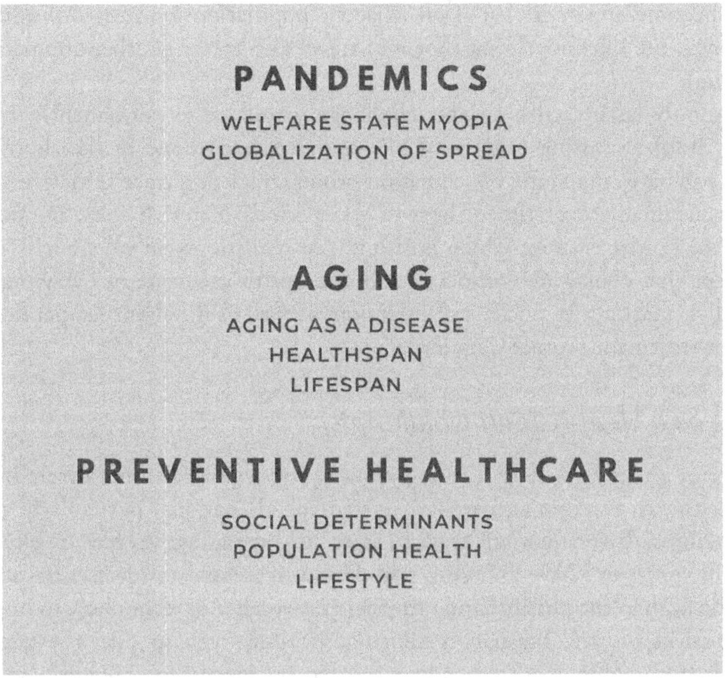

PANDEMICS

WELFARE STATE MYOPIA
GLOBALIZATION OF SPREAD

AGING

AGING AS A DISEASE
HEALTHSPAN
LIFESPAN

PREVENTIVE HEALTHCARE

SOCIAL DETERMINANTS
POPULATION HEALTH
LIFESTYLE

Figure 5.1 Grand health challenges.

counting– shocked the system enough to force a 50% or more increase in tele-health adoption (Koonin et al., 2020), boosted vaccine production and, with that, the entire pharma industry, it has turned the digital health industry into the newest fad and is starting to affect other adjacent sectors as well. There will also be changes to healthcare education, especially because the shortage of trained emergency and ICU personnel has already meant re-training non-ICU personnel very quickly, so they can competently do rounds on the ICU ward under surge infection periods.

The lasting consequences are a bit trickier to tally. The system will, if things get sorted within the next few years, undoubtedly mostly go back to where it was. Right now, many observers feel differently, but they are likely deluded by an optimism (or pessimism) and do not consider the well-established statistical phenomenon of regression to the mean or the fact that natural variation in repeated data at times looks like real change.

One aspect that even my futurist hat renders contingent on a host of factors I cannot yet combine with high confidence of the outcome is whether our healthcare systems will adopt a global attitude or not. Logically, they should, because it has become apparent that if an adjacent population group is unhealthy or infectious, the likelihood that they will travel and infect another population is quite high.

The only lasting cure for this challenge would be to permanently impose stricter border crossing criteria. While that has been done in the short term (e.g. travel bans, mandatory vaccination proofs, track and trace initiatives), they are unsustainable over time. Short of those kinds of restrictions, or shutting down the border entirely, which is also not so realistic, what we are left with is to accept that contagion will occur and attempt to vaccinate our way out of it (globally), mask up in pockets of infection, as well as develop therapeutics and efficient treatment protocols nationally.

Aging as a Health Tech Challenge

We live in an aging society. Demographic aging is poised to negatively impact the healthcare systems and welfare system of all nations, particularly developed nations. There are many ways to start tackling aging; yet few are effective. Basically, once you have an aging population, it is hard to reverse. Because of that, the faith in the possible and imminent emergence of technology to improve both healthspan and lifespan is alluring. It allows you to turn the question around: from aging as a tremendous burden on society to aging as a massive opportunity for growth, quality of life, and a big new market.

Awarding the First Person to Reach Their 123rd Birthday

In 2015, in an effort to motivate the acceleration of the longevity industry, London-based Moldovan investor Dmitry Kaminskiy famously created a $1 million prize for the first person to beat the current lifespan record and reach their 123rd birthday. Kaminskiy, who spent formative years in Moscow, is a co-founder of Deep Knowledge Ventures and a Managing Partner of Longevity Capital. He recently was the Head of International Development for the UK All-Party Longevity Secretariat. Kaminskiy is instigating what he sees as a necessary and immensely fruitful "Manhattan project" for longevity (Kaminskiy & Colangelo, 2020).

That notion may have been laughed off, just a few years ago, but with COVID-19's condensed version of such an ambitious undertaking, it might just work for other pressing pursuits, including longevity or climate-change and eco-system collapse-mitigation.

The reason it might work is the COVID moment (which I tackled in an earlier chapter). I am referring to the race to get (multiple) vaccines for COVID-19, which contained several circus movements in societal invention.

First, it required believing in the idea that the world could move (relatively fast) toward an immensely hairy and audacious societal goal (stop coronavirus in its tracks), as well as accepting the political and social dynamics risk of a potential of fallout (e.g. anti-vaxx sentiment—both deserved and undeserved).

It meant being fiercely aided by sci-tech (which needed a 5+ year step-change in clinical trial speed with the mRNA vaccines of Moderna and Pfizer).

It also meant being in consort with strong political will, accepting drastically increased regulatory risk, including good faith and risk-taking attitudes in the world's regulatory authorities including the FDA.

It implied being aided by both public and private financing (e.g. R&D support and vaccine purchase guarantees).

One thing is (fairly) clear: even without taking on a novel "Manhattan" or "Apollo" project, life expectancy is longer than many of us assume. It has happened due to current sci-tech progress as well as "improved" lifestyle (e.g. getting out of the first and second industrial revolution, out of factories and mines and into cities that we have cleaned up, water that has been processed, vitamins that we eat to compensate for potential mineral deficiencies, and an overall improved diet (apart from an excess of carbohydrates that causes obesity—which we haven't fully dealt with yet).

Either way, on average, young and even middle-aged people of today (unless they are clinically obese, disregard all nutritional guidelines—or are still poor, which we also yet have to deal with), can expect to live 120 years, and even the elderly today can expect to live to 100, they write (op.cit, p. 10). Bracket here, the entire set of UN Millennium and the 13 Sustainable Development Goals (SDGs) for a second—as much as I am not a "progress theorist" (I am quite the opposite). Even I am willing to admit that a lot has already been accomplished in the "living longer" department. To me, though, we have done the absolute simplest things and the hardest—working on social acceptance of limiting growth within societal and ecological limits—remains.

Is Longevity Already the Next Multi-Trillion-Dollar Industry?

When I interviewed longevity optimist and investor Dimitry Kaminskiy for the Futurized podcast (2020), he talked warmly about the Longevity Industry as (already) the next multi-trillion-dollar industry. In fact, he claims, it reached $17 trillion in 2019 and will reach $27 trillion in 2026. That number appears because he defines it at the Intersection of AgeTech, WealthTech, and FinTech, first and foremost, and also including longevity based FemTech and Geroscience R&D. There are lots of acronyms in this description. The newest of them, Femtech (or female technology), is a term applied to a category of software, diagnostics, products, and services that use technology often to focus on women's health. The numbers are formidable, too. Even isolating the AgeTech market, that segment alone will reach $2.7 trillion by 2025, a 21% year-on-year growth driven by the elderly care sector enhanced by digital solutions.

Many companies in these emerging markets will rely on AI. Valo Health, arguably the first "digitally native" pharmaceutical company, created in 2020 and already going public by 2021, is a new type of AI-drug discovery biotech. Its database is massive, its AI models already at 30,000, covering 70 trillion molecules, and already with 17 drugs in the pipeline, a staggering number considering that researchers formerly spent a career on single molecules and that a drug would typically take decades to develop (Vinluan, 2021). Valo Tech integrate human-centric data across the entire drug development lifecycle into a single unified architecture.

The Advent of P4 Medicine

The technologies underlying the longevity industry will be many, and involve biomarkers, regenerative medicine, neurotech, precision health and artificial intelligence (AI), just as the basic premise. Altogether, the combination of the startup innovation acronyms plus the technologies, arguably will create P4 medicine (predictive, preventive, personalized, and participatory), a term coined by Dr. Leroy Hood of the Seattle-based Institute for Systems Biology. Hood, who importantly defines biology as an informational science, is also credited with introducing the term "systems biology", fostering a cross-disciplinary environment which he sees as a fundamental necessity for the biology of the future. Hood has written 700 peer-reviewed papers, has received 36 patents and 17 honorary degrees, and is no slouch.

Hood (b. 1938) is an American biologist who has served on the faculties at the California Institute of Technology (Caltech) and the University of Washington. He coined P4 medicine to demonstrate his framework to detect and prevent disease through extensive biomarker testing, close monitoring, deep statistical analysis, and patient health coaching (Hood, 2013). P4 medicine arguably represents a quantified understanding of wellness and is in sharp contrast to the, often, semi-scientific influences of the overall wellness movement.

Hood, in his later years, particularly applies systems biology to the study of cancer as well as the study of neurodegenerative disease. His overall thrust is exemplified in the movement known as the quantified self, which uses digital devices to monitor self-parameters such as weight, activity, sleep, and diet. Hood was prescient in his observations well over 10 years ago, that P4 medicine will "probably be embraced by the public before it is embraced by the medical establishment", and "Therefore, the driving force will be the social networks" (Hood, 2013). Kaminskiy and Colangelo (2020, p. 18) maintain that limited, controlled stressors (fasting, sauna, cryosauna, short intense exercise, and short psychological stress) can train the immune system and repair age-related damage. Maybe so but is the evidence incontrovertible yet?

The Future of Longevity Science

If we believe Hood (2013), the question then becomes, what is the future of longevity, and can the emerging science live up to these ambitions? Will it be recognized as a science, given that its proactive characteristics differ from traditional "evidence-based" medicine which derives from the rationalist era of professionalized medicine (the one where the doctor is on top of the medical pyramid)? There are more, not fewer measurements, but that also makes it hard to argue what method is more exact, and harder to argue things are "scientific" (in the Vienna school of logical positivism). P4 medicine is also individual-centric (for now) and eventually would aim to stratify individuals into small groups of (perhaps) 50 or so patients. It is also not disease-centric, which brings another element of idiosyncrasy that challenges traditional statistical paradigms. After all, if each man (and woman) is an island one and to himself (and herself), then how can you generalize? And, is generalization even the point at this stage? The P4 medicine movement raises many epistemological questions that are fundamental to the theory of science. And, if the science fails, it affects all of us.

The Complexity of Longevity

Whether people, politicians or industry leaders realize or not, longevity will impact the world in ways we are only starting to consider.

Over the past decade there has been the rise of policy scene for longevity. Politicians have, tentatively, tried to engage with scenario models to imagine what they might be faced with just a few years from now. When Kaminskiy and Colangelo (2020) put their futurist hat on, they do not hold back. They casually state that "many countries will decline and become bankrupt because of the Silver Tsunami". Their rationale is that the phenomenon will cause political crisis and default national financial systems. On the other hand, they seem to project that certain countries already are ahead in their thinking, and Switzerland might become "the first longevity hub", unless another entity, perhaps a "world city" beats the country to it. However, there are many who claim healthspan, not lifespan, is the main goal (and the ethically conscious one), and the techniques used to optimize for each may not be the same.

The Sci-Tech

Sci-tech, particularly mathematical technologies and AI combined with data science will drive healthcare and longevity science. While it is obvious that sci-tech is part of what kickstarts the discussions around longevity (apart from the empirical fact that people are getting older), the next step is not at all obvious. Somewhat abruptly, the authors suggest that implementing longevity technologies will be an immediate fix. I am not so sure. Much more will be needed and technology will only be one, crucial ingredient. Perhaps more interestingly, and relevant to leaders of today, is their prediction that big tech, healthcare, and pharma companies will start to prioritize longevity in their business models. I find that somewhat perplexing.

Social Dynamics

Not all the social dynamics of longevity can be foreshadowed. One that seems obvious is that as people gain healthspan (and lifespan), the previous model of a retirement with pension does lose its meaning. No government would be able to afford it, about that they are correct. Imagine retiring at 70 and living until you are 120—that's 50 years of retirement. Clearly, we need to raise the retirement age. We all know how that song goes, there will be immense protests, especially from people who are not lucky enough to benefit from the evolution in wellness. What we are quite likely to see is a stark divergence between haves and have not's in terms of health and lifespan, closely following socio-economic status, but with some surprising outliers, who get a "second chance to shine" in their later years.

Assessing the Longevity Argument

Kaminskiy and Colangelo (2020) do not operate with very specific timeframes. That is wise from a credibility standpoint (you cannot be wrong) but it also makes their analysis more conceptual and somewhat quasi academic. The task of the futurist, in my mind, is to be able to frame the gradual changes with some accuracy on timelines but depending on the degree to which various key parameters are dialed up or down. Going down that path would take me well into my next book, but I wanted to point this ambition out.

It might seem strange that I have tackled aging and longevity in this chapter and still have another chapter dedicated to wellness. The reason for that will, hopefully become apparent when I get to that chapter. To clarify: what I am concerned about is the opportunities and pitfalls of the natural wellness approach, a quite distinct movement within the broader wellness paradigm. With that, I mean the adherents of a no-biological-intervention approach to maintaining good health. I find that school of thought, while at times synergistic with systems biology, at other times completely at odds with it.

As I hope was apparent, it is not that I consider natural wellness "less scientific". Quite the contrary, because there are strands in systems biology or even in rationalist science and sci-tech that are non-scientific in their approach or even in intent (the emphasis on living longer in the first place strikes me as a rather moralistic goal or perhaps an existentialist ambition, or a humanist quasi-religious longing). Whatever it is or however it is motivated, it transcends scientific thinking and is more of a scientific-religious hybrid (e.g. read Cattell's (1987) book *Beyondism*), which is more than mildly influenced by eugenics.

Without forecasting that chapter I will say this: natural wellness builds on a very strict vision of human nature as embedded in our biological ecosystem and having an unquestioned "natural" place in that ecosystem. I struggle quite a bit with that perspective, much more than I struggle with making sense of systems biology. I wanted to make that disclosure, and those distinctions, before I ventured full hog into "wellness".

Preventive Healthcare toward Chronic Conditions

Preventive healthcare (the medics use a fancy Greek word, prophylaxis, where phylax means "guard"), consists of measures taken for disease prevention. The assumption is that disease is affected by environmental factors, genetic predisposition, disease agents, and lifestyle choices, and are dynamic processes which begin before individuals realize they are affected.

Typical preventive healthcare measures include shots and screening tests. Many of these try to tackle potentially chronic conditions (before they become chronic, ideally). May chronic diseases, including heart disease, cancer, chronic lung disease, stroke, Alzheimer's disease, diabetes, osteoarthritis, and chronic kidney disease, are the leading causes of poor health, disability, and death— things we all want to avoid as long as possible (Levine & Malone, 2019).

Somewhat shockingly, preventive services are so far underutilized, largely as a result of an implementation gap rather than an information gap due to the fact that insurance companies, hospitals, and physicians are paid to treat rather than to prevent disease (Levine et al., 2019). In contrast, payers have every opportunity and incentive to introduce value-based care.

The digital health industry has its premise that health apps are a solution to this challenge because they are marketed mostly toward the consumer and because they are easy to implement. However, without buy-in from all actors in the system, they will merely be band aids that fall off after a while.

How Wealthy Nonprofits Shape Grand Challenges to the Detriment of Other Causes

A small group of governmental and philanthropic funders each spends at least $100m per year on research, and each has a focus on biomedical science or human health.

The Grand Challenges in Global Health (GCGH) is a research initiative launched in 2003 by the Bill & Melinda Gates Foundation in collaboration with the Foundation for the National Institutes of Health (FNIH) in search of solutions to health problems in the developing world. Over the years from 2003 to 2015, Gates injected $200M into the FNIH into 14 scientific challenges in the areas of immunology, microbiology, genetics, molecular biology, cellular biology, entomology, agricultural sciences, clinical sciences, epidemiology, population and behavioral sciences, ecology, and evolutionary biology that, if solved, could lead to key advances in preventing, treating, and curing the diseases and health conditions contributing most to global health inequity. In 2014, the initiative was broadened to global development and renamed Grand Challenges (2020).

The family of initiatives have been criticized for being overly focused on science or technology as opposed to the complex economic, social, and political factors that explain the lack of progress made in these areas. Another criticism is that they focus on spectacular issues to the detriment of others, including an all-disease health system focus (Sharma, 2015).

A similar set of criticisms could be leveled against the UN's SDGs launched in 2015, which involved many ways that were the successor to Gates' Grand Challenges. Despite the apparent simplicity of a small set of goals, the fragmentation of global health factors, up to 200 organizations, counting numerous UN affiliates (WHO, UNICEF, UNAIDS, UN Women) and a myriad of global nonprofits (Global Fund, GAVI) and governmental initiatives (PEPFAR by the US), have led to a dearth of coordinated action. To confuse matters, the Gates Foundation has increasingly become the spokesperson outside specialty circles, yet coordination among the various initiatives, and transparency, is still not happening (Spicer et al., 2020).

Gates Foundation Prioritizes Children, the Young, and Women

Gates Foundation is based in Seattle, Washington, was launched in 2000, and is the second largest private foundation in the world, holding $46.8 billion in assets. Gates Foundation focuses on lifting people out of poverty through education, nutrition, and vaccines. Fighting infectious diseases through science and technology and market-based innovations are particularly in focus. Polio eradication has been a long-term goal. Nutrition, which arguably has been a neglected area of global health, has only received 1% of global foreign aid. Criticism of the Gates Foundation has come from the anti-vaxx movement who see nefarious motives behind the push to vaccinate and use the fact that the Foundation participated in a small pandemic exercise called Event 201 back in 2019 (Gilbert, 2020).

Novo Nordisk and Chronic Disease

The Novo Nordisk Foundation is an international foundation focusing on medical treatment and research, deploying sci-tech insight on proteins and peptides, RNA interference (RNAi), gene editing, and stem cells. In 2019, the foundation had a net worth of $59.89 billion, making it the largest endowment in the world. The foundation is hyper focused on chronic disease, particularly diabetes and produces 50% of the world's insulin supply. Today, 1 in every 11 people in the world has diabetes, a figure that is projected to rise to 1 in 9 by 2045 if action is not taken. The Foundation aims to reach 100,000 children by 2030. They also have a strong focus on obesity, a serious chronic disease with 650 million living with it globally at a global treatment cost of $1.2 tn by 2025 (https://www.novonordisk.com/).

The Wellcome Trust's Three Priorities: Infection, Heat, and Mental Health

The Wellcome Trust (https://wellcome.org/) is a London-based charity established in 1936 to improve human and animal health. As the UK's largest funder of non-governmental funding for scientific research, it is the fourth largest charity. Wellcome has a major stake in cancer research from its historical priorities and has become quite engaged in the fight against COVID-19, notably through genome sequencing work. Its new strategy formulated in 2020 puts renewed emphasis on three areas based on urgency: infectious diseases, global heating, and mental health because each carries the risk of premature disability and death in future generations, and each will be felt most acutely by minorities or resource-poor populations. Interestingly, with that, cancer fell off the priority list.

KFF and "Impartial" Health News

KFF is a US endowed, nonprofit organization arguably filling the need for trusted, independent information on national health issues. Legally, it is a public charity—not a foundation—and is *not* affiliated with Kaiser Permanente, the California-based American integrated managed care consortium (and health plan) which operates 39 hospitals and has 12 million members. Kaiser Health News, started in 2009, is a nonprofit national news service dedicated to in-depth reporting on complex health policy issues. KHN is now the largest health policy newsroom in the US, producing a wide range of journalism for print, radio, and TV, from explanatory stories to features and deep investigations (Altman,

2020). KFF also has a global health policy program, largely supported by the Gates Foundation.

How to Identify Emerging Grand Challenges

What if we want to define the grand challenges of the next decade beyond these three topics? How do we proceed?

There are many ways to identify grand challenges, and established ways of gaining consensus on which to prioritize, but fewer ways to productively make true progress toward solving them. In other areas of society or business, the challenge is often to identify the right focus area, which issue to dedicate our finite resources and attention to, or, in business, simply a matter of deciding which horse to bet on. In healthcare, the opposite is true. The priorities themselves can seem blatantly obvious. Clearly, there are an array of global healthcare issues at any given moment—but there is little disagreement about where the solvable solutions lie at least the ones that could be agreed upon within the current governance paradigms we operate under including nationalism, neoliberalism, and meritocracy. On the other hand, how specifically to make progress on each, without causing major tension or hitting obvious budget ceilings, is not that evident and it is easy to waste money or resources on an issue without making a dent. Having said that, overlapping or uncoordinated activity is also a problem which wastes resources. Lastly, many healthcare issues are interconnected, so that action on one single issue might hamper progress on others. That's why the argument has been made to simultaneously focus on an all-disease approach. However, the challenge is far greater than diseases, they may not even be the biggest issue. Mapping out the true long-term impact of environmental degradation upon next generations' healthspan seems to me far more important, for example. What's needed is a systems approach (Clarkson et al., 2018).

However, describing the overall system is a complex affair with many moving parts, diseases, actors, contexts, and interdependencies. What this system (the global healthcare system) lacks is the notion of a global welfare state, which in the next 25 years should become far more relevant than the notion of any national welfare state. We need a global safety net. We need a global minimum income. We need global health security basic rights. We need a set of technology principles and technologies that can deliver healthcare on a global scale and at a low cost. We need a globalized social insurance system. We need to implement global social rights (not just be content with declarations of such rights). We need a redistribution of healthcare dollars toward where it's the most needed. We need global food subsidies (likely through cash welfare) to guarantee nutrition of all the world's children. None of this is happening in any organized, global fashion as of today.

Once you do establish these rights and start financing the guarantee of such rights being upheld across the globe, systemic priorities become crystal clear because the costs are clear. Only by doing that can we achieve a true, rebalanced notion of grand challenges. Globalization has broken the tenuous social contract that existed between citizens and governments even in advanced, western welfare states (Powell & Chen, 2012). Pandemics exasperate the problem and widen the disparities. Without doubt, the results are about to become disastrous. A fix is needed.

Although many candidates exist as future grand challenges—cancer, nutrition, infectious diseases, poverty, and beyond—a few stand out. If we had to pick, to me, pandemics, aging, and preventive healthcare are the three most important challenges. Pandemics are an obvious and escalating threat where we have made much progress over the past few years alone because of COVID-19, but more must be done. Aging is the invisible killer which gradually eats away at our bodies until we slowly break apart from the inside—and many of us would like to both increase lifespan and improve healthspan.

But to think this way is to resign oneself to the current paradigm. The notion of grand challenges is fundamentally problematic in and of itself. It clouds our

KEY TAKEAWAYS AND REFLECTIONS

1. Do you agree that there are grand health challenges at this time that we can universally agree upon? If so, how should this agreement happen, and at what level (global, regional, local)?

2. Is the welfare state a good national goal to pursue? If not, what else will be helpful toward wider health tech adoption?

3. Say you had enormous personal wealth—and decided to build a healthcare foundation. What would you focus on and how would you set up this entity?

judgment. It becomes unclear when we have met our goal and when to move on to other challenges, that are being left undone in the meantime.

Regardless what part of the world you live in, life expectancy is drastically different depending on social determinants, it is all about resource-based inequality. Preventive healthcare is the ultimate challenge. If we could prevent rather than be forced to act on already existing diseases, we would save a lot of resources in the healthcare system. For the world to progress, we would need to make drastic progress in that domain over the next 25 years.

Conclusion

Having said all that, without building not just "solidarity" as the WHO argues, but perhaps more productively starting to chart how building a global welfare state would float all boats, both boosting healthcare and economic growth, seems quite a lot more pressing to me.

In the next chapter, I'll try to make a dent on one systemic aspect far bigger than the known grand challenges, the gargantuan challenge of interoperability.

References

Altman, D.E. (2020) Explaining KFF, President's Message. Available at: https://www.kff.org/presidents-message/.

Cattell, R.B. (1987) *Beyondism: Religion from Science.* New York: Praeger.

Clarkson, J., Dean, J., Ward, J., Komashie, A., and Bashford, T. (2018). 'A systems approach to healthcare: from thinking to practice', *Future Healthcare Journal*, 5:3, 151–155, Available at: DOI: 10.7861/futurehosp.5-3-151.

Filgueira, F., Causa, O., Fleurbaey, M., and Grimalda, G. (2018) 'Rethinking the welfare state in the global economy', Policy Briefs, G20 Insights. Available at: https://www.g20-insights.org/policy_briefs/rethinking-the-welfare-state-in-the-global-economy/.

Gilbert, B. (2020) 'A bizarre conspiracy theory puts Bill Gates at the center of the coronavirus crisis — and major conservative pundits are circulating it', Business Insider, 19 April 2020. Available at: https://www.businessinsider.com/coronavirus-conspiracy-bill-gates-infowars-2020-4?r=US&IR=T.

Gough, I. and Therborn, G. (2010) 'The Global Future of Welfare States', *The Oxford Handbook of the Welfare State*, edited by Francis G. Castles, Stephan Leibfried, Jane Lewis, Herbert Obinger, and Christopher Pierson, 703–876. DOI: 10.1093/oxfordhb/9780199579396.003.0048.

Grand Challenges (2020) Available at: https://grandchallenges.org/.

Hood, L. (2013). 'Systems biology and p4 medicine: past, present, and future,' *Rambam Maimonides Medical Journal*, 4:2, e0012, Available at: DOI: 10.5041/RMMJ.10112 (Accessed 28 November 2020).

Kaminskiy, D. and Colangelo, M. (2020) *Longevity Industry 1.0.* London: Deep Knowledge Group. Available at: https://www.longevity-book.com/ (Accessed 28 November 2020).

Koonin, L.M., Hoots, B., Tsang, C.A., et al. (2020) 'Trends in the use of telehealth during the emergence of the COVID-19 pandemic — United States, January–March 2020', *Morbidity and Mortality Weekly Report*, 69, 1595–1599, Available at: DOI: 10.15585/mmwr.mm6943a3.

Levine, S., Malone, E., Lekiachvili, A., and Briss, P. (2019) 'Health care industry insights: why the use of preventive services is still low', *Preventing Chronic Disease*, 16, 180625, Available at: DOI: 10.5888/pcd16.180625 (Accessed 28 November 2020).

Powell, J.L. and Chen, S. (2012) 'Globalization and global welfare: a critical excursion', Fast Capitalism, 9.1. Available at: https://www.uta.edu/huma/agger/fastcapitalism/9_1/powell9_1.html.

Sharma, Y. (2015) 'Gates Foundation reviews funding focus after criticism', Scidev.net, 27 January 2015. Available at: https://www.scidev.net/global/news/gates-foundation-reviews-funding-focus-after-criticism/.

Spicer, N., Agyepong, I., Ottersen, T. et al. (2020) 'It's far too complicated': why fragmentation persists in global health', *Global Health*, 16, 60, Available at: DOI: 10.1186/s12992-020-00592-1.

Undheim (2020) *Pandemic Aftermath.* Austin, TX: Atmosphere Press.

Vinluan, F. (2021) "AI-drug discovery biotech Valo Health is going public via a $2.8B SPAC merger", MedCityNews, 9 June 2021. Available at: https://medcitynews.com/2021/06/ai-drug-discovery-biotech-valo-health-is-going-public-via-a-2-8b-spac-merger/?rf=1 (Accessed 6 July 2021)

Wellcome (2020) 'Wellcome Science Review 2020'. Available at: https://cms.wellcome.org/sites/default/files/2020-10/wellcome-science-review-2020.pdf.

WHO (2020) '10 global health issues to track in 2021', WHO, 24 December 2020. Available at: https://www.who.int/news-room/spotlight/10-global-health-issues-to-track-in-2021#.

Chapter 6

The Gargantuan Global Fight for Interoperability

An Epic Story

Seventy-seven-year-old entrepreneur Judy Faulkner, with her flowing dark hair and square glasses with a bluish tint and a characteristic grin, might seem like an unlikely person to be standing between you and better healthcare in the next decade. Yet, as the CEO of Epic Systems, the largest medical records company in the US, throughout this decade she has arguably been actively working to oppose proposed legislation designed to make it easier to share medical information. It is in her company's best interest. She nearly succeeded, in fact she might still succeed, the jury is out.

Faulkner self-founded Wisconsin-based Epic Systems in a basement in Madison in 1979 and subsequently moved it to nearby Verona, population 10,000, with the original name of Human Services Computing with a $70,000 bank loan secured against her house and the sweat equity of a few programming customers (Conn, 2015) and has never sought venture capital or private equity growth capital. She wrote the original code to Chronicles, Epic's precursor, while working alongside doctors and nurses at the University of Wisconsin.

As a University of Wisconsin graduate student in computer science, she took a course on 'computers in medicine' and studied with Dr. Warner Slack who soon moved to Beth Israel in Boston and became the co-founder of the Division of Clinical Informatics at the Harvard Medical Faculty Physicians. Slack, who passed away in 2018, was among the first physicians to envision the essential role that computers would play in medicine and healthcare delivery (Boston Globe, 2018).

Already by 2015, healthcare groups using Epic electronic health records (EHRs) served 54% of patients in the US and 2.5% of patients worldwide (Glaze, 2015) and clients including Kaiser Permanente, Cleveland Clinic, Johns Hopkins, and CVS Health (Conn, 2015). With $3 billion in revenues, 10,000 employees, over 160 hospital clients, and an operating system that touches 40% of the American population (Johnson, 2020), Epic has made Faulkner a billionaire with a net worth of 5.5 billion USD (Forbes 2021), and America's second-richest self-made woman, according to Forbes billionaires list. She still proudly drives an old Audi station wagon and has signed The Giving Pledge, promising to donate 99% of her assets. She clearly has many great qualities and has created enormous value—but with some relatively invisible costs to the health system—and to us.

Epic's Cozy Relationships with the US Government and Leading Hospitals

The privately held company was a major beneficiary of a $48 billion Obama-era federal program to promote the adoption of EHRs (Mandl & Kohane, 2020). To this day, less than 1% of Epic's employees work in marketing because given the entrenched market where everybody knows them, it is simply not needed. Today, 96% of hospitals have adopted EHRs, up from just 9% in 2008, but the system has led to doctors not spending enough time face-to-face with the patient and doctors still resort to transferring medical data via fax and CD-ROM (Schulte & Fry, 2019).

It is universally understood by most that healthcare relies on pre-internet proprietary and non-interoperable software, of which Epic is the most prevalent example (Mandl & Kohane, 2020). The much quoted "drop-down menu problem" with EHRs refers to the fact that database systems typically don't allow you to navigate the way you do on the internet but rather have you scroll through a near infinite number of menus, leading to another expression, "death-by-a-thousand-clicks". That's a lot of clicks, given that Epic supports the medical records of over 250 million patients (Forbes, 2020).

From Massachusetts to Wisconsin and Back—A Story of Billions of Dollars

EHRs have contributed to an epidemic of physician burnout (Schulte & Fry, 2019). This is unfortunate, but not surprising, given that the history of electronic medical records is long and stretches back to the 1970s. Massachusetts General

Hospital, the third oldest hospital in the US, registered the Massachusetts General Hospital Utility Multi-Programming System (MUMPS), or just "M", as a trademark with the USPTO on November 28, 1971. M expanded across the US as the predominant technology for health information systems and EHRs.

In an irony of ironies, Mass General reportedly spent a billion plus dollars on the Epic implementation (MHA, 2019), essentially buying back the right to license and use its 'own' technology. The average cost for large hospitals and clinics seems to hover around $500,000 a year including license and training costs, and most of the leading institutions spend between $20,000 and $30,000 per doctor for training for EHR systems (Costhack, 2020).

Epic's database technology, Caché, a NoSQL database, traces its roots to that 1970s effort but is a proprietary upgrade of MUMPS developed by Intersystems (2020) in Cambridge, Massachusetts, initially released in 1997. Caché runs on a variety of operating systems, including Windows, Linux, Solaris, HP-UX, AIX, macOS, and OpenVMS platforms, the most popular object-oriented data base management systems. It is also used in the VistA system until recently used by the US Department of Veteran Affairs. The VA is now switching to Cerner, spending $16 billion over a few years to migrate (Drees, 2020), another system which also uses Mumps.

It is instructive to look at the origin of EHR systems, which were originally designed for transactional, activity-based, fee-for-service payment methodologies, e.g. billing, not for patient care. How they became used as a patient facing system (in that doctors use it simultaneously as they care for patients) is a long story but an important one. It is the story of poor usability, lack of tech awareness among the medical profession, and scrupulous providers exploiting the situation to their advantage.

There should perhaps be a law against marketing software for a use case it was never intended for, or at least some kind of usability review before software is certified for a specific use? What about another rule that says that a computer program's code must be retired after 30 years? Epic states that none of the founder's original code is present in the current software, yet an engineer who worked there for 2 years stated that there was a "nightmarish accumulation of technical debt continually rolled over since 1979" and moreover that "the tech stack was a real resume killer" (Hacker News, 2017).

According to Johnson (2019a), EHR companies become essential components of their clients' cultures and operations, developing deep trust, co-opting IT departments which implement massive installations with enormous switching costs, which makes them difficult to dislodge. Partners Healthcare in Boston, now calling itself Mass General Brigham, spent $1.6 billion to implement Epic, the majority of which was tech support and lost patient revenues due to training. It is almost unbelievable to think of how much that healthcare system was willing to adapt to its new software overlords.

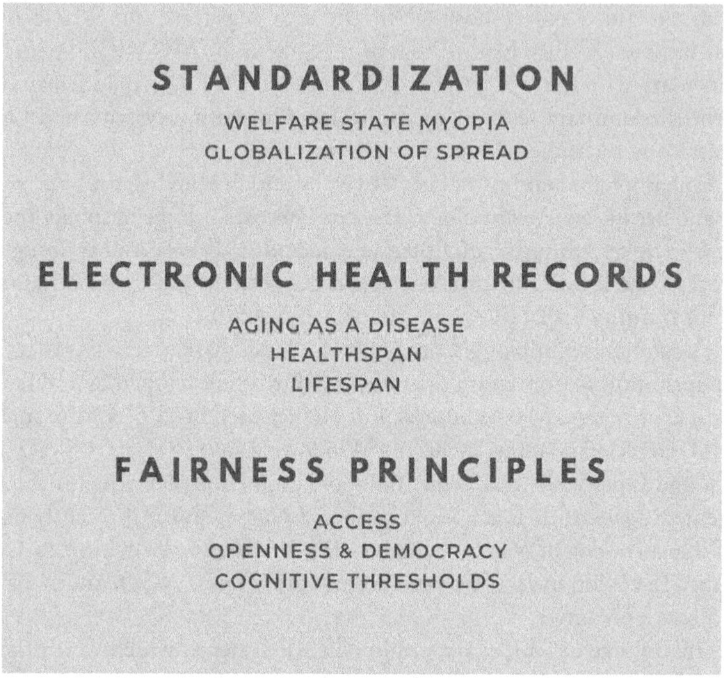

STANDARDIZATION

WELFARE STATE MYOPIA

GLOBALIZATION OF SPREAD

ELECTRONIC HEALTH RECORDS

AGING AS A DISEASE

HEALTHSPAN

LIFESPAN

FAIRNESS PRINCIPLES

ACCESS

OPENNESS & DEMOCRACY

COGNITIVE THRESHOLDS

Figure 6.1 Global interoperability.

Having said that, being a patient of that health system, I have noticed that I suddenly don't have to fill out any paperwork anymore, and that my health login truly does give me access to my medical record and a messaging app that works, so something did change. What we need is a world where "trusted information transforms health and healthcare by connecting people, systems, and ideas", as in the vision behind an organization such as The American Health Information Management Association (AHIMA), a leading voice in health information (Figure 6.1).

Stories of Lock-In Repeat Themselves across Technology

Without an easier way to share medical information, your health record stays with whichever provider produced it and cannot easily be extracted. In short, you do not own your health information in any meaningful way, and you cannot easily share it, switch providers, or get the best medical care based on consumer choice. In addition, it slows down the overall path of innovation in healthcare and stops a tremendous amount of progress in reaping the efficiencies of emerging analytics, including artificial intelligence.

You have heard this record before. Big software company enjoys several decades of cozy relationships with its suppliers and embed their technology with strong lock-in features that are costly to break away from. You could look at the history of IBM, Microsoft, or Apple to find a similar story play out. Bill Gates, who ironically has such a big role in contemporary global healthcare, knows this first-hand. His battle with the US Justice department was televised. Nothing he does in healthcare takes away from having exploited a monopolist situation through Microsoft and having significantly slowed innovation among startups and the entire software vendor community throughout the 1990s and 2000s.

Yet, in healthcare, the situation is worse and even more ingrained relationships have developed. Unfortunately for those wishing for disruptive innovation to take hold, there is, arguably, alignment between payers and providers and a very small set of vendors to ensure that health information does not flow freely. After all, that would mean patient choice, which would mean they could pick different health providers. As we know from any industry, banking, for example, incumbents are slow to release their grip on their customers if they do not have to. Only an avalanche of digital technology combined with a set of banking crises, that necessitated a shrinking of the existing physical infrastructure of bank tellers, brought about the ATM revolution, and subsequently e-banking and online banking. Moreover, the early work of the Society for Worldwide Interbank Financial Telecommunications (SWIFT) in the 1970s defined a standard of interoperability that has enabled messaging between more than 11,000 institutions (Taneja, 2020).

US Health Tech Regulation—Long in the Coming

In the 2004, State of the Union address, President George W. Bush created The Office of the National Coordinator of Health IT (ONC). His vision was to transform healthcare data management from 19th century paper records to 21st century digital records, a laudable goal.

In 2009, in the Obama administration, Congress passed the Health Information Technology for Economic and Clinical Health (HITECH) Act, providing almost $40 billion in funding to digitize health records, accelerate EHR adoption, and promote interoperability. HITECH did accelerate adoption.

Coincidentally in 2009, Epic's CEO Faulkner was appointed by President Barack Obama to a seat on the Health IT Policy Committee representing health IT vendors, the panel overseeing the $19 billion EMR "incentives" program from which her company benefits grandly (Malkin, 2013), where she served until 2014. Faulkner was also part of a White House assembled team of experts tasked by the Office of the National Coordinator (ONC) for Health Information Technology to examine privacy and security in healthcare IT. By 2013, she was dubbed "the most powerful woman in health care" by Forbes.

Lobbying to Keep EHR Dominance

Lobbying has increased over the past 3 years in the runup to this major interoperability proposal (according to Opensecrets.org).

In August 2014, Epic hired lobbying firm Card & Associates, run by A. Bradford Card, the brother of the former White House Chief of Staff under Pres. George W. Bush, to improve the perception of the vendor on Capitol Hill regarding its position on interoperability. Epic's lobbying budget has fluctuated between $148 and $500 thousand (OpenSecrets.org), which is not very much, although the way these numbers are reported typically drastically under-communicates the amount of resource spend. Notably, Epic doubled its budget from 2016 to 2017 which is when the work with the information blocker legislation kicked off. Epic EHR competitor Cerner Corp spent somewhere between $440K and $560 K in the 2017–2020 period.

For comparison, the company I once worked for, Oracle Corporation, is listed with a lobbying budget of $6.56 and $12.9 million (OpenSecrets.org)—and that company has an entire corridor of (very nice) in-house lobbyists. Overall, this proves just how much easier it is to maintain a health IT monopoly which has largely already been sold and implemented (e.g. Epic) than it is to operate with a much broader IT portfolio across agencies and use cases (e.g. Oracle) and with much more formidable competitors (e.g. IBM, Microsoft, Amazon, Google).

The issue of open Application programming interfaces (APIs) is unresolved. The American Health Information Management Association (AHIMA), the American Hospital Association (AHA), the American Medical Association (AMA), the American Medical Informatics Association (AMIA), the College of Healthcare Information Management Executives (CHIME), the Federation of American Hospitals (FAH), and the Medical Group Management Association (MGMA) have all been involved in this process. Many of them, taking Epic's lead and running their errand, as well as for their own reasons, one would assume, have consistently argued that open APIs (another synonym for interoperability) could compromise patient data, even though it is pretty clear that misuse of patient data happens for other reasons, even from EHR companies selling data without the participation of patients (Roth, 2020).

The Electronic Health Record Association (EHRA) is a trade association with 33 member companies. Their October 3, 2019 position statement (EHRA, 2019) on the information-blocking legislation was largely a complaint about intellectual property rights and not a substantial argument in the fight. This is very likely because with so many competitors as members, they had to focus on the common position.

In a January 10 guest column in the *Wisconsin State Journal*, former Wisconsin governor Tommy Thompson, who served as HHS secretary from 2001 to 2005, wrote: "These rules would unfairly harm Wisconsin's health IT industry and, along with it, the Wisconsin economy", [...]. "These rules would compel Epic to give its trade secrets away to venture capitalists, Big Tech, Silicon Valley interests, and overseas competitors for little or no compensation. [...] at the expense of Wisconsin residents" (Roth, 2020).

On February 3, 2000, Epic's CEO Judy Faulkner sent a letter to HHS Secretary Azar with 60 signatures, mostly from Epic health system clients, including a few states. The letter states: "The ONC's proposed rule on interoperability will be overly burdensome on our health systems and will endanger patient privacy" and requests extended timelines. Epic's letter backfired. However, they did manage to dilute the regulations significantly.

US Interoperability Legislation Approved—But Not Implemented

At the end of the day, strikingly, on March 9, 2020, the US Department of Health and Human Services (HHS) finalized two transformative rules that will give patients unprecedented safe, secure access to their health data (HHS, 2020).

The rules implement interoperability and patient access provisions of the bipartisan 21st Century Cures Act (Cures Act), requiring insurance plans to share health data with their patients in a format suitable for their phones or other devices of their choice. It establishes new rules to prevent "information blocking" practices (e.g. anti-competitive behaviors) by healthcare providers, developers of certified health IT, health information exchanges, and health information networks. With the new rule, providers using certified health IT have the ability to communicate about health IT usability, user experience, interoperability, and security including (with limitations) screenshots and video. Notably, it still does not mean that individual users can freely share such information in those formats.

The new interoperability provision would affect "clinical notes", allergies, and medications among other important clinical data and requires health plans in Medicare Advantage, Medicaid, CHIP, and through the federal Exchanges to share claims data electronically with patients.

On October 29, 2020, the Trump administration issued an interim final rule extending the compliance deadlines for healthcare information blocking and interoperability regulations, originally set for April 5, which marks that the second time HHS has pushed back the deadline, which now becomes April 5, 2021, and with new standardized API functionality not required until December 2022 (Landi, 2020).

In the long term, the new data-sharing regulations may advance the use of medical data from consumer devices like the Apple Watch to address chronic conditions and may also help improve population health efforts, as well as, potentially, drive the industry to adopt a new business model that mixes brick-and-mortar services with virtual care (Landi, 2000).

As with many things, it depends. The proposed rule might meaningfully end up enforcing individuals' right to access digital copies of their health records, something that was theoretically possible under the Health Insurance Portability and Accountability Act (HIPAA), but rarely happened (Mandl & Kohane, 2020).

Where Should Consumers Store Their Health Data?

Once you have your health data what should you do with it? Should you put it on a bulletin board at your home, on an Apple HealthKit, on a computer spread sheet, or in a bank vault? Who should you share it with and in what format? The US does not regulate consumer behavior in any way, so this is up to you. What really is an issue is that healthcare and consumer protections differ, but all that means is that there is a need to look at the way consumer health IT is regulated, not that we need to slow down data sharing in healthcare (Johnson, 2020).

The Policy Road Ahead

The Biden administration is likely to take a proactive role on interoperability, if only for an idiosyncratic reason. Biden personally experienced the challenge of getting his son Beau's medical records from one hospital to another during Beau's struggle with glioblastoma (Schulte & Fry, 2019). In 2017, it was reported that then US Vice President Joe Biden and Epic CEO Judy Faulkner exchanged words on the value of sharing medical information with patients, according to which Biden asked her why patients shouldn't have access to their medical records, and Faulkner responded: "Why do you want your medical records? There are a thousand pages of which you understand 10". Biden is supposed to have retorted: "None of your business" (Farr, 2017).

That particular episode alone can mean that interoperability in healthcare will make significant progress during the Biden administration. On the other hand, it can be argued, it was the Obama administration that exacerbated the mess by funding the continuation of the EHR monopoly for another decade. What lessons have they learned? Furthermore, Epic CEO Faulkner was a big donor to Obama's 2008 Presidential campaign and supports congressional Democrats. [I have no data or records on her potential support provided to the Biden campaign.]

Global EHR Markets—More Interoperable?

I have kids born in three countries and my wife and I were each born in two additional countries, which makes us big supporters of portable medical records. Regrettably, it has been difficult, and I reckon my own medical records reside in at least five countries, given my travel, studies, and professional career living in as many. I certainly don't have my Norwegian, Belgian, Italian, or UK records, although I believe I got some Belgian X-rays that I have since lost. As for my US records, as stated earlier, they are with MGH Brigham and I have not yet tried to retrieve them in their entirety, online or otherwise, although I'm looking at them more regularly now that their Patient Gateway has become more user friendly (my eyes glazed over the first few years of its operation).

European eHealth Interoperability

The European Commission's Communication on interoperability for public services (2010) introduces the European Interoperability Framework (EIF), which promotes and supports the delivery of European public services by fostering cross-border and cross-sector interoperability which I am proud to have been part of developing, back in my days as a European bureaucrat-policymaker. The EIF is implemented through the Interoperability Solutions for European Public Administrations (ISA) program.

In 2013, the EU financed a *Study on the eHealth Interoperability Framework* (2013), carried out by Deloitte, which essentially presented a vision of a day when there would be an EU eHealth Interoperability Framework complete with technical, semantic, organizational, and legal interoperability.

The New European Interoperability Framework, part of the Communication (COM(2017)134) from the European Commission adopted on March 23, 2017, gives more specific guidance on how to set up interoperable digital public services, increasing from 25 to 47 recommendations. However, EIF explicitly does not cover eHealth, indeed, the word health is not mentioned since this is a separate policy process and outside of core EU competence.

On February 6, 2019, the European Commission finally adopted a recommendation on a European Electronic Health Record exchange format seeking to unlock the flow of health data across borders with a baseline including patient summary, eprescription/edispensation, laboratory results, medical imaging, and reports, as well as hospital discharge reports (European Commission, 2020).

This is high time because few member states are studying the possibility of data extraction for research, statistics, and other uses serving the public interest and there is not a single common EHR system operating across all EU Member States except for Finland which has a system based on OpenEHR (https://www.openehr.org/) (De Raeve & Jardim-Gonçalves, 2020). However, it is starting to trickle. EHR exchanges are becoming operational in the European Union (EU), starting with e-prescriptions between Estonia and Finland, followed by patient summaries between Luxembourg and the Czech Republic, and eventually Croatia—and will gradually be implemented across 22 EU countries on a voluntary basis, under the auspices of the eHealth Digital Service Infrastructure (eHDSI or eHealth DSI).

Worldwide EHR Market

The worldwide EHR market topped $31.5 billion in 2018, according to Kalorama Information (Landi, 2019). The healthcare industrial complex's key players arguably rely upon lax and beneficial regulation to optimize their market positions and profitability (Johnson, 2020).

Due to its acquisition of Siemens Health Services in February 2015, Cerner, the North Kansas City based provider, has the largest share of the worldwide market with around 17.3% of the market, with Epic second at 8.8% and Allscripts at 6.1%. Cerner has by far the highest non-US revenue at more than $650M in 2019, representing 12% of its business, although Meditech has a similar share starting from a smaller base (Gill, 2020).

Cerner is the leader in large health systems, building on its connections with the US Department of Defense to leverage foreign governments, while Epic is the leader with smaller hospitals and large physician practices. GE Healthcare and Meditech are runner ups (Monegain, 2018). As for regular physician practices, Cerner, Epic, Allscripts but also NextGen, athenahealth, eClinicalWorks, and NueMD compete for market share. Overall, Cerner is strong in the UK, while Epic is strong in the Netherlands (Heath, 2015) and has offices in The Netherlands, Dubai, Singapore, and Copenhagen. About 76% of HIMSS Stage 7 Global Hospitals use EpicCare (Epic, 2020a,b).

Cerner recently made its interoperability connection opt-out rather than opt-in for its customers (Jason, 2020a), that's at least a start.

As we can see, the impact of US-based EHR providers in global healthcare systems is significant. This means that internationally, single countries likely cannot change the interoperability requirements significantly without having the US government on board. Considering that all of the nation's top-20 hospitals use Epic, that would be the way to put pressure on and attempt to align these hospitals on a path toward truly interoperable EHRs. The challenge is that this is not in their own interest as they would potentially lose patients. This is where it becomes complex. In the San Francisco Bay Area, a hotbed of healthcare IT innovation, there is a running joke among healthcare IT entrepreneurs. It goes as follows: Question: "Where do healthcare IT startups go to die?" Answer: "To a hospital".

Do Interoperable EHRs Exist?

Solutions such as Infor's Cloverleaf, Corepoint, or InterSystems achieve data interoperability via published standards (Johnson, 2019). Standards include the Fast Healthcare Interoperability Resources (FHIR), which combines the best features of other standards such as HL7 V2, HL7 V3, and CDA, while leveraging the latest web service technologies.

Epic has not joined the CommonWell Alliance. CommonWell Health Alliance, founded in 2013, is a not-for-profit trade association devoted to the simple vision that health data should be available to individuals and caregivers regardless of where care occurs and whose members include competitors Cerner, athenahealth, McKesson, Allscripts, CPSI, and Greenway Health.

What true interoperability enables is a blank slate to innovate upon. It paves the way for what we have seen in consumer software for decades—highly usable, intuitive interfaces without a correspondingly steep learning curve. In the manufacturing industry, nocode solutions are also making big strides, partly because the older machines have been replaced with newer ones that are easier to tweak. Healthcare, together with finance, the military, and e-government, are the last bastions. Once they fall to the simplicity principle, which is nowhere near as inevitable as it is morally desirable, everything will change more rapidly.

Is Big Tech the Answer to These Problems?

Healthcare is at an inflection point. The challenges in the industry are so numerous, the cost spiraling is somewhat out of control (partly caused by poorly implemented technology), yet the technology opportunity is unprecedented. Could there be an Uber for healthcare? Will there be major aggregator sites or marketplaces for knowledge or transactions or both? Will our medical records ever be able to flow freely (yet securely)?

If the influx of big tech (which is inevitable) happens before healthcare has fixed its interoperability problems, nothing will be gained by big tech's entry. That would be a big shame. In fact, if we think about how big tech typically handled interoperability in the past (thinking of IBM, Microsoft, and Apple's proprietary software), the situation could get worse.

I have seen various folks asking for Google to enter the health records space (Bushler, 2019). But we need to be careful what we wish for. It might solve some problems and create others. Google's Project Nightingale, where Ascension, a nonprofit Catholic hospital system that operates in 21 states, without consent from doctors or patients, gave Google access to millions of patient records, including names and birth dates aiming to build new tools that help doctors extract key information from patients' medical records and deliver more targeted medical treatments (Maddox & MacGibbon, 2019), is also not a great scenario. A better solution would be to level the playing field so that more competition can happen, including from startups, because all technologies interoperate using agreed principles of collaboration.

Conclusion

It must be noted that the only reason Epic lost the regulatory fight in the early spring of 2020 was that other big tech lobbyists are smarter and more numerous. Apple's lobbying budget has consistently fluctuated between $5 and $8 million from 2017 to 2020, whereas Epic's lobbying budget, as previously mentioned, has fluctuated between $148 and $500 thousand (OpenSecrets. org). Apples Health App benefits (somewhat) from interoperability, which is quite ironic given Apple's proprietary history, so they were able to argue both ways (lock-in to award innovation AND interoperability to create and maintain innovation).

KEY TAKEAWAYS AND REFLECTIONS

1. What do you understand by the notion of interoperability?

   _____

2. Describe how lack of interoperability could be seen as a problem for health tech. What other areas are affected by interoperability?

   _____

3. What should be done about big tech, if anything?

   _____

At present, the world's EHRs remain a disconnected patchwork. It has handcuffed health providers to technology they can't stand and has enriched and empowered the $13 billion industry that sells it, at the expense of patient health and primary care work satisfaction, leading to burnout, and most likely, worse effects (Schulte & Fry, 2019). Primary care doctors spend more than 50% of their workday on EHR tasks, American Medical Association study finds (Finnegan, 2017). Is that right? Can it continue?

In the next chapter, I will tackle the mainstream sci-tech of vaccines and the counterculture of anti-vaxxers.

References

Boston Globe (2018) 'Werner V. Slack'. Available at: https://www.legacy.com/guestbooks/bostonglobe/warner-v-slack-condolences/189584973?cid=full (Accessed 28 November 2020).

Bushler, A. (2019) 'How Google EHR could fix one of healthcare's epic flaws', Medium, 19 April 2019. Available at: https://medium.com/design-and-tech-co/how-google-ehr-could-fix-one-of-healthcares-epic-flaws-280036a988e3 (Accessed 28 November 2020).

Conn, J. (2015) 'Q&A | Epic CEO Faulkner tells why she wants to keep her company private', Modern Healthcare, 14 March 2015. Available at: https://www.modernhealthcare.com/article/20150314/MAGAZINE/303149952/q-a-epic-ceo-faulkner-tells-why-she-wants-to-keep-her-company-private (Accessed 28 November 2020).

Costhack (2020) 'How much does epic EMR cost? [Actual rates revealed]', Costhack [Online]. Available at: https://costhack.com/epic-emr-cost/# (Accessed 28 November 2020).

De Raeve, P. and Jardim-Gonçalves, R. (2020) 'Digitalising the healthcare ecosystem in the European Union', HealthEuropa.eu, 25 June 2020. Available at: https://www.healtheuropa.eu/digitalising-the-healthcare-ecosystem-in-the-european-union/100949/ (Accessed 28 November 2020).

Drees, J. (2020) 'Cerner secures potential $161M contract for VA health network go-live', Becker's Hospital Review, 31 August 2020. Available at: https://www.beckershospitalreview.com/ehrs/cerner-secures-potential-161m-contract-for-va-health-network-go-live.html# (Accessed 28 November 2020).

EHRA (2019) 'Congressional briefing summary slides'. Available at: https://www.ehra.org/sites/ehra.org/files/EHR%20Association%20Hosts%20Congressional%20Briefing.%20View%20the%20Summary%20Slides%20and%20Panelist%20Bios.pdf (Accessed 27 February 2021).

Epic.com (2020a) 'From healthcare to mapping the Milky Way: 5 things you didn't know about Epic's Tech', Stories & Snapshots, Epic.com. Available at: https://www.epic.com/epic/post/4871 (Accessed 28 November 2020).

Epic.com (2020b) 'Who uses Epic?'. Available at: https://www.epic.com/community (Accessed 28 November 2020).

European Commission (2013) 'Study on the eHealth interoperability framework', European Commission. Available at: https://ec.europa.eu/eip/ageing/standards/ict-and-communication/interoperability/ehealth-eif_en (Accessed 28 November 2020).

European Commission (2020) 'Exchange of electronic health records across the EU', European Commission [Online]. Available at: https://ec.europa.eu/digital-single-market/en/exchange-electronic-health-records-across-eu (Accessed 28 November 2020).

Farr, C. (2017) 'Joe Biden just brought the debate over medical records into the limelight', CNBC, 7 August 2017. Available at: https://www.cnbc.com/2017/08/07/joe-biden-vs-judy-faulkner-epic-systems-ceo-its-complicated.html (Accessed 28 November 2020).

Fast Healthcare Interoperability Resources. Available at: https://www.hl7.org/fhir/.

Finnegan, J. (2017) 'Primary care doctors spend more than 50% of workday on EHR tasks, American Medical Association study finds', 13 September 2020. Available at: https://www.fiercehealthcare.com/practices/primary-care-doctors-spend-more-than-50-workday-ehr-tasks (Accessed 28 November 2020).

Forbes (2020) '#451 Judy Faulkner'. Available at: https://www.forbes.com/profile/judy-faulkner (Accessed 28 November 2020).

Forbes (2021) 'The Real-time Billionaires List'. Available at: https://www.forbes.com/real-time-billionaires/#39c8cfc3d788

Gill, A. (2020) 'Why international expansion must remain a priority for Cerner, Epic, Allscripts, MEDITECH', HIT Consultant, 24 August 2020. Available at: https://hitconsultant.net/2020/08/24/why-international-expansion-must-remain-priority-ehr-vendors/#.X8ImfGhKiUk (Accessed 28 November 2020).

Glaze, J. (2015) 'Epic Systems draws on literature greats for its next expansion', Madison.com [Online], 6 January 2015. Available at: https://madison.com/news/local/govt-and-politics/epic-systems-draws-on-literature-greats-for-its-next-expansion/article_4d1cf67c-2abf-5cfd-8ce1-2da60ed84194.html (Accessed 28 November 2020).

Hacker News (2017) 'Y Combinator Hacker News', Available at: https://news.ycombinator.com/item?id=13861074 (Accessed 28 November 2020).

Heath, S. (2015) 'Epic EHR use not widespread internationally, survey shows', *EHR Intelligence*. 15 November 2015. Available at: https://ehrintelligence.com/news/epic-shows-inconsistent-ehr-performance-internationally (Accessed 28 November 2020)

HHS (2020) 'HHS finalizes historic rules to provide patients more control of their health data', HHS.gov [Online]. Available at: https://www.hhs.gov/about/news/2020/03/09/hhs-finalizes-historic-rules-to-provide-patients-more-control-of-their-health-data.html (Accessed 28 November 2020).

Intersystems (2020) 'Caché: High-performance database', Intersystems. Available at: https://www.intersystems.com/products/cache/ (Accessed 28 November 2020).

Jason, C. (2020a) 'Epic, Cerner, NextGen top acute EHR interoperability enablers', EHR Intelligence, 12 November 2020. Available at: https://ehrintelligence.com/news/epic-cerner-nextgen-top-acute-ehr-interoperability-enablers (Accessed 28 November 2020).

Jason, C. (2020b) '10 patient data sharing, interoperability principles for providers', EHR Intelligence, 18 November 2020. Available at: https://ehrintelligence.com/news/10-patient-data-sharing-interoperability-principles-for-providers (Accessed 28 November 2020).

Johnson, D.W. (2019a) 'Interoperability battle lines: Data freedom fighters vs. entrenched data blockers', 4sightHealth, 26 March 2020. Available at: https://www.4sighthealth.com/interoperability-battle-lines-data-freedom-fighters-vs-entrenched-data-blockers/ (Accessed 28 November 2020).

Johnson, D.W. (2019b) *The Customer Revolution in Healthcare: Delivering Kinder, Smarter, Affordable Care for All*, New York: McGraw-Hill Education.

Johnson, D.W. (2020) 'Healthcare's epic problem & the audacity of liberating patient data', 4sightHealth, 3 February 2020. Available at: https://www.4sighthealth.com/healthcares-epic-problem-the-audacity-of-liberating-patient-data/ (Accessed 28 November 2020).

Landi, H. (2019) 'Global EHR market hits $31B but faces usability, interoperability challenges', 8 July 2019. Available at: https://www.fiercehealthcare.com/tech/global-ehr-market-hits-31-billion-but-faces-usability-interoperability-challenges (Accessed 28 November 2020).

Landi, H. (2020) 'Trump administration pushes back compliance deadline for info blocking rule', 29 October 2020, Fierce Healthcare. Available at: https://www.fiercehealthcare.com/tech/trump-administration-pushes-back-information-blocking-rule-compliance-to-april-2021 (Accessed 28 November 2020).

Maddox, T.M. and MacGibbon, S. (2019) 'Tech and health care need their own "Hippocratic oath" to make digital health work', Stat News, 23 December 2020. Available at: https://www.statnews.com/2019/12/23/tech-health-care-need-their-own-hippocratic-oath/ (Accessed 28 November 2020).

Malkin, M. (2013) 'Malkin: Judy Faulkner: The Obama crony in charge of your medical records', *Lubbock Avalanche-Journal*, 25 May 2013. Available at: https://www.lubbock-online.com/article/20130525/OPINION/305259922 (Accessed 28 November 2020).

Mandl, K.D. and Kohane, I.S. (2020) 'Epic's call to block a proposed data rule is wrong for many reasons', Stat+, 27 January 2020. Available at: https://www.statnews.com/2020/01/27/epic-block-proposed-data-rule/ (Accessed 28 November 2020).

MHA (2019) 'EHRs have the mumps', Massachusetts Health & Hospital Association (MHA), 19 September 2019. Available at: https://hspeakers.com/h-speakers-blog/2019/9/19/ehrs-have-the-mumps (Accessed 28 November 2020).

Monegain, B. (2018) 'Cerner has almost double EHR global market share of closest rival Epic, Kalorama says', Healthcare IT News, 15 May 2018. Available at: https://www.healthcareitnews.com/news/cerner-has-almost-double-ehr-global-market-share-closest-rival-epic-kalorama-says (Accessed 28 November 2020).

Roth, M. (2020) 'Special report: Epic uproar exposes conflict between data privacy and innovation', Health Leaders, 11 February 2020. Available at: https://www.healthleadersmedia.com/innovation/special-report-epic-uproar-exposes-conflict-between-data-privacy-and-innovation (Accessed 28 November 2020).

Schulte, F. and Fry, E. (2019). 'Death by 1,000 clicks: where electronic health records went wrong', KHN, 18 March 2020. Available at: https://khn.org/news/death-by-a-thousand-clicks/ (Accessed 28 November 2020).

Taneja, H. (2020) 'Announcing commure: A system of innovation for healthcare', *Commure Blog*, 5 February 2020. Available at: https://blog.commure.com/announcingcommure/ (Accessed 28 November 2020).

The Sequoia Project (2020) 'The Sequoia Project - health information exchange network' [Online]. Available at: https://sequoiaproject.org/ (Accessed 28 November 2020).

Chapter 7

The Mainstream Sci-Tech of Vaccines and the Counterculture of Anti-Vaxxers

When I was preparing for my study abroad in Belgium in the summer of 1993, I had read somewhere on a travel site that vaccination certificates were required for travel and study abroad. As a result, I went about procuring World Health Organization (WHO)'s International Certificate of Vaccination or Prophylaxis, in bright yellow color. I spent days gathering all my vaccinations from various sources and putting it all onto an orange, international vaccination card. I arrived in Belgium as probably the only foreign student who had bothered. I was widely ridiculed by my new friends. Clearly, this was not a priority and I had overstated the need.

The International Health Regulations (WHO, 1969), as it turns out, is an ancient protocol. The Yellow card, in theory was meant to act as a safe travel document; the certificate is a kind of "medical passport" that is recognized internationally and may be required for entry to certain countries where there are increased health risks for travelers. The nickname Yellow Card stems from its association with Yellow Fever, a common travel vaccine. Strikingly, until 2020, only a few African countries had digital versions of the vaccination card.

DOI: 10.4324/9781003178071-7

The person taking my stats was writing on a typewriter (not yet digitized, even in 1990), and they never sent me a residence card. This tells you how antique the system was, even then.

Fast forward to 2021, and vaccination cards, this time in the form of a QR code is all the rage (together with proof of having carried out a recent COVID-test).

A Brief Social History of Vaccines

The track record of vaccines throughout human history (smallpox, flu, polio, cholera, Ebola, and coronavirus) is unequivocal—they have largely been successful—although there have been clear misses along the way. Both points deserve to be acknowledged and understood in their full implications.

With over 200 vaccines currently in development and 70 doses required by age 18 according to the Centers for Disease Control and Prevention (CDC)'s required vaccine schedule, vaccines have—depending on your view—come a long way. How did we get here? What does it mean for health tech? Will the future hold more shots, better shots, and what shot do they give us on life itself? As we now know from the popular musical Hamilton, US founding father Alexander Hamilton would "never give up his shot". Smallpox and variolation impacted virtually all of the historical figures represented in Hamilton: An American Musical. These days, a lot of people are, and in public displays of dissatisfaction and anger. Why?

According to The History of Vaccines (https://www.historyofvaccines.org/), a vaccine safety website certified by WHO's vaccine safety net, the timeline for vaccines starts around year 1000 AC with early Chinese inoculation, but it would take until 1661 before there was royal support for inoculation by Emperor K'ang. In 1759, English physician William Heberden wrote a pamphlet called "Some Account of the Success of Inoculation for the Small-Pox in England and America", at the suggestion of his friend Benjamin Franklin. The pamphlet was distributed for free in the American colonies. In 1768, Catherine the Great of Russia was inoculated, which encouraged others to follow suit. In 1777, George Washington ordered mandatory inoculation for the Continental Army if they had not survived smallpox infection earlier in life, possibly as a reaction to the fact that half of the colonial troops has smallpox the year before. In 1796, Edward Jenner successfully inoculated 8-year-old James Phipps with cowpox (genetic analysis has now found it was closer to horsepox), an illness in cattle, and subsequently variolated him with live smallpox virus without him getting infected. Jenner repeated this process with 22 more people and published his documentation of it all in 1798, in a volume called *An Inquiry into the Causes and Effects of the Variolae Vaccinae.* The word "vaccine" was created by Edward Jenner. The word comes from the Latin word vacca, meaning cow.

In 1813, under the Madison Presidency, a US National Vaccine Agency was established. By 1853, the UK Vaccination Act of 1853 made smallpox vaccination mandatory in the first 3 months of an infant's life. A parent's penalty for not complying was a fine or imprisonment. In 1874, a compulsory smallpox vaccination and revaccination law went into in effect in Germany. Over the next decades, smallpox deaths there dropped rapidly.

By 1882, the Anti-Vaccination League of America held its first meeting in New York. Among the assertions made by the speakers at the meeting was the idea that smallpox was spread not by contagion but by filth. This became a popular, though incorrect, argument of anti-vaccinationists.

In 1885, Spanish physician Jaime Ferrán (1852–1929) developed a live, attenuated cholera vaccine. His vaccine was the first to immunize humans against a bacterial disease. During the rest of his career, Ferrán would develop vaccines for plague, tetanus, typhus, tuberculosis, and rabies.

In 1888, Louis Pasteur founded the Institut Pasteur in Paris as a center for rabies treatment as well as for the study of science. Soon Pasteur Institutes in other locations would begin to provide rabies vaccination. Today the Institut Pasteur has 30 international locations and 146 research units, focusing on infectious disease, public health, and teaching.

The first major documented polio outbreak in the US occurred in 1894, but the contagious nature of polio would not be established until 1905 when Swedish physician Ivar Wickman (1872–1914) suggested polio was a contagious disease and that it could be present in people who did not appear to have a severe form of the disease.

The Legal Ramifications of Vaccination in the UK and Beyond

The UK Vaccination Acts of 1840, 1853, 1867, and 1898 were a series of legislative Acts passed by the Parliament of the UK regarding the vaccination policy of the country. It would be far too simplistic to think of vaccinations as simply a public good without taking into account the legal implications of making them mandatory. In fact, the UK (and other countries') vaccination laws "suspended what we might call the natural liberty of the individual to contract and spread infectious disease, in order to protect the community as a whole" (Porter & Porter, 1988).

In 1898, The British Vaccination Act of this year provided a conscience clause to allow exemptions to mandatory smallpox vaccination. This clause gave rise to the term "conscientious objector", in British law (later used to object to mandatory military service) and by the end of the year, more than 2,000,000 vaccination exceptions were issued. Many of these were granted in anti-vaccination strongholds where exemptions outnumbered vaccinations, notably giving relief to working- and lower-middle class anti-vaccinationists, mostly women, from repeated fines and the threat of imprisonment (Durbach, 2004). By 1907, an amended clause made the process easier and resulted in a 25% exemption rate. From this time onward, anti-vaccinationists in England, other parts of Europe, and the US were active in publishing, speaking, and demonstrating about their objections to vaccination.

1905—The Supreme Court Weights In

In 1905, just a few years after a major outbreak of smallpox in Boston, the US Supreme Court in the case of Jacobson versus Massachusetts upheld the constitutionality of mandatory smallpox vaccination programs to preserve the public health. The Court's decision articulated the view that individual liberty is not absolute and is subject to the police power of the state. Although the ruling is regarded as the most important judicial decision in public health, public health practitioners still struggle with Jacobson's basic tension between individual liberty and the common good (Gostin, 2004). Jacobson was judicial recognition of police power, arguably the most important aspect of state sovereignty.

In 1919, dozens of Dallas, Texas, children were sickened and five died from a contaminated batch of diphtheria toxin–antitoxin (TAT) mixture. This has become a factoid used by anti-vaxxers in the US to say vaccines generally are unsafe.

School Vaccination Requirements for smallpox were introduced in many US schools by 1922. Opposition to vaccination continued through the 1920s, particularly against compulsory vaccination. In 1926, a group of health officers visited Georgetown, Delaware, to vaccinate the townspeople. A retired Army lieutenant and a city councilman led an armed mob to force them out, successfully preventing the vaccination attempt.

In 1928, bacterial contamination of the diphtheria TAT mixture in Bundaberg, Queensland, Australia, led to the deaths of 12 children. Five others became critically ill but recovered. Despite this scandal, the same year, the Health Committee of the League of Nations adopts BCG as a recommended tuberculosis vaccine.

During 1929 and 1930, 72 babies in the German city of Lübeck died from tuberculosis out of 252 vaccinated. Many other infants were made ill as a result of vaccination. The vaccine used was later found to have been contaminated with a human tuberculosis strain being studied in same lab where the vaccine was produced.

In 1935, early polio vaccine trials are a widely considered disaster as two separate teams spectacularly fail at developing and testing many subjects die of polio, many were paralyzed, made ill, or suffered allergic reactions to the vaccines (Baicus, 2012).

In 1945, the first four pneumococcal vaccines were introduced but largely ignored due to the advent of widespread penicillin use.

In 1947, a massive vaccination effort was carried out in New York City, some 80% of residents or 6.35 million people, to irradicate smallpox, largely successful, to the point where smallpox is declared eradicated in the US by 1949—although it continued to appear in the rest of the world through the 1970s.

In 1953, Jonas Salk went on the radio to declare that there will be no polio vaccine any time soon, yet gives experimental vaccine to his family. A massive trial of 1.3 million children gets approved in 1954.

In 1957–1958, the Asian influenza pandemic killed 2 million people worldwide, with only 70,000 deaths in the US because of a vaccine developed by Maurice Hilleman (1919–2005), an American microbiologist working at Merck who developed over 40 vaccines throughout his career, and which manufacturers finalized in 4 months. Predictions were the US death toll might have been 1 million without the vaccine.

In 1967, the WHO launched its smallpox eradication efforts. Smallpox was at the time endemic in 41 countries, but the search and quarantine aspects of the program, as well as coercion of quarantined individuals to get the vaccine was later criticized by health and human rights workers.

In 1971, the US government licensed Merck's measles, mumps, and rubella combination vaccine (M-M-R), a live virus vaccine. In an article published in the *Journal of the American Medical Association,* researchers reported that the vaccine induced immunity to measles in 96% of vaccinated children; to mumps in 95%; and to rubella in 94%. Additionally, initial tests in 1968 had already shown that adverse reactions from the MMR vaccine were no greater than from any of the single vaccines. However, a 2012 review article claims that despite its worldwide use, no systematic reviews studying the effectiveness and safety of MMR vaccines are available. That study found no significant association could be assessed between MMR immunization and the following conditions: autism, asthma, leukemia, hay fever, type 1 diabetes, gait disturbance, Crohn's disease, demyelinating diseases, bacterial, or viral infections. However, the caveat noted is the lack of control children not exposed to MMR, due to the population nature of vaccination program. Also, the hypothesis that secondary vaccine failure (waning immunity) could occur is noted as needing to be better elucidated (Demicheli et al., 2012). The lack of MMR control group has become a mantra for the anti-vaxx movement.

In 1976, swine influenza breaks out at Fort Dix, New Jersey. Merck intended to produce 50 million swine flu vaccine doses by January 1977 and delivered about

11 million doses in late September 1976. The nationwide vaccination program, however, ended after vaccination was associated with an increased risk of a condition called Guillain-Barré syndrome (GBS). Also, few cases of swine flu transpired.

In 1977, Merck licensed a pneumococcal vaccine protecting against 14 types of bacteria, developed by Robert Austrian at The University of Pennsylvania. In 1983 Merck expanded coverage to 23 types of bacteria. However, more than 90 types of bacteria produce disease, and it is still hard to know which are more prevalent or probable.

The 1980s—A Vaccine Triumph Decade

In 1980, smallpox is declared eradicated, having ravaged the world for 3,000 years.

In the US, a law passed in 1986 removed liability from the makers of vaccines, a point which the anti-vaxx movement have, somewhat understandably, jumped on.

In 1992, it was uncovered that the French government had been aware of a number of errors allegedly committed in 1985 when collecting HIV positive blood in French prisons and public places frequented by drug addicts, leading to contamination by blood transfusion and hundreds of deaths. More than half of European cases of blood contamination occurred in France (*BMJ*, 1998). Separately, a mass vaccination campaign against hepatitis B in the early 1990s coincided with a jump in multiple sclerosis diagnoses, leading many to link the two. In the late 1990s, an effort in France to vaccinate children against hepatitis B coincided with a rise in multiple sclerosis cases, although it was never proven to be anything but a correlation (Rosman, 2021). These public health scandals tarnished the trust in the French government in matters of health which has translated into vaccine hesitancy.

In 1998, British researcher Andrew Wakefield along with 12 co-authors, published a paper in the *Lancet* claiming evidence of measles virus in the digestive systems of autistic children (see elsewhere in the chapter). Vaccination rates in England drop in response, and this causes a rise in measles cases in England. The paper is retracted in 2010 for ethical reasons and because of scientific misconduct. Despite this and the lack of any evidence to support a link between vaccines and autism, some groups remain convinced of the allegations first raised by Wakefield in 1998.

By 2000, WHO declares a 99% reduction in polio cases from 1988 when eradication began and by 2003, 90% of remaining cases occur in just three countries: India, Pakistan, and Nigeria. In 2007, The Bill and Melinda Gates Foundation gave a $100 million grant to Rotary International to combat polio. Rotary International promised to match the grant over a 3-year period, for a total of $200 million to be used in the global eradication campaign.

In 2014, a West African Ebola epidemic follows previous smaller outbreaks in remote areas but now spreads to crowded urban areas where long transmission chains occur in Sierra Leone, Guinea, and Liberia. In total, 15,261 confirmed, probable, and suspected deaths occurred, including two in the US. More than 28,000 cases of Ebola virus disease (EVD) were reported. EVD has no cure, but supportive care in a hospital setting can increase a patient's chance for survival. Additionally, plasma transfusions from convalescent patients and an experimental antibody preparation have been used to treat certain patients. Several vaccines were advanced rapidly into clinical trials in both African and non-African countries.

In 2019, the FDA approves Ervebo (rVSV-ZEBOV), the first vaccine for Ebola, developed by the Public Health Agency of Canada, with development subsequently taken over by Merck. A 2016 study found it 70%–100% effective, but the study design and high efficacy have been questioned.

COVID-19 Vaccines

The most promising vaccines from an innovation standpoint include Pfizer/ BioNTech which is a joint US-German mRNA vaccine using the genetic code of the virus, approved in the US using EUA in December and rolled out in the EU as well, in limited quantities in 2020. Moderna also produced an mRNA vaccine and proceeded to produce an astonishing 100 million doses in the second quarter, from the starting point of having never run a phase 3 clinical study. On June 23, 2021, the CDC said there is a "likely association" between mRNA COVID-19 vaccines and a higher risk of rare heart inflammation in adolescents and young adults, and it is expected the FDA will add a warning to the label, but said the benefits outweights the risk (Healthline, 2021). The Oxford University/ AstraZeneca vaccine from the UK collaboration between the top university and the big UK pharma company is an adenovirus vector vaccine, using the same virus that causes a cold in chimpanzees. That one was just approved in the UK right before Christmas 2020 and is now being rolled out in the UK although the European Medicines Agency found a possible link to rare cases of unusual blood clots with low blood platelets (EMA, 2021). Novavax is a US protein adjuvant vaccine that also boosts the immune system. Phase 3 trials are ongoing with 100,000 UK volunteers and should deliver in second half of 2021. J&J's vaccine was approved in the US at the end of February 2021 but uses a much more traditional vaccine production approach although the virus vector is the same adenovirus as used by AstraZeneca.

As of 2021, the only remaining smallpox samples/stockpiles are stored in liquid nitrogen vials at the US Centers for Disease Control and Prevention, in Atlanta, and the State Research Centre of Virology and Biotechnology, in

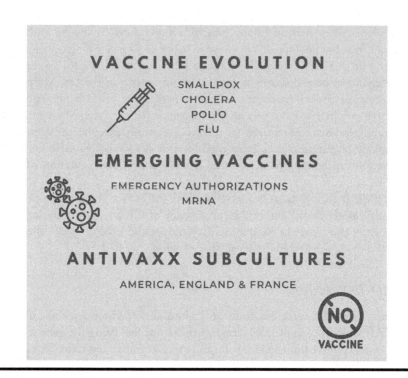

Figure 7.1 Vaccines and anti-vaxx.

Koltsovo, Novosibirsk Oblast, in Russia, both are WHO reference laboratories. The discussion about complete destruction was recommended by the WHO in 1986, with destruction dates set in both 1993 and 1995, but in 2002 WHO recommended against destruction of the virus and had another vote in 2015 with a similar result (Vaccine Safety Net, 2021).

Vaccines are an old remedy that has got miles to go and new approaches will be in the clinic shortly, due to COVID-19, notably Moderna and Pfizer's mRNA vaccines which build on advances in synthetic biology. However, vaccine skepticism has arguably never been higher, and some of the reasoning behind this is sound, due to political influence and incentive that may currently trump sanguine regulatory considerations under more normal circumstances.

A brief synopsis of the history and current status of vaccines around the world reveal a mixed picture—from the relative success of the polio vaccine to the mixed success of the tuberculosis vaccine and others. The safety of child vaccination programs in the US (Maglione et al., 2014) and worldwide is fairly well established (Figure 7.1).

The History of Anti-Vaxx

The WHO in fall 2020 named "vaccine hesitancy" one of the ten health threats facing the world. However, as we have seen the idea of refusing vaccines started back in the early 1800s when the smallpox vaccine was rolling out. Understandably, initially, the idea of injecting someone with a part of a cowpox blister to protect them from smallpox faced skepticism. The criticism was based on sanitary, religious, and political objections. Some clergy believed that the vaccine went against their religion.

Early American Opposition

The Anti-Vaccination Society of America, out of the home of Frank D. Blue, was active in the late 1800s and early 1900s along with other similar regional organizations of overlapping origin. Most of these were started by parents whose offspring had died from smallpox vaccination. Blue was in correspondence with other reform groups at the time, including anti-vivisectionists, temperance advocates, vegetarians, homeopaths, phrenologists, "scientific palmists", and a society for the prevention of premature burial (Youngdahl, 2012).

The English Movement

In the UK, though some of the anti-vaccination movement's leading figures were derived from the upper classes, its activists were largely drawn from the lower middle and respectable working classes. As well as being an effective parliamentary lobby, anti-vaccinationism was a militant mass movement (Fitzpatrick, 2005). In 1876, the Victorian anti-vaccination movement gathered at least 20,000 protesters outside York Castle in Northern England to protest the imprisonment of seven vaccination activists, called the Keighley guardians, because they became emblematic of the protest movement in the Yorkshire industrial town (Durbach, 2004; Earl, 2015).

In her book on the UK anti-vaxx movement that emerged in England in the late 19th century, American historian Nadja Durbach argues the movement was arguably the largest medical resistance campaign ever mounted in Europe but was important also because it clearly articulated "pervasive anxieties regarding the integrity of the body and the role of the modern state" and challenges the notion that resistance to vaccination can best be understood, and thus easily dismissed, as the ravings of an unscientific "lunatic fringe" that invoked the "gothic tropes of the vampire" (Durbach, 2004). As it turns out, the anti-vaccine movement did to some effect use the vampire to depict pro-vaccinators and the medical officers who performed vaccinations, letting the vampire's teeth represent the surgical instruments used to vaccinate the children, the controversy being one over piercing skin. There was the romantic notion of the child as inherently innocent, and God's given gift was not to be defiled, and was, in effect, fulfilling "an apocalyptic prophecy", fearing "monstrous transformation" and "sexual immorality", epitomized in Brad Stoker's 1897 masterpiece, Dracula (Goode, 2018).

Rather, she argues, it must be understood within the broad public debates over medical developments, the politics of class, the extent of legitimate government intervention into the private lives of its citizens, and the battle over the values of a liberal society. For example, she writes, the Victorians (meaning the elites of that society) fundamentally believed that health depended in "preserving the body's integrity", "encouraging the proper circulation of pure blood" [sic] and "preventing the introduction of any foreign material into the body" (Durbach, 2004), a view that echoes within today's global natural wellness elite.

Durbach (2004) points out that cultural resistance to vaccination also happened in India. In that cultural context, the indigenous practice of variolation, which had a ritual component, was attempted replaced with vaccination. The problem was that vaccination was not only practiced by representatives of a colonial state, but incorporated the cow, an animal sacred to Hindus, into the body. Similarly, Ugandans feared they were being deliberately poisoned by British settlers. Mexican nationals who were force-vaccinated upon crossing into Texas in the early 20th century had a similar reaction. In Brazil, working classes felt a 2004 compulsory vaccination represented an attempt by rich Brazilians and foreign capitalists to sanitize and civilize them. All of this, she implies, demonstrates how "disease theory" is not innocent, echoing and evoking French thinker Michel Foucault's work on how modernization represents a biopolitical regulation landgrab to "discipline" the body. Again, there are contemporary parallels to the women's movement's and the evangelicals' opposing view of abortion in the US, in the pro-choice versus pro-life dilemma.

The American Humane Association expanded its agenda to oppose immunizations and use of children as test subjects. Before it became quiescent in the 1930s, the anti-vaccination campaign successfully lobbied many states to ban compulsory inoculations for school admissions.

Contemporary Anti-Vaxxers: Wakefield

In February 1998, Dr. Andrew Wakefield and his colleagues published an article in the reputable medical journal *The Lancet*, entitled "Ileal-lymphoid-nodular hyperplasia, non-specific colitis, and pervasive developmental disorder in children". That article, based on the study of 12 children nine of whom according to their originally published research developed autism from a measles vaccine [the measles, mumps, and rubella (MMR) vaccine], reignited an anti-vaxx movement that had been dormant since the 1960s. Even though it was retracted exactly 12 years later (Eggertson, 2010), and Wakefield was struck off the UK medical register (and moved to the US), the damage was already done, as UK authorities attribute a 2008–2009 measles outbreak to the concurrent drop in children receiving the MMR vaccine.

In 2016, Wakefield directed the anti-vaccination film Vaxxed: From Cover-Up to Catastrophe which was scheduled to air at the Tribeca Film Festival, but Robert de Niro pulled it last moment, causing a stir and a media frenzy ensuring a lot more people became aware of the issue and also watched the documentary. The film is an investigation into how the CDC, the government agency charged with protecting the health of American citizens, arguably concealed and destroyed data on their 2004 study that Vaxxed claims showed a link between the MMR vaccine and autism.

The film featured an interview with Dr. William Thompson, a psychologist employed by the CDC, recorded without Thompson's consent. He was a co-author on a number of vaccine safety studies published by the CDC including the study (DeStefano et al., 2004) that, he claims, omitted a correlation between autism and vaccines. Thompson himself feels misused by the documentary and says in a statement: "Vaccines prevent serious diseases, and the risks associated with their administration are vastly outweighed by their individual and societal benefits" (CHD, 2020; Roser, 2016).

What are the studies published on the safety of vaccines? Vaccinate Your Family's (2020) overview lists 26 studies.

Many consider Wakefield a profiteer and one study after another failed to find any link between childhood vaccines and autism (Mnookin, 2012). For a brief moment, it was the biggest social media story in the world, gathering the interests of "vaccine-injured families" around the US, particularly families with kids with autism (a mysterious diagnosis which leads parents to desperately seek explanations) despite the film makers having no budget, publicity. They got a call from Angelika Film center, a movie theater chain in the US that features independent and foreign films, and were offered to screen it at the Angelika theater in New York for weeks. It turned onto a national tour across America. The film is picked up for distribution by Cinema Libre. The film was given a private screening in Cannes in 2017. There was also a second movie, Vaxxed II, in 2019. The 1:36 hour documentary had 12,018 views on YouTube as of January 2, 2020.

Anti-Vaxx Groups

SafeMinds, an autism advocacy group founded in 2000, claims environmental toxins, notably mercury poisoning, are to blame for the disease. In fact, a landmark report they sponsored went quite far in suggesting mercury as the primary cause (Bernard et al., 2001) (https://safeminds.org/). That line of reasoning has been applied to mercury amalgam fillings as well, for example, in the 2015 documentary film Evidence of Harm (https://evidence-of-harm.com/) which chronicles the lives of three Americans who became health advocates after suffering mercury poisoning released during dental procedures.

A recent review by Kern et al. (2017a,b) suggests there are at least ten environmental compounds suspected of causing autism and learning disabilities, including lead, methyl-mercury, polychorinated biphenyls, organophosphate pesticides, organochlorine pesticides, endocrine disruptors, automotive exhaust, polycyclic aromatic hydrocarbons, polybrominated diphenyl ethers, and perfluorinated compounds. The fact that the impact of neurotoxicants is increasing is hard to dispute, but the causal links are trickier to ascertain, and it seems clear that not all neurodevelopmental disorders are caused by neurotoxicants (Kern et al., 2017a).

Interestingly, the plot thickens around Janet Kern's work. In 2017, she published a similar article (Kern et al., 2017b), but with the explicit aim to show conflict of interest among authors with public health and/or industry affiliation, which was retracted by the publisher (Elsevier) against the will of the authors due to a lack of conflict of interest disclosure beyond a cursory "the authors have been involved in vaccine/biologic litigation", notably that two of the authors are associated with the Council for Nutritional and Environmental Medicine, work on the coalition for Mercury-Free Drugs and one is on the advisory board for the National Autism Association, and finally, one author was involved in amalgam litigation. I should point out that being sloppy about one conflict of interest declaration in a single academic article does not, in my opinion, discredit these authors' entire body of work. This particular case is interesting because it goes without saying that if you are going to accuse a party of conflict of interest (in this case public sector AND industry), you should expect extreme scrutiny on your own part.

Others point out that the bulk of our mercury exposure comes from the organic form which we ingest largely through eating certain fish (Willingham, 2017). In any case, it may the case that the environmental connection with autism is strong enough that natural antioxidants, including letter vitamins E and/or C could have some effect in treating it (Pangrazzi et al., 2020).

Vaccine advocacy finds resonance because of studies such as their 2011 study of the Vaccine Injury Compensation Program (VICP), a US federal program formed in 1989 (Holland et al., 2011), which brought up some unanswered questions and went as far as to suggest a Congressional inquiry into the 83 cases of autism associated with vaccine injury compensation studied (Safeminds, 2011).

In 2015, seeking scientific evidence of a link with vaccines, they found the opposite. Studying thimerosal, a mercury-based antifungal and antiseptic preservative that was removed from most vaccines from the late 1990s, they found no such link (Firger, 2015). The Wakefield (1998) paper is also among the key sources of the prevalent theory of leaky gut (Seneff, 2017). The Internet makes possible wide circulation of songs by the anti-vaccination band The Refusers, a Seattle, Washington rock band performing songs of musical defiance against the establishment.

Is the Anti-Vaxx of COVID-19 Different?

Fast forward to 2020's COVID-19, the anti-vaxx movement, and indeed vaccine skepticism is centered around two issues: (a) the unusually speedy adoption of the coronavirus vaccines (1 year instead of 10 years) which, one could argue, raises safety concerns on its own (even though the speed is mostly due to regulatory expediency not speedier trials) and (b) the advent of the first-in-history mRNA vaccines, which represents a completely new way of producing vaccines compared to the virus vector vaccines that traditionally build on the inactivated adenovirus.

The question now is, to what extent can initial concerns (surveys across the globe indicate between 20% and 50% opposition to taking the coronavirus vaccines—with attitude percentages swinging wildly between surveys) be met and countered by evidence of the safety protocols in place in various national jurisdictions (notably the US FDA, the European authorities, the UK government, as well as the governments of large, densely populated nations such as India, China, and Brazil.

Initial evidence is that vaccine resistance is going to become a serious challenge from the point of view of public health. However, the argument I am pursuing in this chapter is different. I'm instead asking: what is the anti-vaxx argument stating about the relative progress of science, technology, and innovation?

Even the early resistance to vaccination had to do with the introduction of innovations into traditional societies that moved at a much slower pace. What the first vaccines did is to shift the time vectors dramatically and to alter people's conception of disease. Through technological manipulation, something that had been previously seen as inevitable became much more of a cultural choice.

The advent of synthetic biology (Undheim, 2021) has been fast paced yet ongoing for the past two decades at least. Two decades, however, is not enough to situate a technological innovation within the fabric of society. Vaccinations are fundamentally different than other sweeping innovations such as the smartphone, which all its users have a much more direct interaction and familiarity with. Instead, vaccinations are invasive and represent highly episodic occurrences. The rest of the time, synthetic biology is an abstract notion, to most people perhaps it does not even exist as a notion yet. This includes people who might have a fleeting opinion of gene editing, have heard the mention of CRISPR, but haven't yet considered the sweeping change that this technology represents.

The promise of synthetic biology goes far beyond biology as we know it from school over the past 50 years. Rather, with synthetics, biology starts the path toward becoming a true engineering discipline, one where rigor, scalability, and due process are hallmarks. As a result, we are looking at a far different set of results than with what we formerly have known as biological science.

With vaccines, the implication is, for example, that a new vaccine, corresponding to a virus variant, for example, the Delta variant, can be developed in days and weeks, not months and years. Once the principle is accepted (that synthetic biology platforms should be allowed to produce vaccines), the door to pathbreaking medicines will open. As of mid 2021, that's where we are. No government has given a blanket permission, but most countries are about to introduce emergency use authorizations of various flavors. The assumption has to be that the normalization of synthetic biology is underway.

As such, a certain level of resistance is to be expected, in fact it is even warranted. Every new generation of technology should be deeply scrutinized not only for its efficiency but also for its societal, cultural, and humanistic impact. The argument put forward by ethicists, not just by anti-vaxxers of the traditional ilk is that the burden of proof that the mRNA vaccines do not alter human DNA must be on the pharma industry. The issue is whether mRNA cell instructions truly leave your body within 72 hours and never enter the nucleus of the cell so it can combine with DNA. So far, that argument has been pretty convincingly supported by mainstream science worldwide, as well as by the CDC (2020), but one has to be allowed to ask critical questions of any new technology.

Vaccine Attitude Demographics

Before the coronavirus pandemic, there was consensus that anti-vaxxers today are largely upper middle class (Earl, 2015), but this is changing. In fact, the consensus was that parents who are hesitant to vaccinate their children are most likely to be white, female, college educated, and with a family income over $75,000 (Reich, 2016). Mothers who reject vaccines face stigma but receive support on how to manage it from their networks, and their social capital creates subcultural norms that contradicts broader social norms (Reich, 2020b).

However, white adults also more likely to get vaccinated themselves, and substantially more likely than black adults. In fact, only a quarter of African Americans plan to get the coronavirus vaccine and only 37% of Hispanics (Booker, 2020). Why? Perhaps because the latter have less access to medical care, and decades of maltreatment have eroded their trust in the medical establishment (Armstrong et al., 2007). However, vaccine skepticism spans from Goop-reading Californians to the ultra-Orthodox Jews of New York. A recent UK study found the largest predictors of both COVID-19 vaccine uncertainty and refusal were low income (<£30,000 a year), having not received a flu vaccine last year, poor adherence to COVID-19 government guidelines, female gender, and living with children (Paul et al., 2020).

Vaccine hesitancy has been little studied in low- and middle-income countries. One study of Shanghai residents found that about half of parents somewhat or strongly agreed that new vaccines carried more risks than older vaccines, and 71.6% somewhat or strongly agreed that they were concerned about serious adverse effects (Ren et al., 2018).

As many as four in ten adults would refuse or hesitate to receive vaccine for COVID-19, according to participants in a US national survey conducted during the coronavirus pandemic, giving reasons such as vaccine-specific concerns, a need for more information, antivaccine attitudes or beliefs, and a lack of trust (Fisher et al., 2020; Gray, 2020). Many participants in that study and a Reuters poll indicated hesitancy to be among the first to be vaccinated, which will probably delay achievement of high vaccination coverage rates for COVID-19 (Fisher et al., 2020).

Strikingly, I find that viewpoint resonating even with me, given the rushed rollout of this vaccine, my own position as someone who can afford to stay sequestered in my home for another few months as millions of others get the vaccine. The flaw in that argument, including mine, is the lack of a determined endpoint where we would say we have amassed enough evidence of safety. What is the threshold? How long do we wait? Pushing myself to give an answer, I predict that by the time this book is published in the fall of 2021, I will have gotten the vaccine, in fact, I would say by Q2 or Q3 2021, I would see no other option than to take it, but that is not to say that I would feel particularly comfortable about it. This should arguably not be a crime, but should my view be commonplace, even beyond my "elite pocket", it does pose a challenge for the vaccine rollout. (Note: I ended up deciding to get the Moderna vaccine in June 2021, in consideration of upcoming foreign travel to see family, a desire to return to work, and also to protect own family.)

Surprisingly, very few vaccine-hesitant participants indicated a need or desire for a recommendation from a physician, even though positions arguably are well positioned to address misinformation, discuss risk, and convey the seriousness of COVID-19 in a way that is tailored to the unique needs of the individual patient. This is, for example, the approach chosen in France, the only country insisting that those offered the vaccine give their written consent after being informed of possible contraindications (Willsher, 2020).

Informed Anti-Vaxxers

In many circles, it is commonplace to underestimate, belittle or otherwise conveniently gift anti-vaxxers or skeptics with some sort of stupidity bug that would render their arguments moot. I find that not so helpful.

On the contrary, argues sociologist Jennifer Reich (2020a), access to resources, including income, education, time, and cultural capital differentially position parents to challenge (and selectively accept) medical authority and pharmaceuticalization—as well as vaccines. As they do end up in most cases making individualized, active choices, parents struggle with these issues as they clearly recognize when their kids are ill and seek to remedy it through various means that make sense to themselves while still trying to keep the children's best at heart. The result is ambivalence, contraction, trade-offs, and rejection of blindly listening to their pediatrician, teachers, other experts or the medical establishment in the form of public officials or even celebrity doctors. While her research is insightful, her 2020 TEDx Talk (TEDx, 2020) devolves into a less sophisticated argument about the crisis of individualism where she reveals significantly less tolerance for the same folks she wrote about in her science articles and books.

In fact, the 6,161 comments below the article, mostly from vaccine skeptics, were considerably more nuanced, interesting, and insightful. Sheila Ward said: "She doesn't have a clue as to why parents are refusing vaccines". Evan Owen said: "I spend an hour a day studying about vaccines. [sic] It is interesting that the lay people present evidence in the form of studies, papers and articles showing that people have been hurt by vaccines and that they are potentially dangerous. The doctors on the other hand have single anecdotal stories and emotional stories and they cry 'What about the children'. Like they say, trust the science, study their own papers and journals and you will educate yourself. There are three vaccines that I would take, all the rest that I have studied pose too much danger to justify the potential benefit. But we each have the right to choose, just as the government has the ability to kill us. Nobody can force me to do anything. Live free or die".

Third, a long anonymous comment garnered 38 replies and can be traced back to be Dr. Mark Sibley, MD, an anti-vaxx activist. Suffice to say that the anti-vaxx strategy here is clear: respond to key threads where vaccines are debated, such as TEDx talks. It is incredibly efficient, even I stopped and spent more energy with his impassioned, personal, and poignant story than the abstract "socialist" talk of Ms. Reich (and I'm a Scandinavian-born progressive/liberal social democrat).

On the other hand, many times the "personal belief exemptions" (PBEs) in which many states allow parents to opt out of vaccinating their children, tend to occur in pockets, e.g. typically in affluent neighborhoods surrounded by areas with low-affluence, specific geographic contexts where this type of behavior makes sense collectively (the risk is low) even though it collectively is egotistical. Parents right to choose is the rationale, but strong intuitions about what's best for their child and the idea that they know better than medical recommendations by authorities (school or health), weighs heavily. The study (Estep and Greenberg, 2020) was from Santa Monica, CA, but I can personally attest to this place-based logic playing out in my own (current) hometown, Wellesley, MA.

Why would we give any credence to any of these claims? Perhaps because some of them are not as far-fetched as they might seem. For example, there is clear evidence that the agricultural industry knew about the dangers of glyphosate, another contaminant that the anti-GMO activists share with the anti-vaccine agenda but because of their belief that vaccines contain levels of the herbicide glyphosate. They claim that dangerous toxic residues are present in both vaccines and milk. The trouble with these claims, so far, is that the lab studies carrying out the tests come up short in terms of thorough analysis (GLP, 2019). Having said that, as Stephanie Seneff of MIT claims, *if* glyphosate somehow does make it into vaccines (or the food system), or both, it would legitimately raise red alerts for autism and other conditions (Benson, 2015). The issue then becomes to ascertain whether and to what degree this is the case. Seneff (2017) envisions several pathways including through bovine gelatin used to grow the MMR vaccine, hypothesizing "synergistic toxicity" between glyphosate and vaccines, due to glyphosate's ability to chelate (e.g. bond to) metals. The fact is that Monsanto (now owned by Bayer AG) has recently been fined and forced to pay compensation alludes to the fact that its RoundUp product may have had a role in cancer (Zhang et al., 2019; Milne, 2019).

A few autism activists cleverly use science, deeply believe they are doing the right thing and are luddites who fight vaccine technology because they believe it has become a juggernaut. Many different factors have been purported to be linked to autism, including genetic factors, iodine deficiency, vitamin D deficiency, and toxic exposures to a variety of substances, including lead, mercury, aluminum, thimerosal, fluoride, particulate matter in air pollution, to name a few (Beecham & Seneff, 2016).

Examples of autism activist smartness includes the following from one of Seneff's academic articles: "We acknowledge that we have not yet proven that glyphosate/GFH exposure from common food and beverages causes human autism. On the other hand, we have perhaps highlighted glyphosate's/GFH's molecular potential, through a set of deduced mechanisms" (Beecham & Seneff, 2016). That article was published in the *Journal of Autism*, an Open Access journal published by Herbert Publications Ltd. overseen by David Reiss, editor, affiliated with the renowned Imperial College in London.

That being said, I'd say that the autism community naturally would be more receptive to articles that discuss the ailment than any other community (the vaccine community) is. I'd be even more impressed if I found an article expressing similar views in a public health journal (I have not found one yet). There has been significant pushback against Seneff (CFAPHR, 2020). Most studies find no link between the MMR vaccine and autism (Maglione et al., 2014). In fact, anti-vaccine sentiment is strongly associated with conspiracy thinking and protection of individual freedoms, traits that are finding a home among far-right groups (Jarry, 2020).

However, as recently as in 2006, scholars were debating whether there truly was any sense in viewing anti-vaccination groups as social movement organizations as distinct from pressure groups or self-help organizations (Blume, 2006).

Conclusion

Why care about anti-vaxx in terms of sci-tech innovation in health? Simply because a lot of the resistance reflects anti-science attitudes that will impact the progress of overall health innovation at some point in time

KEY TAKEAWAYS AND REFLECTIONS

1. How would you characterize the positions of the scientific establishment versus that of the anti-vaxx movement?

2. Put yourself into the mindset of a parent who has lost a child to autism. Then take on board that there are few good explanations as to why your child has this disease. What would you do to come to peace with the condition and to what extent do you feel any outside party is to blame?

3. Put in place a three-pronged strategy to counter anti-vaxx claims. How would you implement it for greatest effect?

Anti-vaxx sentiments might give clues as to where health innovation needs to be moving in order to stay relevant, e.g. address safety concerns head on, tackle consumerization issues, and be active in online debates to shape the discourse on innovation in health. If that does not happen, many of the wishes we have for progress in health tech, in our healthcare systems, and with wellness as such, simply will not happen as fast as we hope for—or, will backfire.

The next chapter will tackle natural wellness, a major thrust in health innovation, and strikingly also the informed anti-vaxxer's natural remedy to all diseases.

References

Armstrong, K., Ravenell, K. L., McMurphy, S., & Putt, M. (2007). Racial/ethnic differences in physician distrust in the United States. *American Journal of Public Health*, 97(7), 1283–1289. DOI: 10.2105/AJPH.2005.080762

Baicus, A. (2012). 'History of polio vaccination', World Journal of Virology, 1(4), 108-114, Available at: https://www.ncbi.nlm.nih.gov/pmc/articles/PMC3782271/ (Accessed 6 July 2021).

Beecham, J.E. and Seneff, S. (2016) 'Is there a link between autism and glyphosate-formulated herbicides?', *Journal of Autism*, 3, 1, Available at: DOI: 10.7243/2054-992X-3-1 (Accessed 1 January 2021).

Benson, J. (2015) 'MIT doctor reveals link between glyphosate, GMOs and the autism epidemic', Natural News, 20 March 2015. Available at: https://www.naturalnews.com/049065_glyphosate_autism_GMOs.html (Accessed 1 January 2021).

Bernard, S., Enayati, A., Redwood, L, Roger, H., and Binstock, T. (2001) 'Autism: a novel form of mercury poisoning', *Medical Hypotheses*, 56:4, 462–471, Available at: DOI: 10.1054/mehy.2000.1281 (Accessed 1 January 2021).

Blume, S. (2006) 'Anti-vaccination movements and their interpretations' *Social Science & Medicine*, 62:3, 628–642, Available at: DOI: 10.1016/j.socscimed.2005.06.020 (Accessed 1 January 2021).

BMJ (1998) 'Ex-ministers to face trial in French "blood scandal"', *BMJ*, 317:7154, 302.

Booker, B. (2020) 'Poll shows only a quarter of African Americans plan to get coronavirus vaccine', NPR.org, 27 May 2020. Available at: https://www.npr.org/sections/coronavirus-live-updates/2020/05/27/863401430/poll-shows-only-a-quarter-of-african-americans-plan-to-get-coronavirus-vaccine (Accessed 1 January 2021).

Broniatowski, D. A., Jamison, A. M., Qi, S., AlKulaib, L., Chen, T., Benton, A., Quinn, S. C., and Dredze, M. (2018). 'Weaponized health communication: twitter bots and Russian trolls amplify the vaccine debate', *American Journal of Public Health*, 108:10, 1378–1384, Available at: DOI: 10.2105/AJPH.2018.304567 (Accessed 2 January 2021).

CDC (2020) 'Understanding mRNA COVID-19 vaccines', CDC, 18 December 2020. Available at: https://www.cdc.gov/coronavirus/2019-ncov/vaccines/different-vaccines/mrna.html (Accessed 27 February 2020).

CFAPHR (2020) 'Glyphosate and autism: aback to a fake news story'. Available at: https://campaignforaccuracyinpublichealthresearch.com/glyphosate-and-autism-back-to-a-fake-news-story-english-translation/.

CHD (2020) 'The statement of William W. Thompson', Children's Health Defense, 13 February 2020. Available at: https://childrenshealthdefense.org/child-health-topics/whistleblowers/the-statement-of-william-w-thompson/ (Accessed 1 January 2021).

Demicheli, V., Rivetti, A., Debalini, M. G., and Di Pietrantonj, C. (2012). 'Vaccines for measles, mumps and rubella in children', *The Cochrane Database of Systematic Reviews*, (2), CD004407, Available at: DOI: 10.1002/14651858.CD004407.pub3 (Accessed 1 January 2021).

DeStefano, F., Bhasin, T.K., Thompson, W.W., Yeargin-Allsopp, M., and Boyle, C. (2004) 'Age at first measles-mumps-rubella vaccination in children with autism and school-matched control subjects: a population-based study in metropolitan Atlanta', *Pediatrics*, 113:2, 259–266, Available at: https://pediatrics.aappublications.org/content/113/2/259 (Accessed 1 January 2021).

Durbach, N. (2004) *Bodily Matters: The Anti-Vaccination Movement in England, 1853-1907*, Durham, NC/London: Duke University Press.

Earl, E. (2015) 'The Victorian anti-vaccination movement', The Atlantic, 15 July 2015. Available at: https://www.theatlantic.com/health/archive/2015/07/victorian-anti-vaccinators-personal-belief-exemption/398321/ (Accessed 1 January 2021).

Eggertson, L. (2010). 'Lancet retracts 12-year-old article linking autism to MMR vaccines', *CMAJ*, 182:4, E199–E200. DOI: 10.1503/cmaj.109-3179 (Accessed 1 January 2021).

EMA (2021) 'AstraZeneca's COVID-19 vaccine: EMA finds possible link to very rare cases of unusual blood clots with low blood platelets', European Medicines Agency, News, 7 April 2021. Available at: https://www.ema.europa.eu/en/news/astrazenecas-covid-19-vaccine-ema-finds-possible-link-very-rare-cases-unusual-blood-clots-low-blood (Accessed 6 July 2021).

Estep, K. and Greenberg, P. (2020) 'Opting out: individualism and vaccine refusal in pockets of socioeconomic homogeneity', *American Sociological Review*, 85:6, 957–991, Available at: DOI: 10.1177/0003122420960691 (Accessed 1 January 2021).

Firger, E. (2015) 'Anti-vaxxers accidentally fund a study showing no link between autism and vaccines', Newsweek, 2 October 2015. Available at: https://www.newsweek.com/anti-vaxxers-accidentally-fund-study-showing-theres-no-link-between-autism-and-379245 (Accessed 27 February 2021).

Fisher, K.A., Bloomstone, S.J., Walder, J., Crawford, S., Fouayzi, H., and Mazor, K.M. (2020) 'Attitudes toward a potential SARS-CoV-2 vaccine: a survey of U.S. adults', *Annals of Internal Medicine*, 173:12, 964–973, Available at: DOI: 10.7326/M20-3569 (Accessed 1 January 2021).

Fitzpatrick, M. (2005) 'The anti-vaccination movement in England, 1853-1907', *Journal of the Royal Society of Medicine*, 98:8, 384–385.

GLP (2019) 'Moms Across America: 'Consumer' group promotes health scares, targets GMOs and chemicals', GLP Profiles, Genetic Literacy Project, 2 January 2019. Available at: https://geneticliteracyproject.org/glp-facts/moms-across-america-consumer-group-promotes-health-scares-targets-gmos-chemicals/.

Goode, Mary Elisabeth Carter. (2018) 'Dracula: the anti-vaccination movement and urban life in Victorian England', *Tenor of Our Times*, 7, Article 15, Available at: https://scholarworks.harding.edu/tenor/vol7/iss1/15 (Accessed 1 January 2021).

Gostin, L.O. (2004) 'Jacobson v Massachusetts at 100 years: police power and civil liberties in tension', *American Journal of Public Health*, 95, 576–581, Available at: DOI: 10.2105/AJPH.2004.055152 (Accessed 1 January 2021).

Gray, S. (2020) 'UMMS researchers study attitudes toward potential COVID-19 vaccine', UMass Med News, 17 September 2020. Available at: https://www.umassmed.edu/news/news-archives/2020/09/umms-researchers-study-attitudes-toward-potential-covid-19-vaccine/ (Accessed 1 January 2021).

Healthline (2021) 'FDA to add warning on mRNA COVID-19 vaccines about rare heart-related side effect', Healthline, 23 June 2021. Available at: https://www.healthline.com/health-news/fda-to-add-warning-on-mrna-covid-19-vaccines-about-rare-heart-related-side-effect (Accessed 6 July 2021).

History of Vaccines (2021) 'Coronavirus timeline'. Available at: https://www.historyof-vaccines.org/content/articles/coronavirustimeline (Accessed 27 February 2021).

Holland, M., Conte, L., Krakow, R., and Colin, L. (2011) 'Unanswered questions from the vaccine injury compensation program: a review of compensated cases of vaccine-induced brain injury', *Pace Environmental Law Review*, 28, 480, Available at: https://digitalcommons.pace.edu/pelr/vol28/iss2/6 (Accessed 1 January 2021).

Jarry, J. (2020) 'The anti-vaccine movement in 2020', McGill Office for Science and Society, OSS Newsletter. Available at: https://www.mcgill.ca/oss/article/covid-19-pseudoscience/anti-vaccine-movement-2020 (Accessed 27 February 2021).

Kern, J.K., Geier, D.A., Deth, R.C. et al. (2017b) 'Retracted article: systematic assessment of research on autism spectrum disorder and mercury reveals conflicts of interest and the need for transparency in autism research', *Science and Engineering Ethics*, 23, 1689–1690. Available at: DOI: 10.1007/s11948-015-9713-6 (Accessed 1 January 2021).

Kern, J.K, Geier, D.A, Homme, K.G., and King, P.G. (2017a) 'Developmental neuro-toxicants and the vulnerable male brain: a systematic review of suspected neuro-toxicants that disproportionally affect males', *Acta Neurobiologiae Experimentalis*, 77, 269–296. Available at: https://exeley.mpstechnologies.com/exeley/journals/acta_neurobiologiae_experimentalis/77/4/pdf/10.21307_ane-2017-061.pdf (Accessed 1 January 2021).

Maglione, M.A, Das, L, Raaen, L, Smith, A., Chari, R, Newberry, S., Shanman, R., Perry, T., Goetz, M.B., and Gidengil, C. (2014) 'Safety of vaccines used for routine immunization of US children: a systematic review', *Pediatrics*, 134:2, 325–337, Available at: DOI: 10.1542/peds.2014-1079 (Accessed 2 January 2021).

Milne, C (2019) 'Most of these claims about glyphosate, vaccines and cancer are misleading', Fullfact, 4 July 2019. Available at: https://fullfact.org/online/monsanto-glyphosate-cancer-vaccines/ (Accessed 27 February 2021).

Mnookin, S. (2012) *The Panic Virus: The True Story Behind the Vaccine-Autism Controversy*, New York: Simon & Schuster.

Pangrazzi, L., Balasco, L., and Bozzi, Y. (2020). 'Natural antioxidants: a novel therapeutic approach to autism spectrum disorders?', *Antioxidants (Basel, Switzerland)*, 9:12, 1186, Available at: DOI: 10.3390/antiox9121186.

Paul, E., Steptoe, A., and Fancourt, D. (2020) 'Anti-vaccine attitudes and risk factors for not agreeing to vaccination against COVID-19 amongst 32,361 UK adults: implications for public health communications', *medRxiv*, Available at: DOI: 10.1101/2020.10.21.20216218 (Accessed 2 January 2021).

Porter, D. and Porter, R. (1988). 'The politics of prevention: anti-vaccinationism and public health in nineteenth-century England', *Medical History*, 32:3, 231–252, Available at: doi: 10.1017/S0025727300048225 (Accessed 2 January 2021).

Reich, J. (2016) *Calling the Shots: Why Parents Reject Vaccines*, New York: NYU Press.

Reich, J.A. (2020a) 'Vaccine refusal and pharmaceutical acquiescence: parental control and ambivalence in managing children's health', *American Sociological Review*, 85:1, 106–127, Available at: DOI: 10.1177/0003122419899604. (Accessed 1 January 2021).

Reich, J.A. (2020b) '"We are fierce, independent thinkers and intelligent": social capital and stigma management among mothers who refuse vaccines', *Social Science & Medicine*, 257, Available at: DOI: 10.1016/j.socscimed.2018.10.027 (Accessed 1 January 2021).

Ren, J., Wagner, A.L., Zheng, A., Sun, X., Boulton, M.L., Huang, Z., et al. (2018) 'The demographics of vaccine hesitancy in Shanghai, China', *PLoS One*, 13:12, e0209117, Available at: DOI: 10.1371/journal.pone.0209117 (Accessed 1 January 2021).

Roser, M.A. (2016) 'Discredited autism guru Andrew Wakefield takes aim at CDC', Statesman, 23 September 2016. Available at: https://www.statesman.com/NEWS/20160923/Discredited-autism-guru-Andrew-Wakefield-takes-aim-at-CDC (Accessed 1 January 2021).

Rosman, R. (2021) 'Why are so many in France hesitant to take the COVID-19 vaccine?', Al Jazeera, 6 January 2021. Available at: https://www.aljazeera.com/features/2021/1/6/why-are-so-many-in-france-hesitant-to-take-the-covid-19-vaccine (Accessed 14 February 2021).

SafeMinds (2011) '83 Cases of autism', PR Newswire. Available at: https://www.prnewswire.com/news-releases/83-cases-of-autism-associated-with-childhood-vaccine-injury-compensated-in-federal-vaccine-court-121570673.html (Accessed 27 February 2021).

Seneff, S. (2017) 'Wedding out vaccine toxins: MMR, glyphosate, and the health of a generation', MindBody Medicine Center, 28 September 2017. Available at: https://www.healmindbody.com/weeding-out-vaccine-toxins-mmr-glyphosate-and-the-health-of-a-generation-2/ (Accessed 1 January 2021), initially published on 15 August 2017 in Children's Health Defense: https://childrenshealthdefense.org/news/weeding-vaccine-toxins-mmr-glyphosate-health-generation/.

TEDx (2020) 'What I learned from parents who don't vaccinate their kids', Jennifer Reich, TEDxMileHigh, 7 February 2020. Available at: https://www.youtube.com/watch?v=CTj_xoCuhPU (Accessed 1 January 2021).

Undheim, T.A. (2021) Future Tech: How to Capture Value from Disruptive Industry Trends, 153. London: Kogan Page.

Vaccinate Your Family (2020) 'The facts behind the "CDC Whistleblower" accusations spotlighted in the film Vaxxed', Updated September 2020. Available at: https://64gbq3vjl1cj33l2zkxvvl0k-wpengine.netdna-ssl.com/wp-content/uploads/2020/09/Whistleblower_QA012017_updatedSept2020.pdf (Accessed 1 January 2021).

Vaccine Safety Net (2021). Available at: https://www.vaccinesafetynet.org/.

Movie: 2 The People's Truth, 17 May 2020. Available at: https://www.youtube.com/watch?v=3UWNySwlDLg (Accessed 1 January 2021).

WHO (1969). International Health Regulations (1969). Available at: http://apps.who.int/iris/bitstream/handle/10665/96616/9241580070.pdf;jsessionid=070CFE550CE235C394E77467975F4021?sequence=1

Willingham, E. (2017) 'Mercury and autism: enough already!': The science shows that they have nothing to do with each other and never have', Scientific American, 3 November 2017. Available at: https://blogs.scientificamerican.com/observations/mercury-and-autism-enough-already/ (Accessed 1 January 2021).

Willsher, K. (2020) 'Covid: France 'pandering to anti-vaxxers' with slow vaccine rollout', The Guardian, 31 December 2020. Available at: https://www.theguardian.com/world/2020/dec/31/covid-france-pandering-to-anti-vaxxers-with-slow-vaccine-rollout (Accessed 1 January 2021).

Youngdahl, K. (2012) 'The anti-vaccination Society of America: Correspondence', 8 March 8, 2012. Available at: https://www.historyofvaccines.org/content/blog/anti-vaccination-society-america-correspondence (Accessed 1 January 2021).

Zhang, L., Rana, I., Shaffer, R. M., Taioli, E., Sheppard, L. (2019) 'Exposure to glyphosate-based herbicides and risk for non-hodgkin lymphoma: a meta-analysis and supporting evidence', *Mutation Research/Reviews in Mutation Research*. DOI: 10.1016/j.mrrev.2019.02.001

Chapter 8

Welltech—the Opportunities and Pitfalls of the Natural Wellness Approach

Neema and William, a Florida-based couple I know, are what I would call deep naturalists. They fundamentally believe that the body's natural immune system should be allowed to work. In their view, disease happens because you have not taken care of yourself. Neema, who has a science degree from a prestigious institution, regularly frequents healers, therapeutic horse whisperers, herbalists, and even a practitioner of brain integration. Her kitchen cupboard includes at least 50 herbal remedies being taken on a daily or oscillating basis.

William, is a maddeningly successful businessman and an unlikely deep health naturalist. Both are reflective, intelligent, and highly informed. Their choices are made with full awareness of the wonders of modern medical science and, moreover, with ample access to its marvels. They exude healthiness and wellbeing and are positive beings that bring energy to their surroundings. It's hard not to get smitten with their energy. What I don't know is how much of it can be attributed to commercially available wellness and how much is simply their personalities and healthy constitutions.

Given Neema and William's significant reach across the alternative space, their massive circle of friends and connections, and their gracious introductions

DOI: 10.4324/9781003178071-8

to many of these practitioners, my family and I have frequented most of these natural wellness practitioners at least once. This contrasts with an upbringing where the most alternative I can remember was taking only half the dosage of pain killers even if I had a massive headache, a practice my mom continues to this day. Given that, with this new exposure, what have I since learned, about natural wellness, about my friends, about myself?

At the outset, let me just say that lesson one is that it's complex. Far more complicated than what one might think. The alternative medicine space has expanded, bifurcated, integrated, and subsequently disintegrated from contemporary medicine, all in a short span of time. It has also ballooned. I'm not sure it qualifies as alternative anymore if it is the default, unquestioned alternative. What is welltech? What's its promise? What are its risks? Is it scientifically grounded or will it be?

The Promise and the Risk

The Miami-based nonprofit, the Global Wellness Institute (GWI, 2020) founded in 2014, claims we are living in a $4.5 trillion global wellness economy. The industry consists of large companies, startups, emerging companies and perhaps, more notably on an everyday basis, by individual self-help gurus and their associated franchises developed in the 1990s and 2000s.

Self-help gurus for wellness include Oprah Winfrey (her show ran for 25 seasons from 1986 to 2011), Deepak Chopra (his 1993 book *Ageless Body* sold a million copies of the hardcover alone), Tony Robbins (his self-help program "Personal Power" infomercial aired in 1988), Tony Horton (Beachbody's infomercials for the fitness P90X program were at their peak from 2005–2010), or Joel Osteen (who became senior pastor at Lakewood Church in 1999 and grew attendance from 4,000 to 43,000 by 2014), or Chicago-based Joseph Mercola (a top voice in natural health since his website went up in 1997).

Lastly, disgraced celebrity Donald Trump claims he is the "healthiest person ever elected" and whose "extraordinary health" conquered the coronavirus (Caldera, 2020). Yet, while President, he received a type of care unavailable to any other individual on the planet. Also, he may simply have a solid constitution, is clearly clinically obese (as his 2019 medical record states), but otherwise shows no signs of making his situation any better through any other exercise than golfing (with a golf cart). He provides an extremely bad example to follow.

What's the problem here? These folks rely on scare tactics, are inconsistent, overstate the validity of their claims, at times become embroiled in abusing others through their fame, and make massive profits from their own recommendations, recommendations which change drastically over time, just enough to launch new products that capture market share. This, in turn, makes for an unstable market which is hard to predict and track in any rational fashion, which hurts startups and investors in the space. They also contribute to public confusion over nutrition, science, wellness, and happiness.

Preaching Prosperity through Individualism— Tony Robbins, Deepak Chopra, and Joel Osteen

Tony Robbins whose core message seems to be that you should not see yourself as a victim but should view your pain as something you have the power to "destroy", and whose platinum program costs $85,000 a year, has used his fame to ridicule and berate victims of rape and violence, has called the #MeToo movement an "excuse", and has created a sexualized environment during his public appearances (Bradley & Baker, 2019). These are tactics that by now are familiar to those watching other sides of American public life during the Trump Presidency.

The Deepak Chopra's tweets were used in a scientific study of "pseudo-profound bullshit", he claims meditation changes the expression of the human genome, and his Chopra center has released advice on how meditation can heal cancer (Goldhill, 2017). As for Tony Horton, Santa Monica prosecutors say Beachbody made false or misleading claims about products aimed at fighting aging, inflammation, and mental decline and in 2017 he agreed to pay $3.6 million for applying recurring charges to customers without their legal consent (Pierson, 2017). Joel Osteen preaches the prosperity gospel which clouds the persistence of suffering from social inequality and has not found a way to properly respond to human tragedy—as witnessed by his refusal to open Lakewood church's stadium to flood victims after Hurricane Harvey (Bowler, 2017).

The Questionable Dietary Advice of Oprah Winfrey

In 2020, Oprah Winfrey talks the talk about wellness as eating better, moving more, and developing a positive mindset (Krischer Goodman, 2020), on stage promoting a company she owns millions of shares in, WW (formerly Weight Watchers). Yet, she shows no sign of being particularly healthy herself which is not an issue were it not for the fact that she continues giving health and wellness advice based on her own experience, her weight constantly fluctuating by several dozens of pounds.

Winfrey has touted all kinds of diets and advice throughout her 40 years in the limelight, including her 1988 Optifast liquid diet (Benet, 1988), and again in 2005, this time with the mantra "eat less", then with "balanced calories" (Greene, 2007) which brought her to 160 pounds. By 2009, it's all downhill, and she is past the 200-pound mark. She got a hyperthyroidism diagnosis, claims to discover a "food addiction", but ends up claiming all along, she has been "hungry for balance", meaning she was working too hard, playing too little and "craves love" (Winfrey, 2009).

Oprah first bought Weight Watchers stock in 2015 for $43.5 million, which at the height of that stock in 2018 was worth $400 million (La Monica, 2018) and has lately sold quite a bit of it (Liu, 2020). Come 2016, she touts "seafood is your friend" (Sassman & Bulow, 2016), yet by 2017, she advocates to "make peace with food" (Green, 2017), and in 2018, she endorses the "freestyle program" including rosé, pasta, and bread (Ahlgrim, 2018), and in 2019 the "OMD" plan of one meal a day meaning one plant-based meal per day (Sass, 2019) is all the rage and more. Forgive me, but I just don't see how hits journey is at all helpful in helping anyone develop a healthy body image, lose weight, or become truly healthy. The only value gained by asking people to empathize with her roller coaster is to feel better about ourselves for also failing at the same thing, I guess. Perhaps no small thing? I'll leave that door open.

The Anti-Medicine Claims by Joseph Mercola

Joseph Mercola is an American alternative medicine proponent who is internet and marketing savvy. An osteopath by training, e.g. a licensed physician who practices medicine using both conventional treatments and osteopathic manipulative medicine, which focuses on relieving pain and tension in the musculoskeletal system, he has made a fortune selling natural health products, including vitamin C and D supplements. He operates one of the Internet's largest and most trafficked health "information" sites and claims his newsletter has over a million subscribers (Barrett, 2020).

Mercola is controversial for his arguments that most things around us cause cancer and for his disdain for both big pharma and traditional medicine (Satija & Sun, 2019). Mercola is against immunization, fluoridation, mammography, and the routine administration of vitamin K shots to the newborn, claims that amalgam fillings are toxic, and has advised against eating many foods that the scientific community regards as healthful, such as bananas, oranges, red potatoes, white potatoes, all milk products, and almost all grain (Barrett, 2020).

Mercola falsely claims that at least 22 vitamins, supplements (melatonin, zinc, selenium, licorice, astaxanthin, N-acetyl cysteine, and prebiotics, probiotics, and sporebiotics), and other products or substances (ozone) available for sale on his website can prevent, treat, or cure COVID-19 infection, according to a claim filed with the FDA and FTC by the Center for Science for Public Interest (CSPI, 2020). In Mercola's defense, nobody is saying modern medicine is perfect. Big pharma certainly have had its issues with the truth, although transparency has improved. Toxicity can, theoretically, come from near anywhere—but there is something about the volume he chooses to speak at and the high horse position he claims.

The nascent wellness market is still a mixed bag of science, culture, and tribal resistance intermixed.

Making Sense of the Wellness Market

The wellness market, which purports to foster holistic, healthy living, a longer life span, better health span (living healthily longer), with higher mental, social, and spiritual wellbeing—sometimes all of it together can be segmented into a myriad of huge, multibillion dollar global verticals: Personal care, beauty and anti-aging, healthy eating, nutrition and weight loss, supplements, wellness tourism, fitness and mind-body, preventive/personalized medicine and public health, traditional and complementary medicine, wellness lifestyle real estate, spa economy, thermal/mineral springs, and workplace wellness (GWI, 2020). Broadly, when thinking of wellness in terms of health, it represents a shift from treatment to prevention.

Corporate Venture Capital in Healthcare

Corporate venture capital is also starting to make themselves visible but make comparatively fewer bets. BlueCross BlueShield Venture Partners (https://blueventurefund.com/) are highly strategic and invest in healthcare startups that align with their insurance objectives and trends such as "the implementation of the Affordable Care Act, the expansion of retail healthcare and rise of consumerism, new provider payment models, and rapid change in medical technology and the delivery of care". Over the past 8 years, health systems made 184 investments in 105 early-stage digital health companies, with over one-third of health systems making these investments being academic and the majority being nonprofit organizations. Overall, provider health systems are more likely to invest in companies focused on workflow, on-demand health services, and data infrastructure/interoperability (Safavi et al., 2020).

Mayo Clinic Ventures (http://ventures.mayoclinic.org/), founded in 1986, part of the largest private, integrated group practice of medicine in the world, is focused on finding partners that can bring Mayo's inventions to the marketplace. The firm makes venture investments in firms operating in the medical technology, medical devices, biopharmaceuticals, diagnostic, and other healthcare sectors purely within its own network. My Travel Health is an example of an outlier which is based on content licensed from the Mayo Clinic.

Leaps by Bayer (https://leaps.bayer.com/), ironically the same company arguably complicit in the crimes of the Third Reich by producing its medical supplies (Hayes, 1988), combines a focus on healthcare and agriculture based on the notion of Wellbeing Adjusted Life Years (WALY), e.g. "patient-experienced quality of life" (on a scale from 0 to 1), developed with The Happiness Research Institute as a new impact metric to help better prioritize investment in breakthrough innovations. WALY relies on subindicators of subjective wellbeing such as self-sufficiency, depression/anxiety, vitality, optimism, engagement, and loneliness.

There is also Ziegler/Link-age Investment Funds (https://www.linkageconnect.com/ventures/) investing in the aging services of tomorrow, spearheaded by Chicago-based Ziegler, a privately held investment bank, capital markets, and proprietary investments firm, specializing in the healthcare, senior living, and education sectors. GV (https://www.gv.com/) also has a massive health and wellness portfolio.

Greenwich, Connecticut-based LCatterton (http://www.lcatterton.com/) is the leading investor in consumer growth companies. With a portfolio of 200 investments in leading consumer brands across all segments of the consumer industry, they have $20 billion dedicated to growing middle market companies and emerging high-growth enterprises with a strong thesis around health and wellness which "will continue to be a determinant in almost all consumer decisions".

Finally, there is Nashville-based Martin Ventures (https://www.martin-ventures.com/), the family office of Vanguard Health Systems founder Charlie Martin, investing exclusively in healthcare with the thesis that the healthcare system is "flawed in design by focusing on episodic care vs. holistic care". Vanguard was an operator of hospitals and other medical facilities in five US states: Arizona, Illinois, Massachusetts, Michigan, and Texas and acquired by Tenet Healthcare for $4.3 billion in 2013.

The Best and the Worst

At best, wellness helps us balance our lives and live more meaningfully, comfortably, and well, perhaps naturally. There are honest startup entrepreneurs in this space trying to make a difference with experimental behavioral apps that have the potential to do great good. At worst, self-help gurus, each of which have kernels of truth mixed in with, arguably, questionable generalizations and conjecture, make billions selling shaky, at times dangerous notions about our bodies, our priorities, and our mental states.

For example, they consistently overstate the role and responsibility of individuals in shaping their own fate, even though society is founded on systematic inequality and oppression which is the true cause of most hardship. Second, their claims are cloaked in pseudoscientific language speaking of their self-help principles as "laws" of nature. Third, their motivational thrust based on the social psychology of positive affirmation seldom lasts. These are readily established counters that apply to a great deal of wellness priests, but that does not stop the movement. Beyond that, what self-help points to is a great need. Is there a way that we are getting closer to fixing the ails these gurus speak of? Weight gain. Low self-esteem. Victim mentality. Negative thoughts. Eating unhealthy foods? (Cissé, 2020; Williams, 2019).

My Exploration of Alternative Medicine

Back to my forays into alternative medicine. One of the practitioners I went to is a holistic nutritionist. During the session, I was exposed to my body being "listened to" (using what applied kinesiology calls "muscle testing") in order to figure out the right dosage of herbs. I came back with seven different herbal and mineral supplements at a total price of some $750 for a 6-month supply. I started taking them as I was doing my own independent research. Most substances were harmless and perhaps slightly helpful, I don't know. One was not and the dosage was way off. I was given an iodide supplement with 10× the recommended dosage, which most medical sources I consulted claim were toxic at those amounts. Once I figured that out, I drastically lowered my dosage and a lost faith in this particular nutritionist's quality control, methods, and for a time, in the entire herbal effort.

It is only one data point, but I want to note that had I not done my independent research and had I trusted the provider 100%, I would have been destined to taking toxic doses of iodide. Reported fatal doses vary from 200 mg to 20 g, but even ingesting over 1.1 mg/day may be harmful (Southern & Jwayyed, 2020). I think we need to stop thinking of herbs or minerals as harmless or healing, nutritional supplements can be highly virulent—they have medical effects and should be regulated as such. The fact that they are not is a major oversight by national regulatory bodies and shows their ignorance of medical innovation and moreover shows a genuinely worrying lack of curiosity about the progress of their own field.

Does this mean that I'm against nutritionists? Not at all, I think nutritional science will be key to the next medical breakthroughs. However, we need more longitudinal, systematic studies of herbal and mineral interaction effects.

Acupressure—As a Therapy

The sustainability of considerable amounts of wellness approaches hinge on whether the Asia-derived meridian theory can be further supported by scientific evidence. Meridian theory essentially goes like this: illness and symptoms result from alterations in the normal flow of life-supporting bioenergy (qi/ki) that moves along a predictable network of pathways.

The theoretical–functional argument aside, there is considerable anecdotal, prescientific, and a growing body of small-scale qualitative evidence behind the possibility that acupressure (and acupuncture) can be helpful as part of pain management (Ning & Lao, 2015) including migraine, although pain itself is poorly understood in science. Other recognized applications are against nausea and vomiting, as well as against insomnia and fatigue, notably as an ailment for jetlag. The evidence is mounting but not conclusive (Selfridge, 2012). I happen to believe that it will be proven out, but perhaps not until we can access brain waves and even then we might wait until we can truly access the body's bioelectric system through new advanced sensors (my prediction is that these sensors will emerge over the next 10–15 years, at maximum 25 years from now).

I first started exploring acupressure massage through one particular Chinese massage place in Brussels that offered what it called Tui-na massage. I later discovered what they offered was a westernized form that was delivered through oil massage which is not traditionally done. Either way, and not trying to look down at other massage forms, the massage felt much more efficacious than any other massage I had had at that point. As I was trying to investigate the reasons behind the qualitative differences, I started frequenting Chinese massage places wherever I went and have compared and contrasted.

The quality varies immensely, but in the 5% of places that do seem to practice true acupressure by Chinese-born practitioners who have learned this in hospitals and clinics in China using pressure points that correspond to the map of meridian points that I later learned more about, have an effect that cannot seem to be explained by it simply being touching aching muscles.

As my wife suffers from migraine, I have attempted to learn some of the acupressure technique. The method I follow is from the *Massage for Pain Relief* by Peijian Shen, a Chinese–Canadian practitioner (Shen, 1996). What I have found is that the location of pressure points needs to be exact and that this really is location-specific touch applied with a certain forcefulness and repetition, methodically throughout the massage session. The mysterious aspect remains that the impact is not localized as pressure points in the foot might correspond to areas around the body. Wrapping my western mind around that phenomenon is not easy, but I have given up not rationalize it and I simply follow the effects. After some weeks and months, I was able to amplify the impact of pain medication and the speed by which it entered the body by at least 2–5×. This is not miraculous, but it makes a difference for somebody suffering from a migraine. I've also managed to get my kids to sleep faster which, again, was no miracle cure (two of my kids left me with less than 4 hours sleep on a regular basis throughout their childhood—and regularly took 2 hours to go to sleep), but at least kept them (and me) alive.

WellTech's Possible Impact on Wellness

You could be forgiven for wondering if there is a place for health tech in wellness, given all the talk about nature. After all, isn't technology the antithesis to nature? There is nothing more man-made than technology.

Yet, nothing is further from the truth. The wellness-movement is steeped in technology. Lately, there's also an acronym for it—WellTech—the hallmark of startup interest in a space. Others call the wider emerging space the Longevity industry, but WellTech is certainly a somewhat well-defined subcategory. It is confusing, though, because it touches on mental health services that were pre-existing but adds a distinct digital layer and a strong experiential component.

Which Technologies Will Transform Wellness?

A plethora of emerging technologies could transform the wellness market in the years ahead, including 3D printing, wearables, synthetic biology, artificial intelligence (AI), or their combinations. Drugs, supplements, personalized foods, medical devices, human organs and tissues, can all soon, to various degrees be 3D printed. The food processing industry will altogether be transformed by new machines that are more highly attuned, providing increasingly mass-customized foods at greater precision. Gastrograph AI powered by consumer data can predict flavors and preferences at the pre-production stage. Supply chain optimization becomes possible through food sorting robots from Tomra. Augmented workers are benefiting both from software and increasingly in association with collaborative robots, so-called co-bots.

When I held my first foodtech workshop at MIT back in 2016, I was shocked to see the positive response. People came from afar to hear what MIT startups and faculty founders had to say about the topic. However, the interest in food is not all friendly and is likely already leading to food wars (note the attempts to reverse Michelle Obama's healthy school lunch initiative).

The Ascent of Neutraceuticals

It's almost like as long as it is not clinical-grade, it is great and fair play. Neutraceuticals, coined by Dr. Stephen DeFelice in 1989, from "nutrition" and "pharmaceutical", might be the best example (Kalra, 2003). DeFalice is the founder and chairman of FIM, the Foundation for Innovation in Medicine (https://fimdefelice.org/), a nonprofit organization established in 1976 whose purpose is to accelerate medical discovery by establishing a more productive clinical research community.

In 1984, the Japanese government studied foods for specific health uses (FOSHU) and ended up with a new legislative food category and label which requires manufacturers to obtain scientific evidence as to the proposed medical or nutritional link, suggested doses, safety, and composition. In the EU, more stringent regulations tend to prohibit advertising functional food benefits. In the US, there is an evidence-based review system where manufacturers may issue nutrition content claims and function claim, as long as there is no health claim involved, and can include health claims only if effects have been suggested, and with the disclaimer that the scientific evidence behind health claims is weak or has not been assessed. However, without a formal definition of functional foods or neutraceuticals, the category is lost in the US food vocabulary (Martirosyan & Singh, 2015).

Since the early 1990s functional foods have emerged at the boundary between the pharma and the food industry, using three distinct innovation strategies: tech development aiming for B2B adoption (pharma, chemical, industrial, and tech startups), new tech aiming for B2C adoption (food companies, consumer brands, and applied startups), and brand and marketing-heavy mass market consumer products and product extensions from the low-tech food industry (Bröring, 2010).

Either way, with neutraceuticals, you have near-scientific treatments that stop short of going the FDA-approval route in order to make a quick buck, or, according to the founders, make sure their product benefits the users right away. These products use legitimate scientific arguments in terms of the way products were developed but cannot claim medical benefits because their clinical trials are not registered with national agencies. The most famous of which might be MIT professor Guarante's startup, Elysium Health founded in 2014 as a dietary supplement business based on NAD+, arguably "indispensable for life", in any event, demonstrably, levels of this molecule decline as we age.

Many neutraceuticals are nootropics (e.g. cognitive enhancers), which claim to improve cognitive function, particularly executive functions, memory, creativity, or motivation, in healthy individuals. These are typically marketed toward students, professionals, or the elderly. In some cases, they are also used in treating memory disorders, such as Alzheimer's, Parkinson's, and Huntington's diseases, although that is still controversial (Suliman, 2016).

In the natural form, these include caffeine (found in coffee), L-Theanine (found in tea), Siberian ginseng (an inexpensive ginseng variant, an eleutheroside compound of the questionable effect studied by Russian doctor Brehkman in the 1950s), ginseng (widely used in Chinese medicine to boost brain function and immunity), creatine (used in bodybuilding supplements), Ginkgo balboa, nicotine to improve motor function, alertness (found in tobacco), the Rhodiola rosea herb (widely used against stress), and curcumin, which then become elements mixed in with herbs, mineral and other substances.

As synthetic biology comes of age, it will be difficult to argue that something is "natural" versus "synthetic" as many natural substances are being synthesized and many synthetic substances will approximate natural ones. Fitness startups using tech as a core part of their offering fit this bill.

Patient experience startups are a borderline case. Are they within the model of traditional healthcare or are they coming at it from the wellness angle? Chronic health apps definitely straddle this line as well. Tech is not a threat to holistic care, but a means to scale it beyond individualized experiences and getting the benefit of the wisdom, comfort, and community hidden within large pockets of the masses.

Miracle cures do occasionally exist, but when they happen, they are just that, miracles, and miracles can rarely be templated. If they are, they cease to be viewed as miracles, by the way.

Wellness companies almost per definition provide "nice to have" products as opposed to "necessary" ones. It's all about surplus thinking. For that reason, whether these products are recession proof is a serious question mark.

There is a crossover between preventive care and behavioral healthcare for chronic conditions, given that, left untreated, some behaviors turn into chronic conditions, or better said, some behaviors can stem or stop chronic conditions in their tracks. The behavioral approach to healthcare has received massive attention lately, given the uptick of digital platforms to manage such interventions at scale. One figure is there are some 318,000 health-related apps on the market (IQVIA, 2017). There are behavioral apps for better sleep, losing weight, controlling various forms of anxiety, managing depression, preventing suicide, treating trauma, breathing better, meditating deeply, and much more.

Fitness apps have skyrocketed, with a virtual fitness company such as publicly traded Peloton worth near $8 billion at the time of writing. Wellness as a Service

(WaaS) is emerging as an attempt to answer the consumerization of everything through the merger of decentralization and digitalization of care, in the mobile era, with behavioral wellness interventions, and fueled by machine learning and "AI", both as a consumer service and then, gradually, as a health service integrated with health systems, insurance plans, and corporate healthcare provision.

Behavioral health starts chipping at the binary notion of either being sick or healthy, between illness and wellness. In reality, we are all, always somewhere in between. The emerging continuum of healthiness will include a more fine-tuned scale (e.g. diseased, poor health, good health, and optimal health) that not only incorporates degrees of sickness and health for each disease area, and perhaps tuned to different genetic profiles, but perhaps does away with a hierarchy altogether.

Arguably, being completely healthy may not even be the ideal, seeing as it may lead to an absence of meaning, especially for those of us with project identities that constantly get redefined. This is somewhat controversial but not an unthinkable conclusion. Similarly, given that huge swaths of the population suffer from chronic diseases, at what point do they become so endemic that it makes no sense to talk of them as sick—they are merely on the normal spectrum? Finally, most people who die suddenly from some disease had no idea that they had said disease because they had no (discernible) symptom—until they suddenly did. They were considered healthy up until that point. If that needs to change, then very dramatic parts of our conception of what it means to live happily needs to change. After all, depending on how you see it, we may all be ill, suffering from various nutritional deficiencies, significant health issues with the potential to be life-altering, as well as suffering from undiagnosed chronic conditions such as inflammation, depression, and pre-diabetes (Dryburgh, 2016).

Quality of Life and the Limits of Alternative Medicine

In 1997, I was deeply involved with the International Student Festival of Trondheim (ISFiT). Preparing for the influx of 300+ international students to our event, we had been frantically preparing for months already. My tasks were somewhat limited in scope, I don't even recall exactly what I was doing, but the reason for that is somewhat self-explanatory.

Right as students were arriving, my father was, out of the blue, diagnosed with metastatic stage 4 melanoma cancer. I was, naturally, devastated. My counselor at ISFiT, however, was unfazed. She said I should have faith in alternative medicine and advised all sorts of remedies for my father, herbal drinks and the like. The mantra was, your body can heal itself, and you "have to believe" you can get well. We had had lengthy discussions about such things because the theme for the ISFiT '97 event was "Quality of life". In a curious turn of events, I ended up being asked to write the festival song, impromptu as everyone was arriving from all corners of the world.

One phrase that still sticks with me was "Is quality of life housing, butter and rice, or is quality born with the mind?". I performed the song on stage with a full band put together for the occasion, with 300 students ending up standing up, singing it together at full voice. It was a moment to remember. Meanwhile, my father's illness rapidly took a turn for the worse, and in a matter of days, he passed away.

From this earth-shattering experience, I obviously have come out somewhat scarred. I have also become more reflective. For now, I just wanted to point out that if I seem somewhat ambivalent on the power of natural wellness, it is because I do feel it has its limits. Metastatic cancer might be one of the demarcation lines I would draw. In fact, so far, research indicates the use of alternative medicine for cancer has negative impact on survival (Johnson et al., 2018), although the opposite viewpoint has certainly got its proponents, too.

That is not to say, however, that I don't believe there can be great power in natural wellness, far from it. Also, one could readily counter that back in 1997, traditional medicine was not able to save my father either. I do think that this decade will provide some therapies that will make a difference in metastatic melanoma, but for my family this is 30 years too late. And, by the way, I also do believe in miracles. I just don't think you can rely on them (Figure 8.1).

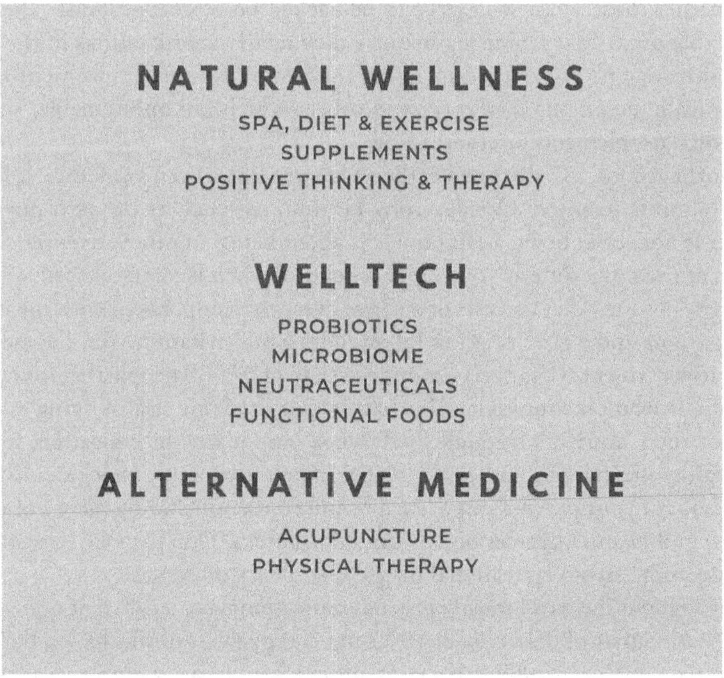

NATURAL WELLNESS

SPA, DIET & EXERCISE
SUPPLEMENTS
POSITIVE THINKING & THERAPY

WELLTECH

PROBIOTICS
MICROBIOME
NEUTRACEUTICALS
FUNCTIONAL FOODS

ALTERNATIVE MEDICINE

ACUPUNCTURE
PHYSICAL THERAPY

Figure 8.1   Natural wellness versus welltech.

The Mixed Blessings of Natural Wellness

Can we fight off disease by being attentive, eating well, getting exercise, talking to people (and therapists), and living supremely healthy lives? The answer is that we sometimes can but not always. Also, it's unclear what the right course of action is for any given ailment or for an individual, family, or community as a whole, and it is far too easy to overdo it.

Moreover, these approaches are *mostly* supplements not replacements. They also heavily rely on the placebo effect (though there is more to it). More worryingly, they act as escape hatches from social responsibility. This is not to say that some traditional medicine approaches involving pills and engineering efforts such as surgery should not be supplemented or even replaced by less invasive and wiser approaches. However, each natural wellness step tends to accumulate and create the exact same kind of drag that too much traditional medicine will do. Watch your wellness efforts!

I find myself in an interesting situation. As an investor, the welltech space is promising (although risky), but as a futurist I see a discrepancy between the lofty promises and the significant shifts the proposed remedies will undergo even over the next decade. It is not at all clear neither who the winners are likely to be nor whether those winners deserve to be backed on ethical grounds. There are niches that are wildly promising because they rectify shortcomings in the existing health system's understanding of key social groups—such as women's health or ethnically conscious medicine, and others which are questionable, such as nutritional supplements or cryotherapy.

For the record, as I disclosed earlier, I have at times been swayed by celebrity self-help gurus (e.g. Joel Osteen, Tony Horton) as much as the next guy. This chapter is not about being a saint but it is about being an innovative, yet careful skeptic at the same time as you can be a believer when it matters most.

Right now, my diet consists of a coffee every morning, taken with my home-made granola and a glass of water followed by a multivitamin. Yes, I'm aware of the relatively recent 6-year NIH-founded study of 37,000 people that found that individuals who take multivitamins have about the same risk of dying as those who got their nutrients through food, when you adjust for education, income and healthy lifestyle (Kantor et al., 2016). In fact, that study concludes listen to the "advice of your parents", e.g. "eat a balanced diet, including plenty of fruits, veggies, and healthy sources of calcium and protein. Don't smoke. Use alcohol in moderation. Avoid recreational drugs. Get plenty of exercise".

Throughout the day, I mostly just add more granola or a different non-sugary cereal, with bursts of dark chocolate during energy lows, until I have a hot meal around six, which generally either contains chicken, meat or simply veggies. The important thing is that I have tried to eliminate processed foods. I realize this is not fanciful, certainly not ideal, but neither is it completely negligent. From time to time, I experiment with various natural supplements (ginseng, letter vitamins, experimental concoctions of various sorts) but I never stick to it over time, partly because I worry about the long-term consequences, partly because it is expensive, and partly because I rarely see any systematic effect. I think it's fair to say that this is where we are at this point in time. We know there's more to it, but we don't have the scientific (or everyday) apparatus to measure and prove it. I try to keep in mind that most things consumed in excess have the potential to cause adverse effects.

Great parts of the wellness industry is just a bit too much most of the time. Fundamental wellbeing shouldn't be this complicated, expensive, and exclusive. At least not if it is to be considered natural, accessible, and reachable for most of humanity. You don't need a spa experience at a mountain resort, running on indoor treadmills with oxygen vaporizers, burning sticks of imported palo santo, the aromatic wood used in South American spiritual rituals, getting regular seaweed wraps, cryotherapy, and detoxify diets in order to feel alive. If we do, we have bigger problems than wellness efforts can fix. The idea that we can individually manage health takes away from the truer notion that health inequality is often caused by systemic factors outside of individual control, such as how much you earn, where you live, and who your friends are (all of which have an element of social constraint baked in).

Relying on natural wellness in the form of diet, exercise, sleep, spirituality, and surroundings to cure all your illnesses and as a remedy of serious diseases is asking too much of wholistic medicine. It is also asking more than even its most ardent providers ever promise. Why this is still out there in popular culture, eludes me, but I'm also not immune to it. It seems intuitively believable, fancifully wonderful, and yes, somewhat magical in that magical reality kind of way that we all love to indulge in through fiction and fantasy. It is just not true in a medical sense. Having said that, neither is scientific medicine. Medicine of the more traditional ilk has a similar history of overuse of placebo. It works exactly the same way. If you believe something will work, it may just do so. Only that it may not.

Asking for less medical miracles from our efforts to manipulate diet, sleep, spirituality, and surroundings may actually in itself be emancipatory. We then realize that these things are part of life, naturally part of life, that is, and we can with this new insight relax in the renewed faith in the power of the mundane. The New Testament's Paul had a proverbial thorn in the flesh, a mysterious illness, likely an eye disease, and dealt with it as a (hu)man, he embraced it as a corrective reminder. I've reflected on that fact many times and find comfort in what's less than ideal dealt with correctly can make you stronger.

Paradoxically, it may be in the mundane, non-magical practice of daily rituals that we experience the most reliable therapeutic effects. Eating a green vegetable a day may indeed help keep the doctor away, if only because it indicates other good practices are also being followed. Going to sleep and getting up at the same time every day may indeed help with regularity which is a key to so many good things. Praying at regular intervals throughout the day or at least at the beginning and/or the end may well provide the kind of grounding and reflection that anybody needs to feel whole and composed. Frequenting familiar places and engaging with them as surroundings that have a more innate meaning because of their usefulness as sources of fresh air more than anything more fanciful, could indeed be a profound therapeutic activity that reminds you of where you are but perhaps also of who you are and aspire to be. It need not become a grounding exercise tied to earth's electromagnetic field.

There are both opportunities and pitfalls of the natural wellness approach to life much like there is with attempting to follow the straight-edge medical approach to life. I'm not sure that either is significantly more scientific or powerful than the other. They may follow different laws of nature, but they are surprisingly similar both in their practice and in their effects, which is to say that they tap into equal parts mystical and factual realities, each and the other. Returning to my friends, Neema and William, the deep naturalists, I think the assessment is that they might be precursors but as such they are pre-scientific (or perhaps simultaneously post-scientific) in their beliefs, which is fine. Science is being dragged into the debate, though, and I suspect it will be more so, throughout the entire wellness value chain. Science is not perfect, in fact it is designed to fail most of the time, that's the way it works. If scientists are certain about something, it is only because they are deluding themselves. True science does not produce certainty, only hypotheses.

I predict there will come a day, for instance, where the medical establishment realizes that the function of a non-placebo pill is equally psychological as physiological or at least that the two may or indeed must mutually reinforce each other for a successful treatment to occur. Equally, the day may come when most of the practices now bundled into the category of natural wellness will find their scientific explanations, whether favorable or unfavorable as to the reliability of its treatment effects over time and under systematic scrutiny with the right measurement variables and control groups.

In fact, whether it comes to the healing power of touch, the life enhancing value of regenerative diets, or the intrinsic benefits of micro-electrostimulation in the form of acupuncture, I'm fairly confident that science will prove out their hypothesis within this decade alone. The reason is that more advanced experimentation is emerging and we will have had longitudinal studies that can once and for all confirm whether the effects are measurable and provable under any acceptable scientific method. Many other alternative therapies are likely to be debunked. There is no either or, the answer is contingent. What it does mean is that we have to be cautious. Cautious as individuals trying out all of these traditional or experimental therapies. Cautious as medical professionals opining on them based on scant evidence and quite a lot of aggregated skepticism and, I dear say, prejudice. Cautious as regulators whose task it is to approve some of these therapies for medical reimbursement, acceptance as medical therapies, or debunked as pseudoscience.

Conclusion

The borderline between quackery and medicine is a thin one. It is important to realize that one reason behind the ascent of natural wellness is that a lot of bad medicine is allowed within the boundary of that professional, certified, and protected human practice—not all of it scientific in nature or practice. Medical doctors would do well by being humbler about the limits of what they know.

Similarly, in an age where mass events might be curtailed by coronavirus for a while, self-help gurus may find that their skill sets are better applied to selling real products and not snake oil. Still, many fine scientists, from Louis Pasteur to Linus Pauling were initially or even ultimately accused of quackery. One person's quack is another person's guru—even within friendship groups. I'm sure that goes for my friends, as well, no matter how highly educated they might be.

KEY TAKEAWAYS AND REFLECTIONS

1. Please define natural wellness and explain its main tenets.

2. Try to think of three positive and three negative things with a huge focus on natural wellness as the basis for family life.

3. What's your sense is the pharma industry or the supplements industry more ethical? Which institutions around you do you feel are most helpful in keeping these two industries in check? (governments? nonprofits? competitors? friends? social media? influencers?)

Seldom has science and pseudoscience been so closely pitted against each other with such disastrous results. Equally, seldom have stakes been higher for the successful reintegration of science and holism.

In the next chapter, I will discuss the needed system reboot in health governance.

References

Ahlgrim, C. (2018) 'Oprah Winfrey's diet lets you eat pasta and bread — but you still may find it surprisingly annoying', Insider.com, 2 March 2018. Available at: https://www.insider.com/oprah-winfrey-weight-watchers-meal-plan-experiment-2018-2

Barrett, S. (2020) 'Dr. Joseph Mercola ordered to stop illegal claims', Quackwatch, 27 July 2020. Available at: https://quackwatch.org/11ind/mercola/ (Accessed 30 December 2020).

Benet, L. (1988) 'Oprah's Liquid diet: a tough act to follow, Los Angeles Daily News, 26 November, 1988. Available at: https://www.orlandosentinel.com/news/os-xpm-1988-11-26-0080360273-story.html (Accessed 6 July 2021).

Bowler, K. (2017) 'Here's why people hate Joel Osteen', The Washington Post, 29 August 2017. Available at: https://www.washingtonpost.com/news/acts-of-faith/wp/2017/08/29/heres-why-people-hate-joel-osteen/ (Accessed 30 December 2020).

Bradley, J. and Baker, K.J.M (2019) 'Leaked records reveal Tony Robbins berated abuse victims, and former followers accuse him of sexual advances', BuzzFeed News Investigation, 17 May 2019. Available at: https://www.buzzfeednews.com/article/janebradley/tony-robbins-self-help-secrets (Accessed 30 December 2020).

Bröring, S. (2010) 'Innovation strategies for functional foods and supplements—challenges of the positioning between foods and drugs', *Food Science and Technology Bulletin: Functional Foods*, 7:8, 111–123. Available at: DOI: 10.1616/1476-2137.15996 (Accessed 31 December 2020).

Caldera, C. (2020) 'Fact check: Fake Trump quote about battling coronavirus, his body', USA Today, 8 October 2020. Available at: https://www.usatoday.com/story/news/factcheck/2020/10/08/fact-check-trump-quote-virus-his-body-fake/5925710002/ (Accessed 30 December 2020).

Cissé, A. (2020) '10 most blinged-out celebrity self-help gurus', The Talko. Available at: https://www.thetalko.com/celebrity-self-help-gurus-rich/ (Accessed 27 February 2021).

CSPI (2020) 'FDA and FTC urged to bring enforcement proceedings against Joseph Mercola for false COVID-19 health claims', Center for the Science in the Public Interest (CSPI), 21 July 2020. Available at: https://cspinet.org/news/fda-and-ftc-urged-bring-enforcement-proceedings-against-joseph-mercola-false-covid-19-health (Accessed 30 December 2020).

Dryburgh, L.S. (2016) The 3 pillars of wellness as a service (WaaS): human-computer integration, redefinition of health & decentralization of healthcare', Hyperwellbeing. Available at: https://blog.hyperwellbeing.com/the-3-pillars-of-wellness-as-a-service/ (Accessed 27 February 2021).

Greene, B. (2007) Oprah's 7-Day Food Diary, Oprah.com. Available at: https://www.oprah.com/health/oprahs-seven-day-food-diary

Goldhill, O. (2017) 'We asked Deepak Chopra, the guru of sayings that mean nothing, to fact-check his own tweets', Quartz, 5 March 2017. Available at: https://qz.com/917820/we-asked-deepak-chopra-the-guru-of-sayings-that-mean-nothing-to-fact-check-his-own-tweets/ (Accessed 29 December 2020).

Green, M. (2017) '"I'm finally at peace with food": Oprah Winfrey tells people how she lost 42.5 Lbs.!', People, 11 January 2017. Available at: https://people.com/bodies/oprah-winfrey-tells-people-how-she-lost-42-5-lbs/ (Accessed 30 December 2020).

GWI (2020) 'Wellness industry statistics & facts', The Global Wellness Institute (GWI). Available from: https://globalwellnessinstitute.org/press-room/statistics-and-facts/# (Accessed 28 December 2020).

Hayes, P. (1988) *Industry and Ideology: I. G. Farben in the Nazi Era*, Cambridge: Cambridge University Press.

IQVIA (2017) 'The growing value of digital health', 7 November 2017. Available at: https://www.iqvia.com/insights/the-iqvia-institute/reports/the-growing-value-of-digital-health (Accessed 27 February 2021).

Johnson, S.B., Park, H.S., Gross, C.P., and Yu, J.B. (2018) 'Use of alternative medicine for cancer and its impact on survival', *Journal of the National Cancer Institute*, 110:1, Available at: DOI: 10.1093/jnci/djx145 (Accessed 30 December 2020).

Kalra E.K. (2003) 'Nutraceutical--definition and introduction', *AAPS PharmSci*, 5:3, E25. DOI: 10.1208/ps050325.

Kantor, E.D., Rehm, C.D., Du, M., White, E., and Giovannucci, E.L. (2016) 'Trends in dietary supplement use among US adults from 1999–2012', *JAMA*, 316:14, 1464–1474. DOI: 10.1001/jama.2016.14403.

Krischer Goodman, C. (2020) 'Oprah and Lady Gaga: diet myths busted as attention focuses on wellness and total health in 2020', South Florida Sun Sentinel, 3 January 2020. Available at: https://www.sun-sentinel.com/health/fl-ne-weight-watchers-20200103-tk2y76ksrzfy5ihtg2uzcmwqce-story.html (Accessed 30 December 2020).

La Monica, P.R. (2018) 'Oprah has made a killing on Weight Watchers stock', CNN Business, 4 May 2018. Available at: https://money.cnn.com/2018/05/04/investing/weight-watchers-oprah-winfrey/index.html (Accessed 30 December 2020).

Lin, E. (2020) 'Oprah Winfrey sells millions of dollars of slumping Weight Watchers stock', Barron's, 13 June 2020. Available at: https://www.barrons.com/articles/oprah-winfrey-sells-millions-of-dollars-of-slumping-weight-watchers-stock-51592046004 (Accessed 30 December 2020).

Martirosyan, D. and Singh, J. (2015) 'A new definition of functional food by FFC: what makes a new definition unique?', *Functional Foods in Health and Disease*, 5, 209–223, Available at: DOI: 10.31989/ffhd.v5i6.183.

Ning, Z. and Lao, L. (2015) 'Acupuncture for pain management in evidence-based medicine', *Journal of Acupuncture and Meridian Studies*, 8:5, 270–273, Available at: DOI: 10.1016/j.jams.2015.07.012.

Pierson, D. (2017) 'Santa Monica fitness brand Beachbody is fined $3.6 million over automatic renewals', Los Angeles Times, 29 August 2017. Available at: https://www.latimes.com/business/la-fi-beachbody-20170829-story.html (Accessed 28 December 2020).

Safavi, K.C., Cohen, A.B., Ting, D.Y., et al. (2020) 'Health systems as venture capital investors in digital health 2011–2019', *npj Digital Medicine*, 3, 103. Available at: DOI: 10.1038/s41746-020-00311-5 (Accessed 28 December 2020).

Sass, C. (2020) What is Oprah's latest diet? A nutritionist explains the OMD plan, Health. com, 28 January 2020. Available at: https://www.health.com/nutrition/oprah-diet

Sassman and Bulow, A. (2016) Today. Available at: https://www.today.com/health/oprah-winfrey-s-5-go-diet-tricks-weight-loss-t80966

Satija, N. and Sun, L.H. (2019) 'A major funder of the anti-vaccine movement has made millions selling natural health products', The Washington Post, 20 December 2019. Available at: https://www.washingtonpost.com/investigations/2019/10/15/fdc01078-c29c-11e9-b5e4-54aa56d5b7ce_story.html (Accessed 30 December 2020).

Selfridge, N. (2012) 'Acupressure: the evidence presses on', Integrative Medicine Alert, Relias Media [Online], 1 June 2012. Available at: https://www.reliasmedia.com/articles/78333-acupressure-the-evidence-presses-on# (Accessed 28 December 2020).

Shen, P. (1996) *Massage for Pain Relief*, London: Gaia Books Limited.

Southern, A.P. and Jwayyed, S. (2020) *Iodine Toxicity*, Treasure Island, FL: StatPearls. Available at: https://www.ncbi.nlm.nih.gov/books/NBK560770/ (Accessed 27 February 2021).

Suliman, N.A., Mat Taib, C.N., Mohd Moklas, M.A., Adenan, M.I., Hidayat Baharuldin, M.T., and Basir, R. (2016) 'Establishing natural nootropics: recent molecular enhancement influenced by natural nootropic', *Evidence-Based Complementary and Alternative Medicine*, 2016, 4391375. Available at: DOI: 10.1155/2016/4391375 (Accessed 31 December 2020).

Williams, R. (2019) 'The problem with the self-help movement', Medium, 5 October 2019. Available at: https://raybwilliams.medium.com/the-problem-with-the-self-help-movement-ab972ef58728 (Accessed 27 February 2021).

Winfrey, O. (2009) '"How did I let this happen again?"', The Oprah Magazine, January 2009. Available at: http://www.oprah.com/spirit/oprahs-battle-with-weight-gain-o-january-2009-cover/all (Accessed 30 December 2020).

Chapter 9

System Reboot in Health Governance

My medical records are spread in five countries. I had the same primary care physician (PCP) the first 20 years of my life and developed a valuable personal relationship that benefited my health. Then, I had a decade with many different doctors. I have had another PCP for the last 20 years of my life, a person who I know and trust. I have been deeply privileged in my access to healthcare. But the only common denominator in my health has been me. Regardless of how many healthcare interventions I've had—a knee operation at 15, an elbow operation at 43—the sole comprehensive authority on my health has been me, and I find that to be a problem. Why? Because I'm not a medical professional.

On the other hand, it is also possible to see this as an opportunity. Precisely because I'm not a certified medical professional, and because I deeply care about my own body and self, I am able to see myself more objectively and I'm able to dedicate the amount of time, energy, and dedication it takes to keep myself in a healthy, working condition. Let's be honest, that task was never possible for a professional who had to count the minutes they spend on me. And my case is that of a relatively well-off person living in between two of the healthiest health systems on the planet (e.g. the health system available to the US elite and the excellent public health system of oil-rich Norway). In many ways, my experience is unsustainable and even if it was the perfect system (which it is not), for the sake of the rest of the world, this level of in-person personalization of care cannot continue.

DOI: 10.4324/9781003178071-9

Let's leave me for a second and consider Pedro, who lives in Rocinha, the Brazilian shantytown (favela) in Rio di Janeiro, in the hills above the São Conrado neighborhood's Fashion Mall, the shopping mall of the Rio's elite (full disclosure, I bought a nice pair of jeans there back in 2002). Rocinha, population 70,000, is a highly internally mobile community where kids constantly move in and out with parents and relatives depending on the volatile family situation. The assigned family doctor was useful in his childhood, but Pedro is now 18 and currently has no healthcare option. Moreover, that one family doctor was absent (he was on holiday) when Pedro broke his nose in a bicycle accident. The doctor was with another patient when Pedro got a stray gunshot wound last year. There is no accessible, written medical record for Pedro. His records amount to a messy pile of paper files in a file cabinet in a run-down little room at the ground floor of a busy building at the bottom of the favela.

The Brazilian National Immunization Program is recognized for promoting free vaccinations with more than 15 antigens (Sato, 2018). However, Pedro has missed most immunizations because his mother doesn't believe in vaccines, a legacy from his grandfather who marched in the Vaccine Revolt in 1904, and there is nobody questioning his stance (Pinto et al., 2017; Sato 2018).

The opportunity of e-health in Brazil is vast. Around 40% of the population inhabit areas distant from urban centers. These groups are low-income and susceptible to chronic diseases. The basic health network is already decentralized. Until a few years ago, no technology was used. Hospital trips are costly and often not undertaken, or not possible in time for timely intervention. Despite this, Brazil on the whole has good cell phone coverage and most people have cell phones (Hummel, 2016).

I would submit that neither myself nor Pedro have an optimized access to health and that both of us would greatly benefit from a transformation of the health system. That being said, Pedro has more to gain, as he might add years to his life through better systems. I might add months. However, both of us could have far better healthspan, meaning a better quality of life, if we had access to the right data about population health and were offered advice on where to spend our time, what to eat, and what to do in order to maximize our health. Depending on his ills, Pedro's life might, for example, be transformed by a few health apps. Say he develops a mental condition. By having access to an inexpensive online therapist, he might benefit greatly. Similarly, say he develops chronic diabetes. Again, there might be online apps that could teach him to live well with his disease. I could myself benefit from similar solutions, but given my existing access to a great medical system, the benefit would be smaller. Should there be transformational insight available in each sub-field, all of us would benefit from having access to the top expertise. Such would be the case in terms of specialized cancers that would require tumor sequencing, personalized medicine, access to invite-only clinical trials, and expertise only available in a few hospitals.

The discrepancy between Pedro and my access to healthcare would not all resolve through the use of technology. Our economic differences would persist. My physical proximity to Boston's hospital ecosystem would outstrip the value of his access to Rio's medical system although the best in Rio is also very good. My digital skills would mean I could find any published scientific article on my possible illness or could quickly master any app available to monitor a chronic disease, should I develop one. My economic resources would enable me to pay for treatments even if experimental and not covered by insurance. My vast professional network of medical professionals, scientists, and innovators would mean I could rapidly consult experts around the globe for myself or my immediate family. However, in designing a new global health system, we should consider how to even out these differences as much as we can. Is that at all possible, you ask?

How Would It Happen and What Would a Health System Reboot Mean?

First off, my assumption is that we will be able to rapidly digitize the health system, even in remote areas of poorer countries. Even though reboot is a metaphor, it is not simply the act of turning on and off a computer, since without digitalization, no reboot. A system reboot would mean a new approach to the financing, education, information exchange, delivery, and accountability of health. The key tenets of a meaningful reboot would build on the principles of federated data sharing globally, heavy reliance on lowcode or nocode applications, distributed delivery, and wide deployment of inexpensive, interoperable e-health applications. It would also mean a radical upskilling of non-traditional healthcare workers to do 99% of the job, leaving specialists to conduct the 1% of activity having to do with research, monitoring advanced robotic surgery, and analyzing population level health data to design future system wide interventions and system tweaks.

Others, such as Harvard's Regina E. Herzlinger (2021), argue that the consumerization of health, in itself will transform the system. That the personalization of care will have a big effect, is without doubt, even according to current healthcare thought leaders (Pereau, 2019). Changing the incentives, the business models that govern the healthcare system have been part of the moment toward so-called value-based care. As is widely known, the US healthcare system does not incentivize keeping us healthy. Whether or not it makes us better, insurers, employers, the government, and individuals pay for every procedure, prescription, and laboratory test (Lee, 2020).

Yet others feel that it is the mix of consumerism, technology, and the pandemic that are accelerating the future of healthcare (Marx & Padmanabhan, 2020). It is true that the post-COVID reality forces a complete rethink. However, that rethink needs not only to be informed by the latest sci-tech and industry providers but also by behavioral science.

Entrepreneurship and innovation have also been proposed as changemakers in healthcare. Part of my thesis in this book is that this is real. Digital health entrepreneurs and medical professionals, who are keenly aware of needed tweaks to laws and regulation to enable their innovations, and able to influence them, who make use of clever IP protection, mindful of cybersecurity, and with smart business models will indeed make changes possible faster than many realize (Wulfovich & Meyers, 2020).

Some countries have better healthcare than others (Emanuel, 2020) and that may equally well be an inhibitor to innovation. Merely being the best now, or even for the past three decades is not necessarily a perfect predictor of the future, although it is, of course, a strong indication. Note that both the US and the UK have had among the poorest outcomes for COVID-19 so far, despite appearing near the top of most healthcare system rankings for health security in the years prior to the pandemic, for example, ranking 1 and 2, respectively, on the GHS Index (2020). What will happen now to that health system in terms of performance improvements is anybody's guess. My bet is on a systemic shift toward true systemic excellence, and a painful set of parliamentary and Congress reports on what went wrong, but for that to fully permeate the mighty but dinosaur-like NHS, or the federalized and privatized healthcare system of the US, will take time, organizational change, and the influx of resources.

Systemic change in national and global health based on public/private partnerships and new governance paradigms that have global reach but local legitimacy are not only needed but also potentially transformational. Either way, as a matter of fact, global health now must be part of national security policy. The close connection between global health and national security has been visible for decades. Ebola was perhaps the first global scare in this regard, and it was a close call (Afolabi et al., 2020). Had the disease started spreading in urban areas in Africa, we would have soon seen it on European, US, and Asian shores, too. Regrettably, the lessons learned from Ebola were short-lived. The world rapidly moved on as if nothing had happened. Pandemic preparedness plans continued to emphasize the influenza epidemic and not other pandemic threats (Undheim, 2020). At long last, the Biden administration will treat epidemic and pandemic preparedness, health security, and global health as top national security priorities (The White House, 2021).

What forces currently comprise the medical profession and its institutional infrastructure? Essentially, the entire system is built out of seven basic components. First, physicians play a central role as arbitors, orchestrators, and authority figures on what constitutes quality care, health assessment, and optimal treatment plans. Second, the primary practice which also includes a small set of nurses and administrators, the institutional setting of mass delivered urgent care in the form of a hospital system of physical buildings and health workers of various types. Third, an industrial complex of pharma companies as well as an associated supply chain which also includes the industries involved with maintaining the current physical infrastructure of hospitals and primary care facilities. Fourth, a set of technologies, medical devices, and machines and the engineers who operate them, as well as the tech industry and occasionally startups who innovate and produce these technologies and devices. Fifth, a system of reimbursement (either publicly or privately financed) including insurance companies. Sixth, a group of people defined as "patients" who frequent the system in two ways, either as part of annual checkups or as part of urgent care episodes (injuries and diseases). Seventh, the final component is a regulatory system that governs the legal relationships between them.

The fact that the primary care profession (and the medical profession overall) might not be as essential to public health as they themselves (and their lobby) think is a politically sensitive topic. Yet, given their low numbers in proportion to other health factors, the loss of a pivotal role of PCPs in the increasingly important everyday delivery of behavioral health or chronic care by health apps as well as telehealth nurses, there can be no hiding of the fact that four groups are far more important to the future of global health.

First, the emerging cadre of (a) innovators (sci-tech engineers) are already bringing step-up change in the speed, intensity, and impact of data in healthcare. Their role is equally important as intrapreneurs and as entrepreneurs. Second, upskilled nurses, who may—in greater numbers—be able to take on many or most of the functions in primary care, have shown tremendous agility and utility in the COVID-19 pandemic as they are hugely more determinant in the outcome than doctors not only because of their numbers but because of the skills that they have in basic healthcare as well as their empathy skills. Third, empowered patients, who, to a large degree must (and can) bring "healthcare to the edge", meaning to themselves, much the same way that has happened to technology at large with the Internet of Things revolution. Individuals are the last mile of healthcare apps, they go on the internet to check what their medical symptoms mean, to get instructions on how to take medication or how to live with their chronic diseases. In short, healthcare can only scale when it is 99% carried out by the people who need the care, not by a caretaker. Fourth, the emergent category of health AIs in the form of behavioral health apps, which need far less practitioners to run, although the human design and monitoring role remain important.

The core tenet of this proposal is that it depends on convincing the current health profession that their role will need to become significantly less dominant in the health system of the future. This does not necessarily mean a loss of privilege, salary, or prestige, but it does mean that they need to step aside to a far greater degree and get out of the way of progress. Global society simply cannot educate enough doctors to meet the demand, if by a doctor you mean; somebody schooled for 5–8 years and trained on the job for 2–6 years depending on the country's system. One study found 16 African countries with no medical school (Boulet et al., 2007). There is also no need to maintain that barrier. A great many tasks could be accomplished much faster, safer, and with far superior impact with a system without this bottleneck.

This shift needs to happen in three ways. First, by letting computers carry out the vast majority of clinical decision making, e.g. screening who should see a doctor versus who should be diagnosed at a distance by a chatbot, digital health app, digital therapeutics behavioral solutions, or a nurse practitioner. Second, by outsourcing 90% of the remaining work to medical intermediaries who are trained online, part time, and part of a distributed health workforce. This, in addition, to training many more community nurses to ensure that a gradation of health competence is available on every patch of the globe. Third, by augmenting individuals to perform most of their own healthcare as empowered selfcare.

These three shifts can only happen on a global scale if there is political will, buy-in from patient groups, support from industry, and if the medical profession supports it. In addition, experiments need to be carried out regionally as to what would happen once such a system starts to scale. The first bottleneck is not just the physician scarcity, but its uneven global distribution, as well as the necessary backlash from the profession itself. However, I'm confident that can be dealt with given the stakes. What new bottlenecks will start to appear and how to address those? The systemic constraints are likely to be combination of technical, skills based, and medical.

The Role of Technology Augmentation

Many are those who feel a single makeshift change would—or will—transform healthcare. Often, they put their faith in sci-tech to be the salient factor. In *Deep Medicine*, Topol (2019), himself a medical doctor and a researcher, argues artificial intelligence (AI) can transform everything doctors do, from notetaking and medical scans to diagnosis and treatment, greatly cutting down the cost of medicine and reducing human mortality. That may be so.

Yet, AI alone cannot transform anything. AI-hype cannot either. People can. Intelligence-based medicine (Chang, 2020) which makes use of both AI and human cognition may stand a chance at transforming clinical medicine and healthcare overall. The disruptive forces driving change in the healthcare industry include new operating and business models in response to profound changes that include real-world data from electronic medical records, health wearables, Internet of Things, digital media, social media, and more (Elton & O'Riordan, 2016).

Technology must be used in a wise, sustainable manner in order to have that effect. Likewise, even the sum of all tremendously interesting e-health applications out there could fail to transform the healthcare system. Evidence for my claim is that e-health has been available for decades already, and even though individual companies and apps and use cases are beginning to make themselves noticed, each of them is only slowly transforming the system. The tech change must be part of an overall approach of systemic change and mindful of the various hard-to-control aspects of system dynamics once all such disruptive forces are unleashed. You need no futurist to tell you that telehealth will become up to 50% of healthcare short-term and will start to approximate 80% of healthcare fairly shortly, unless the system enacts irrational self-protective measures to protect former monopolies and power relationships. Some of that is likely to happen but not likely to prevail for many decades, given the opening up of medical platforms for all to judge for themselves. Interoperability is likely the biggest barrier and a far more tricky issue than technology or even the resistance to telehealth by health practitioners because of the skill gap or gradual perceived power loss (in reality, physician experts will not lose power but will merely shift roles toward becoming hybrid engineer–consultant–scientists).

However, to enact this change, the medical profession needs to allow it (or be convinced of its merits) and technology needs to become fully self-service while still connected to the major institutional nodes that will make sensors and monitoring effective and connected, and who will ensure the upskilling and reskilling of nurses, community health personnel, and individuals engaged in taking care of their own health. Truly distributed healthcare is one thing, but truly distributed health tech is a whole another thing. Without usable, re-configurable, hot-pluggable tech that can be operated by locals with minimal training, less technology is often better than more technology. This does not mean that the technology itself needs to be simple, far from the case (which is why the old development adage of "appropriate technology" is questionable). Rather, it means that the way it is implemented needs to be well thought out and cannot just be a foreign government donor grant directly to a national government or a NGO-project without local embedding.

What Is Lowcode or Nocode and Why Does It Matter to Health Tech?

I have used the phrase "lowcode or nocode" a few times by now, and I might need to quickly explain what I mean. First consider what Microsoft's Excel did for advanced statistics. Statistical software in the 1980s required not only deep statistical insight but also in-depth knowledge of software coding and computer interfaces. I know this because back then, as a teenager I was helping my father execute such analysis using SPSS, the proprietary statistics program initially released in 1968 and much later (in 2009) acquired by IBM. Back then, SPSS was gradually implementing a clunky graphical user interface, but advanced modeling still brought back the coding window.

Enter Excel on Mac in 1985 (and on Windows in 1987), which didn't replace SPSS but made advanced statistics available to the rising class of financial traders on Wall Street, thousands of whom would not have had the patience to fiddle with computer code since their main motive was to analyze data in order to execute trades. Fast forward to 2006 and Google Sheets took sharing and convenience to another level and by 2012, the Google Docs suite changed document collaboration forever with a web application doing the same. Importantly, it should be noted that these Google products were results of acquisitions and did not originate within Google. Soon others followed suit, Airtable (2012), Notion (2016), and Coda (2019) have all become nocode trailblazers in the social database space, creating a "nocode movement" (Choudhury, 2020).

By 2003, Wordpress issued its blogging software which enabled building websites capable of content management (of blogs and associated content) without coding skills. Its initial focus was on aesthetics, web standards, and usability. Wordpress today powers near 40% of the internet. Fifty thousand Wordpress plugins extend the capabilities of the site and increase its complexity (Choudhury, 2020). Because it paved the way and has become a victim of its own success, there are now far simpler ways to build a website than Wordpress, but that's another story.

Over the last 5 years, lowcode and nocode have begun to permeate visual interfaces to integrate apps and automate workflows in industrial automation as well. You can now run a wide variety of robots on Ready Robotics' Forge/OS operating system which includes a lowcode toolkit (a so-called SDK) on which they managed to retrain coal miners to program robots within days. This was a task that previously would have taken engineers months to do.

Finally, I should point out that whether an end-user application (or an app platform) is built with code or without, there is always an element of code. Furthermore, as the CEOs of Ready Robotics as well as the CEO of Vention, an automation company, shared with me in a podcast interview

(Augmentedpodcast.co, 2021), if you want to be an innovator in the emerging workforce, you still need coding skills (or at least the coding mindset of tinkering) to be at the forefront of building new applications. I try to impart this fact to my children.

Is There a Role for e-Government in Health?

Most people would somewhat rightly consider e-government complex and prone to failure (Undheim, 2008). E-health is infinitely more complex because health is not to the same extent as other necessary services controlled by the government. In some countries, a vast majority of the system has been privatized. Even if the system as a whole is based on public healthcare, the delivery is quite often outsourced to private providers. The systems are by now almost exclusively built by private contractors, which is largely a good thing, because the monolithic internally built health systems of the past were massive drags on efficiency and had extremely poor usability.

Paradoxically, because health and e-health are so complex, the rationale for change is even greater, and the promise of technology to tackle the most persistent and fickle of the system's problems is far greater than with other services of public interest.

The role of government in health is the first and foremost in setting standards, fostering interoperability between health tech providers, and in stimulating innovation to ensure health systems catch emerging waves of innovations before their current systems go stale. This is an ongoing process with faster cycles than ever before. To perform that role well, governments must procure the expertise to do the job. Most of the expertise can be accessed through advisory councils, although in the crucial middle layers of the bureaucracy, there is no substitute for excellence, otherwise bureaucratic procedures abound and start to cripple the system.

In addition to interoperability, one sweeping move which is within the powers of government would be to mandate (or at least strongly recommend) that all health apps should be lowcode or nocode, so that nobody using them, whether it be hospitals, primary care practices, or behavioral health app startups ever get locked into a code base they cannot themselves adapt and tweak using their own product developers and operators. Part of the problem with infrastructure-scale technology of any flavor is that it rapidly becomes too monolithic, too big to fail, and attains a complexity that belies the functionality it serves. Even creating a service as simple as booking an online appointment or allowing people to check a test result online can become a huge technical challenge if a practice area is locked into a health record system where the user interface and code base were developed decades ago with the explicit intent to lock in the client (Figure 9.1).

Figure 9.1 System reboot.

Reshaping Multi-Tiered Governance in the Middle of a Global Crisis

With increased reliance on distributed behavioral technology across jurisdictions and in a hybrid scenario of online and in-person delivery for liminal cases, healthcare needs highly advanced multi-level governance to work well, at global national, regional, local, and individual levels. If that sounds complicated, that's about right. However, it is not impossible, and here's how to proceed the way I see it.

Reforming the WHO's Functions

Global healthcare needs to be connected to diplomatic, foreign aid, security, research, and military capability in a networked fashion, with immediate response capability worldwide, regardless of where the health infraction occurs and from whom or what. Right now, that function is carried out by the World Health Organization, a treaty-based organization. The last time that treaty was updated was in 1948 when the organization was created, 3 years after the United Nations (UN) itself.

Despite the ongoing pandemic, there is now growing dissent around the WHO (Babones, 2020) and for good reason. The organization is unfit to carry out the increasingly pressing global health challenges it is confronted with. Part of that challenge is that the UN itself is an organization in desperate need of a full overhaul, not a reform but a reconstitution. The keywords describing its ills are well known: lack of transparency, layers of bureaucracy, and lack of accountability to the citizens of the world (given that the UN is only accountable to member states not to individuals).

Criticizing the WHO is not the same as abandoning it. We are in the unfortunate situation that we need to fix the ship while it is at sea. Short-term, the WHO needs to quadruple its budget, needs 100% coverage of all the world's nations, and needs a big army of labs distributed across the world capable of virus sequencing to the tune of millions a day. There really is no point in not coordinating such sequencing globally, even if connecting up labs doesn't need to mean relocating lab resources but rather connecting dots digitally. The fact that different nations have different speed and capacity of virus sequencing is not helping anybody.

Long term, the mission of the WHO is too narrow in scope, too limited in its operative capability, and lacks enforcement mechanisms sufficient to match a global pandemic, even a relatively minor threat such as COVID-19 (minor only compared to health threats that are looming in the next decades). Moreover, its mandate is not viewed as sufficiently representative of individuals. It is, rightly so, viewed as a vehicle of its member states. But citizens of various nation states don't have empathy for member states (which in the case of WHO includes authoritarian states such as North Korea), they have empathy of other individuals—even if they live somewhere else on the planet. A renewed WHO, or a future iteration with a similar remit, cannot be treaty based, it must have a basis in true representative democracy. Think that is a radical thought? Far from it, arguing for a reboot is a fairly conservative sentiment, it may be the only thing that could save remnants of the status quo that conservatives so treasure: history, legacy, tradition, even the nation states so revered by some. The most probable scenario, e.g. the lack of such a reform, would only mean we are marching steadily toward a collapse of the current world order as opposed to an orderly transition to a global state of sorts.

Reorganizing National Healthcare

National healthcare needs to be decoupled from short-term political concerns and needs to go into a decade plus long planning cycle that is protected from election friction. Most countries have elections of various shapes and forms at regular timeframes, 2–8 years apart at most. That timeframe is both too short and too long for the challenges facing us now. Transforming national healthcare has been underway in every nation state for as long as they have had health systems. There is a need to decouple health from politics. One way to do so is to create national health endowments that have a longer governance cycle and is run by boards, perhaps as listed public benefit companies, and not by politicians alone. We need to bring the leadership resources of all parts of society to bear on health. Likewise, national voluntary health organizations can be helpful, but without coordinating their efforts with other players, they are inefficient and risk diverting health spend to the wrong disease or cause. The solution to this problem is to run public debates on what the priority should be any given decade, obviously readjusting slightly to surprising challenges (such as a pandemic).

For example, a small island country territory such as the UK should be able to eradicate diseases, even fully manage serious chronic diseases, if they simply prioritize a few of them each few years. The effects would be stunning. Imagine getting a handle on the obesity challenge within 2 years alone. Then, one could move into maintenance mode and move on to other challenges. The savings to the overall health system would be tremendous. What I'm saying is that the "grand challenges" logic and approach that has been tried for global health essentially, as a short-term fix, now also needs to be tried for national health.

In the process, I think we will also find out how paternalistic this type of "grand challenges" thinking can be at the national level (imagine you are an African country being told by the Gates Foundation or others that the priority of health resource spending from international donors for the next decade is going to be Malaria when your own Cabinet had wanted to spend it on West Nile or Influenza). The way out of paternalistic health policy is debate. The debate should be on questioning a tacit assumption that prioritization leads to greatest impact. Once that's clarified, the only debate is on the sequence of action, not on the budget spread across each initiative or disease.

If governments continue to use regulation as a wedge to unlock healthcare efficiencies, the way they have paved the way for COVID-19 emergency use authorizations and fast tracking of clinical trial approvals for vaccines, this may unlock and rewire entire value chains across healthcare both nationally and globally. It is notable that not only does this benefit huge players like Pfizer, but because of their collaboration with German startup BioNTech, that startup has been lifted into a new sphere as well. Similarly, MIT spinout Moderna, founded all the way back in 2010, who had not got any therapies approved yet, now has their moment and given that their mRNA platform has been EUA-approved for COVID-19, are poised to benefit greatly also for all of their other clinical trial tracks.

Regional Healthcare Empowerment

Regional healthcare needs to be viewed in connection with, and should be run by, the institutions that actually deliver the care, not as an administrative level. If there are regional levels that don't correspond to the adequate level of health delivery, these levels should be abolished or drastically revamped and empowered by larger governance units, national, or supranational (e.g. a revamped WHO). For example, a regional level (sub national) that is not responsible for, or does not run a hospital system, and without a substantial telehealth capacity that reaches every citizen with messaging, advice, medicines, and care 24/7, has no meaning as a governance unit. What this could mean in practical terms is that if a regional government depends on a privatized hospital system, the owner of that hospital system needs to take on governance discussions on parity with that government, with not only equal amount of transparency requirements but also with the benefit of the health political power that comes with such increased responsibility.

Regional levels can take a crucial role in redistributing local resources and coordinating logistics and supply chains, as well as in being keepers of shared, expensive infrastructure and machinery, such as gene sequencers, supercomputers, and the like. This function will be especially powerful if those shared infrastructure items are made available either digitally or for shared use in a lab environment, and even more so if the regional level takes a role in reskilling and upskilling. However, in terms of health, such levels have no legitimacy if they do not possess crucial infrastructure assets. Should weaknesses be spotted at this level, and you can look at any health benchmark report to find it, that's where WHO or its emerging equivalent, needs to play its role.

A truly globalized view on regional healthcare might mean that the WHO comes in to build a lab, even a hospital and diverts resources from another region in order to even out the health coverage. Those labs could be virtual or in-person but would need to be ambulatory and mobile given the enormity of that task. Truly egregious health inequity, such as one currently can observe in sub-Saharan Africa, is ultimately destructive to the world order that the multilateral system was supposed to protect. It is also morally reprehensible, and it goes against common sense for humanity as a whole. That much doesn't require much democratic debate, although the implications do.

Local Healthcare—The Harbinger of Distributed Health

Local healthcare must be upgraded to certain minimum requirements around the world, if not by total service level, at least with sensory and alert capability at speeds and sophistication that almost matches that of the most advanced healthcare system. Otherwise, we get a race to the middle where nobody is happy with the level of care or the ability to respond to public health crises and where local epidemics rapidly spill over to become regional, national, or global concerns. For this to work, highly advanced technology sensor networks as well as financial incentives that bypass existing local, regional, or national constraints need to be put in place.

The question of how this is to be financed is clearly a complex one. Financing schemes will have to be devised in which there are sufficient externalities for all parties who chip in. MIT economist Andrew Lo has recently come up with a plethora of suggestions toward global healthcare finance (https://alo.mit.edu/topic/healthcare-finance/), many of which are worth scaling up. For example, Lo and his collaborators speak of the potential for subscription schemes for portfolios of vaccines instead of awaiting single-payer solutions for individual shots. Also, previous chapters have indicated the need for specific types of pervasive sensors that are or soon will become available, whether in the form of wearable sensors (pulse, movement, etc.) or in terms of sensors embedded in smart cities and public infrastructure (air quality, etc.). In addition to being developed as licensed technologies on behalf of startups or industrial players, it is conceivable that they could be available as subscription plans for national governments and multinational corporations which have an interest in monitoring the globe to increase the chances of their own survival, and for increased resiliency and visibility of emerging shocks to the system.

Local healthcare is also to a wide extent the delivery level where interventions either need to be physically delivered (did the item make it, was the service executed?), monitored (is it proceeding correctly?), or verified (did a certain intervention take place?). Where one might think that automation is the salient feature of this emerging system, it is increasingly a mix of automation and augmentation that will make the biggest difference.

When individuals are enabled through being augmented through technology, they stand a chance at far greater efficiencies, better outcomes, and certainly less chronic illness because they are embedded in a system that can compensate for individual or local constraints, can provide just-in-time advice or training, and may even be able to deliver medical care and equipment through 3D printing.

Incidentally, the biggest healthcare discrepancy of all, that of a highly differentiated ability to pay, can also best be remedied at the local level, and if not that, at the regional level. Even in deprived areas, there are resources that are misaligned. Moreover, compassion is widely dispersed throughout the globe. If we can use technology to make healthcare needs much more obviously visible, that will generate and channel compassion more efficiently. For example, if you knew that a child who lives on your street cannot afford a critical medical treatment this week, you would be incented to contribute financially to that child's treatment. On a wider scale, one could envision a global buddy system where each child was connected to multiple others (and to adults) in a chain that would ensure that no person truly was an island left to their own concerns. We already possess the technological capability to put such a system in place, although we need to resolve some privacy concerns and scale up and pay for the functionality to go live.

Finally, distributed healthcare must be highly tech enabled so that personalized responsibility for one's own health is not only an option for the wealthy, but for anyone. To make that happen, we need to make progress in Augmented Reality, IoT-enabled health devices, Personalized medicine, and Remote population health monitoring specifically. Costs for the above need to be drastically brought down through financing R&D, collaboration, and executing joint procurement initiatives across countries and governance levels.

Population Health on Steroids

Population health is a much talked about and poorly understood area, perhaps because it initially referred to periodic statistics which was a great innovation when they arrived (and allowed generals, mayors, and health ministers to monitor and intervene based on some level of data) have been only incrementally improving every century or so.

Now, with the potential of big data streams emerging from IoT devices in people's hand, there is the prospect of true, always-on monitoring which might in some not so distant future result in always-on triage of patients, anticipating when patients will deteriorate and benefiting from comparisons to large numbers of patients in similar conditions. The promise would be to achieve a level of proactivity that would lead to prevention, not intervention based on disease deterioration, which is the case now.

Individual Healthcare's Trust Imperative

Part of the progress also depends not only on innovative service provision (e.g. of digital therapeutics) but also depends on individual willingness to experiment with, use, and maintain their usage of novel digital health services. For that, trust has to be developed, not only with individual providers but also with the health systems individuals are part of. That process ebbs and flows and will depend on perceived benefits of being engaged. There is no shortcut to success with trust, it evolves over time, and can be taken away in an instant in case of a legitimate (or even illegitimate) trust concern. This is why the anti-vaxx movement needs to be taken seriously as a bundle of concerns that cannot be ignored, whether it comes from an elite of US mothers with children who have contracted autism, from a French electorate

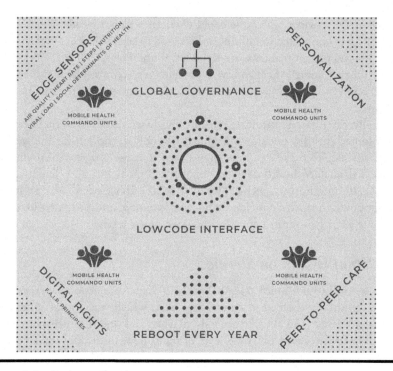

Figure 9.2   System reboot process.

having experienced public health scandals where the government demonstrably was to blame, from disadvantaged ethnic minorities who mistrust the government for historically legitimate reasons, from elite natural wellness fanatics who operate in a post-scientific paradigm, or from conspiracy theorists who have grievances stemming from other injustices that they bundle together in vaccine hesitancy and fake news. This is why privacy scandals have to be remedied immediately by assurances, punishments, and confirmed changes in technology. This is also why big tech needs to be kept in check by a proactive regulator way before they become "big" or worse, too big to fail. Already today, tech is medicine and medicine is tech.

That dynamic is not in place in any existing jurisdictions at present but is also not rocket science. With the right vision, incentives, public–private partnerships and strategic and tactical rollout, it can happen within this decade alone.

The Health Reboot Process

A health system reboot cannot begin bottom-up, top-down, or nationally. Those partial reboots would be like trying to reboot a computer by simply turning off the screen or unplugging the keyboard or webcam. The parts of the system are mere accessories. The system is far greater than the sum of its parts. The system dynamics are such that we have to start with the system itself. How do we do that?

First, we have to build the case that change is needed. I've spent this book doing so, and many others have argued convincingly for years. The COVID-19 pandemic as well as the probability that other pandemics, possibly far worse, could ravage the earth, as well as the impending ecological cataclysm which brings environmental health to the forefront of human health and longevity, have all helped this cause. I'm not going to spend more time on this now. Suffice to say: even if change is needed, that's not enough. COVID-19, for all its ramifications, has so far only led to a partial reboot of society and its healthcare setup. I think one of the universal conclusions from COVID-19 is that the global healthcare system just isn't there. The problem isn't even that it's not working. It is non-existent. Whatever patchwork we have in place certainly does need a reboot, but only after there are some new components installed. Merely rebooting the embryonic system would simply open it up again to the numerous systemic vulnerabilities were are currently experiencing (drastic variability of healthcare delivery and service levels across the globe and even within cities and communities purely based on socio-economic status).

Second, there has to be a credible plan. I believe this little chapter contains the embryo of such a plan. There are details to work out. There is agreement to be had. There are systems dynamics to be figured out. There is an entire global health profession to convince. There is work to do among the world's governments, donors, industry, and patient organizations. But it's all doable and important. Also, we currently have a global healthcare crisis which provides a testing ground for how a system like this would work. We need a system like this, not in 5 years, not in 15 years, but today.

The core of my suggested plan is first, to agree that the system needs to change, to be willing to rebuild the system from the ground up, and to take the consequences of the sunk costs hat invariably will be lost in the restructuring process. For this process to work, we have to put in place near term incentives both for incumbents, disrupters, and individuals. Part of that incentive structure could be organized through a blockchain ledger. I don't want to minimize the importance of getting this first part right. I'm not suggesting that every individual has the potential to transform the global healthcare system. But I am suggesting that with the right incentives, individuals will drive the healthcare economy in a much better direction than when the system was run by oligarchs (whether of governmental or private origin).

What does it mean to "agree"? I'm talking about a converging opinion (not too wide disagreement) among a plurality of voices representing each of the key

disruptive forces—sci-tech, policy/regulatory, business, and civil society organizations and movements—that we need to move forward with a reboot of the
global healthcare system. The reboot process is as much a mindset change as it is
a software and hardware upgrade.

Furthermore, I need to point out that what I'm suggesting here has nothing to do with socialism. It is not socialist to suggest that health is a political
instrument and has political consequences, it is common sense. This is a caveat
that needs to be inserted to any book published in the US because of the toxic
and misguided ideological debates that are raging here this decade where health
is unfairly politicized. Health is by default political, no question, but political
health needs to be no less toxic of a topic than political economy itself. As a
reminder, throughout the last three decades, the intertwining of politics and
the economy have been understood by political scientists and economists as so
closely related that they cannot be studied or acted upon in isolation, and so the
concept of studying the political economy as a whole was born. We are slowly
about to experience that health and tech, in combination, are being added to that
mix. Over the next few decades, we are moving into a *healthspan-empowering
political economy* of sorts powered by sci-tech advances (not an elegant phrase
but bear with me).

Over the past decades, it should be clear that with globalization, infectious
diseases, and pandemics, the same is becoming true about the need for a politics
of health (Bambra, Fox, & Scott-Samuel, 2005), or indeed we need to build a
notion of political health (Bias, 2020). To my US readers, what I'm suggesting is
compatible with furthering individual freedom of the all-American ilk. In fact,
it might be the only thing that can salvage individual freedom in an age where
it is being threatened from all sides.

Second, we have to rebuild a healthcare system from the edge and up, meaning it has to first become a distributed system built like Lego bricks and blocks
so that the sum of its parts communicate with the rest until it becomes a global
system. This is not the way things are now. It is, however, the way other fields
of society are moving, even manufacturing. What this will require is to build
healthcare tools that can be operated with minimal skills, essentially near consumer grade applications or at least nocode type apps that can be worked on by
engineers without a medical degree. For that to happen, medical professionals
will have to redefine their role in the system. They can no longer be the central
nodes, for that they are too few and too inconsequential in the overall system.
Rather, they have to be the glue that keep it together and the consultants and
shepherds of a new process where human expert medical advice is only one of a
tenfold of processes that need to work for the system to operate at global scale.
We don't have to wait for pervasive AI to make this happen, suffice to refocus
medical attention on crafting and advising systems instead of representing and

protecting the monopoly of interventions by a medical establishment that inevitably can be destructive bottlenecks.

Third, even if the strategic plan and objectives are shared and established, there also has to be a joint implementation plan. What needs to be said is that when I say "plan" I don't mean a document concocted by politicians or business leaders. I mean a broad agreement developed in civil society between enough actors who have taken part in debates, media, and policy meetings, that the end result is to begin a stepwise process to make the needed health reboot a reality.

At this point, I should clarify that a reboot would benefit innovators the most. What that means is that the industry as well as the professional establishment might not come to the realization that a reboot is needed, or may not have the flexibility of mindset to realize the benefits involved by increasing the pie as opposed to trying to take a bigger piece of the existing pie.

However, the possibility of expanding healthcare across the globe opens up so many business models and an unprecedented scale, that big tech, for one, will not let that opportunity sail by. I'm not the first to observe that the next goal for big tech is healthcare dominance, having first established their hegemony over content, media, and political speech. Established industry giants that don't embrace health tech are unlikely to be significant players 20 years from now. Nation states that either hang onto their national welfare states, attempt to build welfare states at this late stage in the game, or simply ride out their power surge, will similarly find themselves rapidly outgunned. The power structures of the future are relatively squarely aligned with ownership of the production and execution of health.

Conclusion

Some might think that this chapter has expressed visions without basis in political economy realities. If you are one of those people, you have not spent enough time at the World Economic Forum in Davos, in university lunch rooms, in patient corridors during COVID-19, watching the US Capitol riots, in the locker rooms of youth sports—or on TikTok. Change is coming as surely as stasis has built up over time. The only question in my mind is timing. I could be off by a decade or two, but whether it happens swiftly or slowly, it likely cannot be stopped. Not because I'm a technology determinist, far from it. It is the combined forces of disruption (social, political, economical and technological) that have set in motion this process, but technology can help alleviate some of the negative fallout by smoothing out the asymptotes and creating more value through the painful transitions.

A health system reboot does not have to rely on altruism. The positive externalities are starting to pile up and are visible to all. Technologies have matured to a level where unprecedented changes will be realized within this decade alone, even if interoperability stalls. The effect of inaction, however, would be detrimental to the world's poor, and already is. It will also come back to bite the elites and faster than many think. Markets would shrink, consumer purchasing power would dwindle, and people would continue to be in the COVID-induced survival mode throughout the decade. Is it possible that we choose this option? I'd say it is 50/50 at this point.

Similarly, the current military–industrial complex, and even the G-20 or G-7 countries, have started to realize that they have reached their apex. This much was already stated by the Club of Rome's Limits to Growth back in 1972, 1 year before I was born. Human beings currently have a resource use beyond the carrying capacity of the planet. That cannot continue, even though it did last 50 years longer than the elite prophets at the Club of Rome had hoped. There is no doubt in my mind that health tech is part of the solution to ecosystem collapse. If we implement pervasive health tech platforms in this decade combined with global constitutional reform that ensures the accountability of a reboot, there is still hope to retain parts of the current world order (for those who have that goal). For me, I would simply want to ensure that my children's children live on a planet that I would recognize would I still be alive.

KEY TAKEAWAYS AND REFLECTIONS

1. Try to describe in your own words what is meant by a "reboot in health governance"?

2. Examine Figure 9.2. System Reboot Process. How would such a process get off the ground? What are the selling points toward governments, private sector, nonprofits, and citizens?

3. Assuming you think health tech is a positive force overall, what should be done to accelerate it? What is the role of governments versus the role of industry versus the role of consumers?

4. Imagine a health system that is drastically simplified. Try to name a few principles it would be based on?

One of the big items to figure out is whether health is the issue that the shift needs to begin with, or whether this is all part of an even bigger picture of global governance. I happen to think that there is a need to overhaul global governance more generally, but that's a wider discussion which I'll tackle in a forthcoming book on the future of global democracy. Having said that, I will already tackle some of the ramifications of that stance in my conclusion to the book, which is what I'll turn to next.

References

Afolabi, M.O., Folayan, M.O., Munung, N.S., Yakubu, A., Ndow, G., Jegede, A., Ambe, J., and Kombe, F. (2020) 'Lessons from the Ebola epidemics and their applications for COVID-19 pandemic response in sub-Saharan Africa', *Developing World Bioethics*, Available at: DOI: 10.1111/dewb.12275. Advance online publication.

Augmentedpodcast.co (2021) 'Augmented – the industry 4.0 podcast'. Available at: https://www.augmentedpodcast.co/.

Babones, S. (2020) 'Yes, blame WHO for its disastrous coronavirus response', Foreign Policy, 27 May 2020. Available at: https://foreignpolicy.com/2020/05/27/who-health-china-coronavirus-tedros/.

Bambra, C., Fox, D., and Scott-Samuel, A. (2005) 'Towards a politics of health', *Health Promotion International*, 20:2, 187–193. Available at: DOI: 10.1093/heapro/dah608.

Bias, T. (2020) 'Public health is always political', Think Global Health, 5 May 2020. Available at: https://www.thinkglobalhealth.org/article/public-health-always-political.

Boulet, J., Bede, C., McKinley, D., and Norcini, J. (2007) 'An overview of the world's medical schools', *Medical Teacher*, 29, 20–26. Available at: http://citeseerx.ist.psu.edu/viewdoc/download?doi=10.1.1.469.1843&rep=rep1&type=pdf#.

Chang, A. (2020) *Intelligence-Based Medicine*. Cambridge, MA: Academic Press.

Choudhury, A. (2020) 'A brief history of no-code', Medium.com, 2 March 2020. Available at: https://medium.com/@iCanAutomate/a-brief-history-of-no-code-59c532d90b7f (Accessed 15 February 2021).

Elton, J. and O'Riordan, A. (2016) Healthcare Disrupted: Next Generation Business Models and Strategies. New York: Wiley.

Emanuel, E.J. (2020) *Which Country has the World's Best Health Care?* New York: PublicAffairs.

GHS Index (2020) 'Global Health Security Index, joint project of the Nuclear Threat Initiative (NTI) and the Johns Hopkins Center for Health Security (JHU) developed with The Economist Intelligence Unit (EIU)'. Available at: https://www.ghsindex.org/.

Herzlinger, R.E. (2021) *Innovating in Healthcare: Creating Breakthrough Services, Products, and Business Models*, New York: Wiley.

Hummel, G.S. (2016) 'Brazil eHealth – overview, trends & opportunities. Consulate General of the Kingdom of the Netherlands'. Available at: https://www.rvo.nl/sites/default/files/2017/01/Brazil%20Healthcare%20-%20Guilherme%20Hummel.pdf.

Lee, V. S. (2020) *The Long Fix: Solving America's Health Care Crisis with Strategies that Work for Everyone,* New York: Norton.

Marx, E.W, Padmanabhan, P. (2020) *Healthcare Digital Transformation: How Consumerism, Technology and Pandemic are Accelerating the Future,* London: Productivity Press.

Pereau, K. (2019) *The Digital Health Revolution.* TranscendIT Health.

Pinto, L.F., Harzheim, E., Hauser, L., D'Avila, O.P., Gonçalves, M.R., Travassos, P., and Pessanha, R. (2017) Primary Health Care quality in Rocinha - Rio de Janeiro, Brazil, from the perspective of children caregivers and adult users. A qualidade da Atenção Primária à Saúde na Rocinha – Rio de Janeiro, Brasil, na perspectiva dos cuidadores de crianças e dos usuários adultos', *Ciencia & saude coletiva,* 22:3, 771–781, Available at: DOI: 10.1590/1413–81232017223.33132016.

Sato, A. (2018) 'What is the importance of vaccine hesitancy in the drop of vaccination coverage in Brazil?', *Revista de Saude Publica,* 52, 96, Available at: DOI: 10.11606/S1518–8787.2018052001199.

The White House (2021) 'National Security Directive on United States Global Leadership to strengthen the international COVID-19 response and to advance global health security and biological preparedness', The White House, 21 January 2021. Available at: https://www.whitehouse.gov/briefing-room/statements-releases/2021/01/21/-national-security-directive-united-states-global-leadership-to-strengthen-the-international-covid-19-response-and-to-advance-global-health-security-and-biological-preparedness/.

Topol, E. (2019) *Deep Medicine.* New York: Basic Books.

Undheim, T.A. (2008) 'Best practices in eGovernment–on a knife-edge between success and failure', *European Journal of ePractice,* 2:2, 23–46. Available at: https://www.slideshare.net/epracticejournal/undheim-presentation.

Undheim, T.A. (2020) *Pandemic Aftermath.* Austin, TX: Atmosphere Press.

Wulfovich, S, Meyers, A. (2020) *Digital Health Entrepreneurship,* New York: Springer.

Chapter 10

Conclusions— How to Capture the Health Opportunity Window to Reboot

This decade's health tech alone may provide the biggest opportunity to transform healthcare that we have seen in a century. That fact does not determine that the commensurate impact will be felt by everyone, indeed even by anyone. That window may also close, and once it does, we are stuck with pockets of excellence and pockets of mediocrity (or worse), which is only damaging to the whole system over time.

Throughout this book, I have pointed out how tech alone does not accomplish anything. It remains true that tech tees up the opportunity and provides the opportunity to leapfrog decades worth of legacy processes in the healthcare system, but if we don't do it right, tech can in the end prove destructive and damaging to the healthcare system. As I've pointed out, doing tech right means doing tech with people in mind. But before summarizing the best practice, let's summarize what there is to know about bad practice, which is often more instructive.

Tech can lock us into procedures that are cumbersome, vendors who exploit and balloon overall costs, or worse further obfuscate computer systems which provide cybersecurity vulnerabilities that not only endanger privacy but also threaten to destroy confidence in healthcare provision and the authority of healthcare

DOI: 10.4324/9781003178071-10

providers. That's why the system reboot I suggest will encompass changes to governance structures and processes at all levels—global, national, and regional—and will take participation from all sectors (government, private, and nonprofit).

The possibility to conduct a reasonable amount of healthcare implementation "magic" is very real but hinges on the technology-enabled business models and incentives that can be put into place by creative solutions with short-time horizons for visible return of investment. That's why learning from pilots quickly and scaling up so one does not get stuck in "pilot purgatory" is important. Partnering with startups who have a quicker pace and different thinking is equally important. Being willing to scrap much of the existing system is also crucial but has real cost and is painful to incumbents. Instead, I'm advocating stepwise installing significant new features and then doing regular reboots—enabling us to benefit from both existing functionality and new enhancements. Done right, the payback could be measured in millions of lives, billions of healthspan years, and increased lifespan for the world's population.

What might a reboot look like in more concrete terms? What I have in mind would be: upskilling the health workforce to become more interchangeable, flexible, and hybrid (remote, in-person, and everything in between), periodically shuffling global health priorities to avoid a myopic focus on grand challenges, digitizing the entire healthcare value chain, embedding open technology platforms across healthcare so that it does not get dominated by two to three incumbents in any potential bottlenecks of the chain (science, supply chain, education, tech development, medical devices, delivery of services, monitoring, and innovation), globalizing the information exchange and establishing a democratically elected execution agency for global health that could respond to health emergencies but beyond that provide reliable population health monitoring using inexpensive sensor technology, ongoing analysis of patient-created health summaries and diaries, online behavioral health services available to the entire world's population, and a host of other smaller enhancements of the current system.

Setting more ambitious, globally agreed interoperability criteria for all health software, hardware, and data is the only way to ensure a good combination of bottom-up, middle-out, and top-down governance. Standards setting is a game all can get involved in and once you succeed, the ground rules are the same and ensure a broad set of interest benefit. Big tech in the space need to be regulated (and self-regulate) as if they were responsible governance entities with wide responsibilities for fairness, access, and openness. For data specifically, the FAIR movement gets it right—Findable, Accessible, Interoperable, and Reusable (GoFair, 2021).

The reboot would both be literal and metaphorical. Literal in the sense that because the fundamental infrastructure would be digitized, the system could literally be regularly rebooted and new features, services and apps could be added—ideally many of them lowcode or nocode so that a great part of the world's engineers and healthcare workers— as well as wellness advocates—could take part. That way, healthcare would likely shift toward being the main occupation of 20%–40% of the world's workers rather than the 5%–15% it currently constitutes around the world. The reboot would also have to shift the delivery of healthcare toward a gender-neutral balance and with added DEI monitoring for all possible sources of lack of diversity, equity and inclusion. The metaphorical aspect of the reboot would entail a perspective that no strategy or tactic would be set in stone. Instead of today's ossified regulatory environment, any opportunity to tweak the system would be taken up without question if it surfaced. Leaving the possibility open for metaphorical reboots would only happen if the world's governments built in far greater transparency (and simplicity) in terms of healthcare budget allocation and allowed for simplified pricing and value-based care at all levels of the system.

One failure mode in sci-tech-enabled medicine is to assume that we all want the same thing. However, simply because progress can be made does not mean that there won't be people who are willing to shortcut progress to make a quick buck, slow progress to keep making a buck, or speed up progress to avoid dealing with something else. Industry interest tends to diverge. As much as there have been ebbs and flows of an imperfect paradigm of multilateralism, and there is a notion of "public health", governments want different things. In many ways, health services are not so much "public" as they are, largely, services of the less involved notion of "human interest". And human interests, both those of the elite and those of the people, vary. Social dynamics are fickle, too. Social movements may prove to be a necessary corrective to sci-tech or industrial complex excesses, but also invariably goes too far. There are few controls on a social movement aside from censorship and jail time, both of which are somewhat controversial ways to limit free speech and political action.

The science of longevity, and a healthcare strategy based on abundance, not scarcity, is now moving into a phase of possibility and choice. Which path will we choose as a human civilization? Without determination, we will slide into a continuation of existing structures of governance, innovation, and health systems until some external (exogenous) factor either hollows out an existing function in the system so that it collapses or until one of them starts to dominate by sheer power of its own superiority over the other systemic components.

For example, I could envision how COVID-19, or more likely a next, even more serious pandemic, becomes the mantra that enables such an increased level of scientific coordination that it pushes the system into global mode as the dominant logic within which all other systems fold in.

I could equally well envision a set of innovations, most likely from the sci-tech domain, render all other approaches so inferior that the adoption of the new sci-tech-enabled approaches become a matter of the path of least resistance and biggest (economic and social) gains. Such is the promise of cell-based therapies, for instance, or equally the promise of population-level health monitoring using advanced and inexpensive wearable distributed sensors—or both in some combination. It is indeed possible that sci-tech is easier done in a multilateral fashion and with the global coordinating layer of science simply underlying the superstructure of political veneer as it largely has been over the past few decades.

Finally, I could imagine, as well, that enough national health systems implode on their own and would throughout this decade and the next become replaced by superior ones, not created out of the ruins of existing systems, but built on the foundations of new and emerging technologies, governance structures, community-based delivery mechanisms, and other good things. In some ways, the persistence of global health tech companies that provide products and services—and platforms—across borders is already evidence of this scenario playing out.

Those three scenarios would, largely, be a good thing in and of themselves, but they are not the only possible scenarios. I also see a quite credible one where a few big tech companies (and most pharma players will also become tech companies within this decade so they would be included in that category) increasingly control the majority of health delivery and where governments cease to play even a significant coordinating role in health. One could readily imagine how dwindling public budgets, lack of scientific or regulatory expertise and increased outsourcing of healthcare leads the public to conclude that governments are largely irrelevant to their health outcome. In that scenario, it is not clear what will happen to the speed of innovation. It might initially speed up but would likely inevitably slow down because of less transparency. There is, of course, the possibility that these major tech companies would start to become somewhat indistinguishable from governments and would start taking on more and more of traditionally government specific functions (e.g. system governance, healthcare delivery, system maintenance, etc.). This could happen in partnership with or even in direct opposition to governments. Time will show.

I would offer this warning. The opportunity window for a speedy and efficient transition to a global healthcare system that, ultimately, will benefit the most people and create not only longer lifespans but also better healthspans that will likely close within this decade alone. The reason is that the benefits awaiting those who take even a small part of the increasing pie of the global healthcare market amount to the biggest financial opportunity in the world. Once that opportunity crystallizes, big actors make their moves, and the shift becomes obvious to everyone, opportunities for change will rapidly ossify. Especially, if we don't bake in interoperability—which would give us the option to periodically reboot as a feature not a fix.

For the global health market, there are many takers. What is not going to happen is inaction by financially savvy innovators—both among current tech giants and among emerging startups, or even opportunistic governments (likely within the G7). A new systemic shift is on the horizon, the only question is whether we want to have some sort of plan that is transparently discussed and where pros and cons, implementation paths, and a fair chance of democratic governance is maintained. The reason is that the inextricable link between health and economics has been proven out and will increasingly manifest itself as the effects of COVID-19 shake out around the globe. With a globalized society, national economies are interdependent. Undoing this independence is not feasible. The natural consequence, at least medium term, is increased coordination not less.

The other impact of COVID-19 might be the shattering of the notion that the current societal governance structure can ever provide health equity. Social determinants of health are even more skewed than even those studying it imagined even 3 years ago. The differences in life expectancy between the rich and the poor even within western societies is astounding. The ability to affect one's outcome in the lottery of COVID-19 depends largely on one's social background, financial resources, contact network, and physical location (down to a neighborhood). What seems clear is that disadvantaged groups from across the globe have exponentially worsened their situation.

The question many will start to ask themselves is whether global economic coordination is legitimate or democratic without a corresponding layer of democratic control and transparency at the global level. At this point, the shaky foundation of global justice, health, economics, and coordination rests on a multilateral treaty system. It will increasingly be revealed as inefficient, patchy, undemocratic, and piecemeal. Health, public health policy, global health challenges, and opportunistic health tech coordination will likely be the wedge that drives that lesson home.

At the end of the day, with my futurist hat on, I get the sense that the coming years will be shaped by a growing demand for a global constitutional convention to take place. Contrary to any such process in history, it will not happen by letter correspondence (e.g. Federalist papers) between a few founding fathers who all know each other from face-to-face struggle against a common enemy (e.g. as in the US Founding fathers uniting against colonial Britain). There is a common context, e.g. post-COVID-19 realities, but that context is not shared. The impact has been so skewed. For some, and not only to the super rich, the years of crises which we have experienced have amounted to an unprecedented boom. For others, it has represented utter devastation.

Obviously, a huge part of the governmental establishment will try to resist anything beyond multilateralism in world affairs. However, similar to the events leading up to the 1989 fall of the Berlin Wall (Sarotte, 2009), as contemporary actors, we do not have enough context to know whether we are in the middle of an even bigger wall folding—that of the nation states. More likely, we are looking at a hybrid process of white papers, teleconferences, summits, and political discourse spread out over time and across existing and novel arenas. It will be more diverse than conventions in the past in that women, minorities, youth, other marginal populations will have to have a voice. The process itself may already have started in 2020 with COVID-19, at least in terms of the acceleration of global, open science, with the increased acceptance of public discussion and decisions based on prepublications of scientific knowledge. The next phase of the pandemic, whether it intensifies in force throughout 2021 and 2022 (at minimum in the poorer health systems around the world), which I find fairly likely, or slowly dissipates, which I hope for, will determine that outcome.

The continuation may very well be through an escalation of the climate change discussion both in scientific, political, and civil society arenas. Its climax may well be related to x factors not yet visible or understood, such as the appearance of regional tyrants, social movements of increased force and supported by grassroots across geographical boundaries (related to race, the environment, vaccination, or some such thing that motivates scores of people to civil unrest), or some other element (even extraterrestrial in nature, such as a meteorite, an awareness of other civilizations beyond earth, or some other such thing, even deeper knowledge of ourselves through neuro-inspection by invasive probes such as Elon Musk's Neuralink).

The global (and all national) health systems are in need of a reboot, a fundamental re-set with new software, hardware, and mindsets installed across the board. This is not so much a technical challenge as an organizational one and it might depend on citizen activism, as well as on whether the COVID-19 reboot itself is enough to establish the principle of a reboot which would have beneficial effects on all other global societal challenges as well.

Should I be wrong about the possibility of gaining consensus around regular societal reboots, in the sense that Thomas Jefferson felt was needed every generation, the sensible thing, considering that you, as a reader of this book, presumably share in common with me the increased awareness of systemic risks, is to start properly planning for a near unequivocally assumed to be negative-laden future emergent which has become so apparent to so many of us in such a short period of time.

Let me, however, end on the upbeat. Health tech can be part of a solution to the world's ills, especially if we bake in full digitalization of global health platforms, true interoperability, and enable a wide array of global health apps run by a wide variety of companies and nonprofits large and small, which gives the option of a periodic reboot as a feature not a bug. The emerging system also has to be inclusive, since leaving people out, is both ethically and economically unwise. Exactly what role natural wellness can play in this emerging system depends on how the therapies play out. For sure, regulatory agencies need to take "alternative therapies" and integrated medicine upon themselves. Left unregulated, they are

---

KEY TAKEAWAYS AND REFLECTIONS

1. Try to summarize the main messages of this book, specifically those that resonate with you. Could you name three ones in particular?

_____

2. If you were among the "Founding Parents" of a new global constitution, with emphasis on health, what would you write in the first paragraph?

_____

3. Assuming this book has left you with some new thoughts, how are you going to implement those thoughts going forward? Try to write down at least five actions you aim to take.

_____

---

not part of the systemic reboot. We need to consider how sci-tech can play a role in validating both traditional and emerging therapies and extending the benefits to the edge of the global health system, where only low-cost solutions can scale. Regenerative diets? Brain health? The healing power of touch? Let's prove it in the next decade—or leave it behind. Our future is going to require a heightened moral imagination, but we cannot keep tolerating not knowing for certain.

The world needs new software, hardware, and mindsets "installed" on a regular basis, not by degree, but by constantly evolving our governance in response to systemic changes. Governance, in this sense, is the sum total of all discussions had—democratic or not—that impact the way the world runs. Think about it, you might have a governance discussion at your workplace tomorrow and the result might be lasting change.

It remains true that even flexible health tech will not be the only salient ingredient in becoming a healthier society. If you are left with only one message from this book, here's my version of it: it is only in deeply considering the limits of technology that we can fully embrace its true opportunities.

References

GoFair Foundation (2021). Available at: https://www.gofairfoundation.org/

Sarotte, M. E. (2009). 1989: The Struggle to Create Post-Cold War Europe. Princeton: Princeton University Press.

Appendix

Health Tech Startups

1. **AI/ML Platforms**—including *Analytics & Clinical Intelligence & Enablement* (current health, Innovaccer, Element Science, BioIntelliSense, sema4, BrightInsight, Change Healthcare, Health Catalyst, HealthJoy, Oncology Analytics, Vicarious, VIM, Valencell, Vesta healthcare, saama, Vail, Unite Us, tytocare, Quartet, CMR Surgical, Nuvo, Mahmee, Xealth, Sophia, wellth, gyant, AiCure, Babylon Health, Babyscripts, Behold.ai, Benevolent AI, CloudMedx, Corti.ai, DeepMind, Enlitic, Twistle, Wellth, Quartet Health, Unite Us), MySense.ai, Binah.ai, DocDoc, Suki), *Drug R&D and drug discovery* (AbCellera, Atomwise, celsius, Healx, Ilof, Insilico Medicine, Insitro, Owkin, ProteinQure, Recursion, XtalPi, Valo Health), decentralized clinical trials (Medable) and digital twins (Unlearn), and real-world evidence (Verana Health, TriNetX, nference), *Medical back-office analytics & workflow* (PetalMD, Phreesia, Siilo, SOC Telemed, Xealth), *Healthcare specific Software platforms & Services* (Benchling, Change Healthcare, Veeva, Prime Therapeutics, Teledoc), *Health plans, insurance & benefits management* (alan, bend, Bright Health, Brightside, Carrot, Devoted Health, League, Lyra, Oscar), *Pharma supply chain* (Alto, Capsule, MPharma, Vineti, MediTrust Health, PharmEasy,Truepill), *Clinical trials* (DNA Nexus, Medable, Science 27, Unlearn)
2. **Digital Therapeutics** and *Disease Management* (Adherence Tech, Biofournis, CureApp, Sonar MD, Hinge Health, Dreem, Oura, Omada, Mojo, Happify health, cala health, bigfoot, Proteus Digital Health, Virta, Cognoa, etectRX, Pear Therapeutics, Akili Interactive Labs, Kaia Health, Voluntis, Welldoc) and *Digital health devices* including wearables or portable diagnostics (AioCare, Alivecor, BeatO, Butterfly Network, Clarius, Hearscope, MC10, Fitbit, Medwand, Misfit, Mocacare, Wahoo, Polar, Garmin, Acurable, Dexcom, D-Eye, Ekuore, Eko, Elive, Empatica,

Eyeque, HeraBeat, Liftware, Medtronic, Mojo Vision, Muse, Nemura Medical, Nima, Omron, Oura, Philips, Pilleve, Propeller Health, Viatom, Withings) as well as *Personal health/Self-care startups* (Activ8rlives, Ada Health, GetWellNetwork, HealthVector)

3. **Emerging & Nascent Categories or Markets**—using analytics, including *Chronic conditions* (Catalia Health, Livongo—now part of Teladoc health—the combined company becomes the only consumer and healthcare provider partner to span a person's entire health journey http://go.teladochealth.com/livongo/), *Women's Health* (Fertility care: Carrot Fertility, indbody, and Modern Fertility, Maternal health: Babyscripts, Mahmee, and Nuvo and Virtual care services: Maven Clinic, Hims & Hers, Folx Health, and Ro, Home care (AlayaCare), *Population health* (Health Catalyst), and *Interoperability* (Ciox), and *AR/VR* (Applied VR, Augmedics, Firsthand Technology, Foundation Medicine, Medical Realities, Osso VR, Psious, Surgical Theater, Virtually Better, MindMaze, Oxford VR, Touch Surgery, zSpace, Vicarious Surgical), and *Genetics and Genomics* including *Immunotherapy* (23andme, Atlas Biomed, BioNTech, CureVac, Dante Labs, Flatiron Health, GC Therapeutics, Generation Bio, Genocea Biosciences, Ginkgo Bioworks, Immunocore, Moderna, MyDNA, Oncompass Medicine, Sana Biotech, Thryve, Veritas), Robotics (Cyberdyne, Ekso, Hocoma, Intuitive Surgical, Rewalk Robotics, Veebot, Xenex), Real-world Evidence (Tempus, nfrerence, Aetion, rd-md, evidation, Verana Health, Komodo Health, Medbanks, Concert AI, TriNetX), *Nanomedicine* (Bio-Gate, iCeutica, Keystone Nano, NanoBioSym, Nanomedical Diagnostics, Nanocarrier, T2 Biosystems, Zylo Therapeutics)

4. **MedTech**—including *Medical (3D) Manufacturing* (FabRx, Cellink, Natural Machines, Not Impossible Labs), *Screening & diagnostics* (Arterys, Viz.ai, Modern Fertility, Winterlight, ChromaCode, cue, onera, LetsGetChecked, icometrix, Subtle Medical, qure.ai, Lunit, Healthy.io, zebra, Caption Health, InferVision, Karius, Perspectum, freenome, Grail, Mammoth Biosciences, Thrive, Path.ai, Paige)

5. **Telemedicine**—including Telesurgery, Virtual care delivery & Remote care (Cloudbreak Health, i-GP, iPlato, Push Docto, 98point6, Halodoc, and Galileo Health including telemedicine platforms (Heartbeat Health, Doctor On Demand, Livi, Tencent Trusted Doctors), Remote monitoring & diagnostics (Oura, Element Science, and Dental Monitoring), Therapy & coaching (Omada Health and Virta Health), *Health management and remote care* (Akouos, AmWell, Ava Health, Babylon Health, Bonzun, Diabelloop, Florence, Ginger.io, Headspace, iDoc24, Imaware, INTouch, HealthMaven, Kallyope, Lark, MySugr, Natural Cycles, Omada Health, OneRemission, Oscar Health, Patients Like Me, Ro,

Sensely, Skinvision, Smart Patients, Urbandroid, Woebot) Teladoc https://www.healthline.com/health/best-telemedicine-companies

6. **Traditional specialties being disrupted (using the telemedicine model mostly)**, including *Primary Care*—networks and innovative approaches (Carbon Health, Citiblock, Doctor on Demand, Iora Health, Livi, Medically Home, One Medical, Village MD), Emergency care (dispatch), the *ENT space* (Lyra Therapeutics), *Medical Imaging* (Arterys, Qure.ai), Screening, and Diagnostics, *Other Specialty care* (Axial, Cricket Health, Heartbeat, mindbloom, kindbody, Somatus)

7. **Wellness** (Peloton, Vida Health, HealthKick, BurnAlong, Magic Fitness)

Index

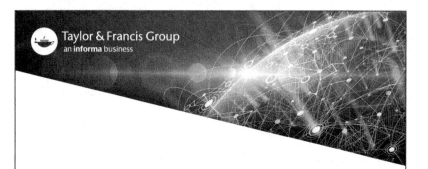

Printed in the United States
by Baker & Taylor Publisher Services